HUMAN MIGRATION

CROOM HELM SERIES IN GEOGRAPHY AND ENVIRONMENT
Edited by Alan Wilson, Nigel Thrift and Michael Bradford

A GEOGRAPHY OF THE
LIFEWORLD
Movement, Rest and Encounter
DAVID SEAMON

CONCEPTS AND TECHNIQUES IN
URBAN ANALYSIS
'BOLA AYENI

REGIONAL ECONOMIC
PLANNING
Generation of Regional Input-Output
Tables
R.C. JENSEN, T.D. MANDEVILLE
AND N.D. KARUNARATNE

TRANSPORT NETWORK
PLANNING
PATRICK O'SULLIVAN, GARY D.
HOLTZCLAW AND GERALD
BARBER

INFORMATION THEORY AND
URBAN SPATIAL STRUCTURE
M.J. WEBBER

THE LARGE INDUSTRIAL
ENTERPRISE
Some Spatial Perspectives
H.D. WATTS

REGIONS IN CRISIS
New Perspectives in European
Regional Theory
EDITED BY JOHN CARNEY, RAY
HUDSON AND JIM LEWIS

URBAN HOUSING PROVISION
AND THE DEVELOPMENT
PROCESS
DAVID DRAKAKIS-SMITH

URBAN TRANSPORT PLANNING
Theory and Practice
JOHN BLACK

HUMANISTIC GEOGRAPHY AND
LITERATURE
Essays on the Experience of Place
DOUGLAS C.D. POCOCK

PLANNING IN THE SOVIET
UNION
JUDITH PALLOT AND DENIS J.B.
SHAW

CATASTROPHE THEORY AND
BIFURCATION
Applications to Urban and Regional
Systems
A.G. WILSON

THEMES IN GEOGRAPHIC
THOUGHT
MILTON E. HARVEY AND BRIAN
P. HOLLY

REGIONAL LANDSCAPES AND
HUMANISTIC GEOGRAPHY
EDWARD RELPH

CRIME AND ENVIRONMENT
R.N. DAVIDSON

HUMAN MIGRATION
A Geographical Perspective

G.J. Lewis

CROOM HELM
London & Canberra

© 1982 G.J. Lewis
Croom Helm Ltd, 2-10 St John's Road, London SW11

British Library Cataloguing in Publication Data

Lewis, G.J.
    Human migration
    1. Migration, Internal
    2. Emigration and immigration
    I. Title
    304.8'09   HB1951
    ISBN 0-7099-0007-4

Printed and bound in Great Britain
by Billing and Sons Limited
Guildford, London, Oxford, Worcester

CONTENTS

To my Parents

FIGURES

List of Figures

PREFACE

Since man's emergence on the earth's surface he has constantly moved from place to place, over long and short distances, in search of improvements in individual circumstances and environmental conditions. The very act of migrating, in turn, often creates changes, individual, local and regional, which in certain instances create acute social problems. Despite the recognition of the significance of the migratory process in any understanding of society, as evidenced by a vast literature, those involved in guiding communities, and economies, whether it be local or national governments, exhibit considerable ignorance of its workings and likely effects. Too often policies which led to migration have resulted in considerable individual and community difficulties; on the other hand, policies aimed specifically at encouraging a shift in population have foundered because of the policymakers' failure to consider the personal and institutional constraints which influence migration potential.

All of the social sciences are, to a greater or lesser extent, concerned with the migration of people. By bringing its own particular perspective to bear each discipline sheds different light on the causes and consequences of migration. Here, however, one perspective, the geographical, will be of prime concern; thus the emphasis will be upon the spatial patterns, and underlying processes, involved in human migration, as well as its role as an agent in the development of the spatial organization of society. Over the last two decades geographers in their study of migration have developed several different methodologies: aggregate, behavioural, structural and consequential, and this volume attempts to integrate them in such a way that it might be useful for undergraduates studying any one branch of human geography at universities, polytechnics and colleges of higher education.

In the writing of this book I am indebted to the assistance of a number of people. Emeritus Professor E.G. Bowen and Professor W. Kirk, who initially guided my interests in human geography and matters associated with migration and, at the University of Leicester, Emeritus Professor N. Pye and, more recently, Professor J.H. Paterson, have provided me with the opportunities and facilities to develop these ideas within undergraduate courses in geography. Many thanks

Preface

also go to Ruth Rowell, Kate Moore and Claudette Foo for drawing the maps and diagrams so expertly, to Terry Garfield for supervising the cartographic and reprographic procedures, to Elaine Humphries for typing the manuscript so speedily and efficiently, and to several of my former research students, Rod Allon-Smith, Jack Balderson, Wil Balderson, Judith Budd, Dave Maund, John Nokes, Steve Royle and Ken Sherwood, whose labours appear scattered throughout the following pages. One of these graduate students, John Nokes, commented on earlier drafts and provided much valuable assistance. Special mention must be made of my wife Vivien, who encouraged me to undertake this task and provided the 'peace and quiet' so necessary for its completion. Finally, this book is dedicated to my parents, as a token of gratitude that is genuinely felt but too rarely expressed.

ACKNOWLEDGEMENTS

The author and publisher gratefully acknowledge permission received from the following to modify and make use of copyright material in diagrams: American Geographical Society, Figure 2.5; American Sociological Review, Figure 4.2; Edward Arnold Ltd, Figure 5.3; Association of American Geographers, Figures 2.4, 3.5, 4.3, 8.3; M.J. Boyle and M.E. Robinson, Figure 8.10; Economic Geography, Figures 7.2, 7.4, 8.11; Geografisha Annaler, Figures 2.2, 2.8, 2.9, 5.6; Geographical Analysis, Figure 2.10; Institute of British Geographers, Figures 7.3, 7.5; Lund Studies in Geography, University of Lund, Figures 4.1, 5.7; Methuen (ABP) Ltd, Figure 2.6; New Zealand Geographical Society, Figure 6.4; Population Association of America, Figures 7.1, 8.4; Regional Studies, Figure 8.7; D.T. Rowland, Figures 5.5, 5.6.

1 INTRODUCTION

> Man is a mobile creature, capable of enquiring, susceptible to
> suggestion, and endowed with imagination and initiative. This
> explains why, having conceived the notion that his wants
> might be satisfied elsewhere, he may decide not merely on
> going there but also on the means by which his project can be
> achieved. (Beaujeau-Garnier, 1966, 171)

Such movements of individuals and groups from one home location to
another, has been taking place since the origin of man. It has even been
claimed that 'one of the distinguishing characteristics of *Homo sapiens*
is his tendency to migrate, and the frequency and distance of these
movements make him alone' (Du Toit and Safa, 1975, 1). In fact,
during recorded history, migration has not only increased in volume but
has also involved steadily lengthening distances. Many of the world's
most acute social problems are associated with migration. Bogue (1969,
752) has suggested that if the problem of fertility was not so critical
today, it is almost certain that the plight of the migrant, especially in
the third world, would be listed as priority for research and action.

Migration is a major cause of social change, since it can be viewed as
an independent as well as a dependent variable in the examination of
change. An area may grow in population size by an inflow of people or
it may decline by an outflow of its members, and it is now recognized
that migration is usually the most important factor in differential
population trends (Clarke, 1965; Woods, 1979). Differences in natural
increase, indeed in birth-rates and death-rates, between areas are often
smaller than differences in migration rates. If such movements are
selective of individuals in terms of age, sex, economic or social
attributes, then they will determine the differences in the demographic
and socioeconomic composition of an area's population. Moreover, the
migrant can initiate further change in his new place of residence by the
introduction of new ideas, values and skills. In other words, migration
is a two-way process: it is a response to economic and social change and
equally it is a catalyst to change for those areas gaining and losing
migrants.

Of the three components of population change migration is,
however, the most complex and the most difficult to analyze,

particularly in a comparative fashion. Unlike the two vital processes, births and deaths, there is no agreed definition of the terms migrant and migration, and so any enumeration of migratory movement can be highly problematic. 'Strictly speaking, the term migration should be reserved for the movement of persons from one place to another for the purpose of permanent settlement. However, the movement of labour — and also of refugees — intended as a temporary shift may well result in permanent change of residence' (Broek and Webb, 1968, 459). Clearly, the distinction between migration and other forms of mobility cannot always be made. Further difficulties arise because any one migratory move can be assigned to a variety of origins and destinations because of the myriad alternative ways of grouping individuals. Since migration is a 'voluntary' action societal values and norms are involved and, therefore, the manner in which these are manifest in individual and group behaviour, in relation to both migrant and non-migrant, must be considered. Also migration has widespread consequences for the individual migrant, for the community of origin and of destination, and for the society within which the movement takes place. All of these consequences must be differentiated and analyzed both separately and in combination.

With the increasing volume and diversity of migration, there has been a corresponding increase in the desire and necessity to identify and explain such movements. According to Simmie (1972, 9-10), there are at least four reasons as to why an understanding of human migration is important:

1. In any attempt to predict population growth an understanding of migration is vital since 'of all the uncertainties which plague population forecasting for local areas the greatest relate to migration as a source of change' (Lowry, 1966, 21).
2. Migration itself may influence many other forms of spatial behaviour. The place of residence chosen largely determines the set of locations available for daily activities and whether this movement be over short or long distances it forms the basis of how people sift and sort themselves residentially in space.
3. For those involved with urban development an understanding of why families change their place of residence is fundamental. With such knowledge they will be in a better position not only to guide private and public housing schemes but also to reduce the socio-economic problems caused by haphazard residential developments (Clark and Moore, 1980).

4. How and why employers and employees move from one region to another is of crucial importance in any explanation of differential economic development. With such knowledge economists and regional analysts are better able to channel development into desired localities and regions.

Such claims have been most succinctly summarized by Claeson and Egero (1972, 1), when they pointed out that 'a knowledge of population movement, representing as it does both a cause and effect of societal processes, remains of fundamental importance to a complete understanding of social change, economic development and political organization'.

The realization as to the importance of migration in any understanding of human organization is reflected in the extensive and detailed literature that is available (Pryor, 1971; Shaw, 1975; de Castro Lopo, 1975; Sharma, 1978). The genesis for much of the study of migration lies in Ravenstein's (1885, 1889) analysis of late-nineteenth-century migrations in Britain and Western Europe. Despite these early beginnings Welch (1970) has claimed, however, that there was a dearth of substantial migration studies until the 1950s; after that date there was a massive growth of interest in the field, possibly reflecting the emergence of several distinctive social science disciplines as well as the realization by planners and policy-makers of the necessity to identify and understand the migration process (Clarke, 1973). Most of the social sciences are involved, to a greater or lesser extent in the study of migration, each discipline bringing its own distinctive perspective to bear on the process. For example, economists have approached the study of migration in terms of jobs and economic opportunities (Thomas, 1954; Shaw, 1975; Todaro, 1976), whilst demographers have been more concerned with the role of migration in population growth, particularly population forecasting and projections (Bogue, 1969). On the other hand, the focus of attention of the sociologists has been upon the character of the migrants (Jansen, 1970; Mangalam, 1968; Jackson, 1969) and that of the anthropologists upon the problems faced by migrant groups within a host community (Spencer, 1970; Brandes, 1975). The geographer's main contribution has been to emphasize the spatial patterning of migration and the locational decision involved (Hannerberg, 1957; Kosinski and Prothero, 1975; Lewis, 1974a). Despite these different approaches the development of migration studies owes much to interdisciplinary efforts and, in general it is difficult to draw sharp distinctions between the different contributions (Richmond and Kubat, 1956; Brown and Neuberger, 1977; McNeill and Adams, 1978). Such studies have taken place at many different scales of analysis, including world movements (B. Thomas, 1961), those within countries, for example, Western Europe (Salt and Clout, 1976), United States (Roseman, 1977), Eastern Europe (Kostanick, 1977), Australia (Rowland, 1979), and even at the urban scale (Simmons, 1968; Moore, 1972; Clark and Moore, 1978). Only of late has extensive research into migratory movements in the third world been undertaken, resulting in a plethora of studies (see essays in Du Toit and Safa, 1975; Safa and Du Toit, 1975; May, 1977; Pryor, 1979b). A parallel development involves the consideration of the migrations of specific groups, such as the elderly (Allon-Smith, 1978), farmers (Nalson, 1968) and minorities (Richmond, 1973) within an areal context.

A major problem in migration analysis is the lack of a sound theoretical basis upon which to frame a study (Willis, 1974). According to Goldscheider (1971, 274), 'without adequate theories it is not clear what guidelines would be involved to determine the types of migration and social and economic data to be collected or how such information would contribute to the cumulative undertaking of migration processes'. Stemming from Ravenstein's (1885, 1889) descriptive 'laws of migration' several efforts have been made to develop such theories, but their efficacy cannot be fully assessed because of a lack of adequate data. This, along with the needs of the policy-makers, has led several researchers to call for a diversion of interest from theoretical work so 'the emphasis in migration [should] ... be placed on the design of studies to collect data not available from census and other administrative sources' (Haenszel, 1967, 261). Bearing in mind the success of interdisciplinary contributions to migration study this book will, however, focus upon one particular perspective – the geographic, although inevitably reference to other perspectives will be necessary from time to time. Since migrants move from place to place then the study of migration is a fundamental spatial process. Such a perspective involves the consideration of at least three distinctive themes: the spatial pattern of migration, the locational decisions involved, and the impact of the migrants upon places, each of which form a major part of this book. In geography the traditional approach to migration study tends to use aggregate ideas and concepts. This large-scale analysis involves economic theory which assumes a homogeneous potential migrant population, so any pattern of migration is considered to be the result of differences in opportunities between areas. More recently, however, it has been realized that various groups react differently to available opportunities and, therefore, many geographers have adopted a more behavioural approach to the analysis of migration. This involves a disaggregation of the population into groups and individuals in order to disentangle the factors involved in the decision whether to move or stay. By such an approach a greater understanding is achieved as to how different people make decisions, thus emphasizing that beyond a few 'general' reasons the migration decision is a highly complex one. But, of late, many students of migration have criticized behaviouralism for its failure fully to take into account that all decisions are made in a highly constrained situation (Ward, 1980). In other words, some individuals have greater choice than others. For a more meaningful understanding of the migration process, therefore, it is argued that consideration must be given to the structure of society since it provides the context of all migrations. The prime focus of this approach has been upon the ways that governments, organizations and institutions by their decisions can determine employment and housing opportunities and, therefore, an individual's migratory potential. Nonetheless, all three approaches are necessary for a full explanation of migration, and so all three will be interwoven in this book as we attempt to show how individual locational decisions (Chapters 6, 7, 8) sum to aggregate patterns (Chapters 4, 5) of human migration within a highly constrained situation (Chapter 9). The resultant migration has a marked consequence for the individuals, communities and regions involved (Chapter 10).

Although the emphasis will be on concepts and methods of analysis, a variety of case-studies will be introduced to illustrate the worldwide application of these ideas. Lines of further enquiry and more meaningful methods of analysis, rather than definitive answers, will be suggested. As a backcloth to the main theme of the book the next two chapters will, respectively be concerned with definitional and conceptual problems involved in migrational analysis (Chapter 2), and a 'broad-brush' account of migration in time and space (Chapter 3).

2 DEFINITIONS AND CONCEPTS

Any review of migration literature will quickly reveal that there are a number of false or inadequate conceptions concerning the nature of migration, and these have led to unsatisfactory definitions of the phenomena. Much of the resultant confusion is due partly to the fact that each discipline has viewed migration from its own particular perspective and partly to the variability of the data sources available for study (Courgeau, 1976). Within the field of migration there are also a number of well-established concepts and measurement techniques in regular use, yet, the manner in which they are defined and used have crucial repercussions for the findings of particular studies. In any study of migration, therefore, it is necessary to define precisely the phenomena being considered as well as deriving a framework within which to conceive the analysis. This chapter will attempt to highlight some of these operational problems; by so doing many of the misconceptions, hopefully, can be resolved.

Definitions

The term migration seems clearest when defined in the light of the demographic balancing equation:

$$Pt = Po + B - D + IM - OM \tag{1}$$

where:

Pt   = population at the close of interval
Po   = population at the beginning of the interval
B   = number of births in the interval
D   = number of deaths in the interval
IM   = number of in-migrants in the interval
OM = number of out-migrants in the interval

Simply, the equation envisages a population system in which the population at time Pt is equal to the population at the earlier time, Po, plus or minus changes due to births (*fertility*), deaths (*mortality*) and migration in the interval between Pt and Po. Clearly a *migrant* is a person entering (*in-migration*) or leaving (*out-migration*) a place by means other than their birth or death, and the total *gross* increments caused by such entrances or departures constitute migration. The difference between births and deaths is often referred to as *natural change* and the difference between the in-migration and out-migration is referred to as *net migration*.

Many have argued, however, that such a definition of migration is too narrowly conceived, since migration involves a whole series of additional dimensions to that of change of residence. At least five are relevant to a geographical perspective. Firstly, in order to define the migrant precisely some territorial schema has to be adopted; for example, an administrative unit, hence:

> . . . we will use the term 'migration' for the change of residence of an individual from one parish or commune to another. (Hägerstrand, 1957, 28)

Further, such migration has to be specified by some time interval, usually the interval between the date of arrival and the date of departure; thus Weinberg (1961, 265–6) stated that:

> . . . migration is the changing of the place of abode permanently or, when temporarily, for an appreciable duration . . . It is used symbolically in the transition from one surrounding to another in the course of human life.

The third dimension is one emphasized by sociologists and anthropologists. They argue that since migration involves a move to a new social setting then migrants will experience a change in their interactional system. Such interactional changes involve a weakening of social and cultural attachments with the place of origin, and the creation of new ties and values in the place of destination. Thus migration has been defined as:

> . . . the physical transition of an individual or a group from one society to another. This transition usually involves abandoning one social setting and entering another and different one. (Eisenstadt, 1953, 1)

Also is has been argued that migration is a form of motivated behaviour, for example:

> migration is defined . . . as the movements (involving change of permanent residence) from one country to another which take place through the volition of the individuals or families concerned. (Thomas, 1954, 510)

If migration is an act of volition it implies decision-making based on some underlying criteria, which usually involve a hierarchy of values. A definition of migration which incorporates all of these dimensions was that suggested by Mangalam (1968, 11):

> Migration is a relatively permanent moving away of a collectivity, called migrants, from one geographical location to another, preceded by decision-making on the part of the migrants on the basis of a hierarchically ordered set of values or valued ends and resulting in changes in the interactional system of the migrants.

This definition distinguishes migration from that of the more general term of *mobility*. Mobility includes all kinds of territorial movements, both temporary and permanent, over various distances whilst migration is much more restricted and relates to a permanent change of residence. Zelinsky has urged, however, that such a distinction should not be overemphasized:

> Genuine migration obviously means the perceptible and simultaneous shifts in both spatial and social locus, so that the student cannot realistically measure one kind of movement while he ignores the other. . . . Ideally, we should observe shifts in both varieties of space in tandem but given the dearth of techniques and data for handling purely social movement, we are forced to rely solely on territorial movements as a clumsy surrogate for total mobility. (Zelinsky, 1971, 224)

Such an approach not only allows the consideration of a variety of migration flows but also reflects the diversity of contemporary studies of migration. Within this volume, therefore, no attempt will be made to follow one uniformly strict definition of the term migration.

Over the years researchers into migration have built up a standard set of terms, which facilitate the collection of data and the testing of hypotheses. A knowledge of these terms is a necessary prerequisite to an understanding of the principles of migration; a brief review of some of the major terms will now be undertaken.

Migration and Geographical Scale

The relative significance of the natural change and the migration components of population change varies with the geographical scale being examined. At a world scale, all population change is accounted for by the relative importance of births and deaths and, even country by country, natural change remains the predominant component determining fluctuations in population. However, when we examine population change *within* countries, migration is usually a more important factor than place-to-place variations in natural change. This reflects the tendency for variation in migration levels between places to be much greater than differences in births and deaths; yet it must not be overlooked that these three components of population change are not independent of each other. Differential migration can either accelerate or attenuate natural change, just as natural change can affect the propensity of people to move.

Migration and Areas

Since migration is defined as a change of residence it is usual within studies of migration to adopt some territorial schema, more often than not an administrative unit. The size and shape of that unit is of considerable significance in determining the number and proportion of persons who are defined as migrants (Figure 2.1). For example, in the United States in 1970, 63 per cent of those classified as residentially mobile moved within counties; on the other hand, only 37 per cent moved between counties, 18 per cent between states, and 12 per cent between regions (US Bureau of Census, 1973: Table 180). From Figure 2.1 it is also evident that the location of people within the defined areas will affect migration totals. For example, where the population is concentrated near a boundary, inter-area rates will tend to be high and those within the area low. Conversely, where a population is concentrated toward the centre of an area, intra-area moves will tend to be relatively higher than inter-area ones.

Migration and Time

Since migration occurs in time as well as space it is necessary, therefore, to specify the interval over which migration is to be recorded. The longer the interval length, the smaller the size of the average annual number of migrants, because those individuals who entered and left an

Figure 2.1: The Size and Shape of Areal Units which Directly Affect those
Defined as Migrants

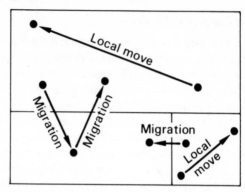

area during the interval will not be recorded. Therefore, any sets of
migration data collected for unequal intervals of time are not
comparable, even if they are reduced to an average annual basis.

Migration Area and Destination

The area from which a migrant departs is termed the area of origin and
that at which he arrives is termed the area of destination. Migrants who
depart from a common area of origin and arrive at a common area of
destination during a particular interval constitute a 'migration stream',
and, where there is a flow in the opposite direction it is termed a
'counter stream'. A portion of all streams will include return migrants,
that is, those returning to their area of origin (Rowland, 1978).

Migration Rates

The rate of migration is similar to that used in other branches of
demography; it is the number of migrants divided by the population
exposed to the possibility of migration. Thus:

$$m = \frac{M}{P} \cdot K \tag{2}$$

where:

  m = migration rate
  M = number of migrants
  P = population at risk
  K = constant, usually 100 or 1,000

Similar rates can be calculated for in- and out-migrants, and gross and net migrants:

$$\text{Out } m = \frac{O}{P} \cdot K \qquad\qquad \text{In } m = \frac{I}{P} \cdot K \qquad\qquad (3,4)$$

$$\text{Net } m = \frac{I - O}{P} \cdot K \qquad\qquad \text{Gross } m = \frac{I + O}{P} \qquad\qquad (5,6)$$

where:

O = number of out-migrants from an area
I = number of in-migrants to an area

Also the rate of migrants can be expressed in probabilistic terms:

$$\frac{M}{P} + \frac{N}{P} = 1 \qquad\qquad (7)$$

where:

N = non-migrants

In all these rates the population at risk is defined according to the needs of the study; for example, in a study of migration between two areas, i and j, the population at risk is usually defined as that residing at i at the beginning of the period. Thus:

$$m\,i\,j = \frac{M\,i\,j}{P\,i} \cdot K \qquad\qquad (8)$$

All of these rates can be computed as 'specific' rates, where both the numerator and the denominator refer to the same particular sub-group of the population. So rates that are specific for age, marital status, occupation, educational attainment, income, etc, may be computed. Despite the diversity of procedures available for measuring migration their success depends largely upon the availability of suitable data; in view of the fact that the methods involved in deriving migration data have been considered in detail elsewhere only a brief description of the main ones is necessary here.

Methods of Deriving Migration Data

A variety of sources can be used as the basis for deriving information on migration and, to a large extent, the quality of that information determines the procedure of analysis adopted by the researcher (Shryock and Siegel, 1971 and 1976). For those concerned with international migrations, 'official' statistics, whether produced by individual governments (Jenkins, 1976) or estimated by the United Nations (1978), are the main source, whilst studies of internal migration can usually resort to a variety of sources (United Nations, 1970; Welch, 1971; Rees and Rees, 1977). Basically, these sources involve two methods: *direct*, or a simple count of individuals who move across a defined boundary within a given time period; and *indirect*, or the estimation of the migrants from vital rates tables (Haenszel, 1967).

To obtain migration data by means of the direct method, the most common source is the *national census*, which provides the basis of most of what is known about modern migratory movements. By comparing the place of enumeration with the place of residence at some earlier date it is possible to distinguish between 'movers' and 'non-movers' as well as in- and out-migrants for different places. By then cross-classifying area of origin with area of destination it is also possible to derive the flows of migrants between areas, whether they be regions, counties, districts, etc. Some countries have only recently collected information on migration; for example in Britain it was not until the 1961 census that questions on migration were first asked, and then only moves which had occurred in the year, or five years, before census-taking day were recorded. The most significant weakness of the census is the void created by the time interval between successive censuses. However, this officially can be overcome if a country has a law, as Scandinavian countries do, which requires each person who changes his residence to report the fact to the local council. *National registration* tables, derived from such reports, provide a detailed dossier on the number and characteristics of migrants, though, unfortunately, not all countries have such a scheme (Van den Brink, 1954). Britain does not have a national register, although its annual register of electors does provide a means of determining the 'gains' and 'losses' experienced by an area. As a means of determing migration electoral registers are weakened by their failure to distinguish between out-migrants and deaths among the 'losses' and between in-migrants and those reaching voting age among the 'gains' (Dunn and Swindell, 1972; Ward, 1975). Despite these shortcomings there are at least two ways in which the registers have been used as a source of migration data: first, after the decision to abandon the proposed sample census in 1976 several local authorities collected some information, including that on changes in residence, by inserting additional questions on the electoral forms (Leicester City Council, 1980) and, second, by means of careful questioning of 'well-informed' residents it is possible to identify for small areas the migrant component among the 'gains' and 'losses' (Jones, 1965). Quite often the information provided by the census and the registers is not sufficient for the needs of a particular research project. In such cases, geographers have had to resort to *social surveys* which, in general, tend to involve samples of the population for limited areas. Despite their restricted nature, however, they do provide a valuable insight into the complexities of the migration process.

The most common form of indirect method of measurement is to compare within the national census the place of birth with the residence of the persons at the time of enumeration (Rees, 1976). Such *place of birth statistics* provide useful indications of the directions of migration flows and inter-censal net migration can also be estimated by comparing the statistics of two subsequent censuses:

$$M = (Io - It) - (Oo - Ot) \tag{9}$$

where Io, Oo is the total number of in- and out-migrants respectively at the beginning of an inter-censal period, and It, Ot is the total number of in- and out-migrants respectively at a subsequent time t. In many third world countries place of birth statistics are the only source of information (Goddard, Gould and Masser, 1975) and for those interested in past migrations they are often the prime source (Drake, 1972; Lawton and Pooley, 1978). However, these statistics do suffer from a number of shortcomings, in particular their failure to identify return migrations to places of birth and being usually available only for large area units.

If only statistics on birth and deaths are available, it is possible to estimate net migration by subtracting reproductive population change from total change between two successive censuses (Siegel and Hamilton, 1952). More simply this *vital statistics* method may be expressed by the equation:

$$M = (P_t - P_o) - (B - D) \tag{10}$$

where:

M is the net migration during the inter-censal period
P_t and P_o are the population at the end and beginning respectively
of the inter-censal period
B and D are the number of births and deaths respectively during the
inter-censal period

A similar approach is adopted by the often used *survival ratio method*. This estimates the number of individuals at one census period still being alive and resident in the same location at the succeeding census if there were no migration. The number of migrants is calculated by subtracting the estimated number of people still alive from the actual census count at the second census. Such an estimate is obtained by multiplying each age group of the first census by a net 'survival ratio', which is a statistical estimate of the proportion of that age group who will still be alive at the next census:

$$M = P_t - P_{os} \tag{11}$$

where P_t and P_o are as defined above, except that they refer to age groups, and s is an estimate of the proportion of the age group who will survive from one census to another. In this estimate allowance is made for the fact that the survivors grow older during the inter-censal period and at the subsequent census are enumerated in a different age group than at the first census (Tarver, 1962). This procedure can be employed at several scales of analysis; for example, House and Knight's (1966) estimate of the role of migration in northeast England during the sixties.

If information on birthplaces or births and deaths are not available then the researcher has to resort to the less sophisticated *national growth method*. This involves a comparison between the rate of growth in a given area and the national average, the difference being interpreted as resulting from migration:

$$M = \frac{Pt - Po}{Pt} - \frac{NPt - NPo}{NPt} \tag{12}$$

where NPt and NPo is the national population respectively at the beginning and at the end of the period, and Pt and Po is the population of an area respectively at the beginning and at the end of the period.

These measures and data sources have been used by geographers in a variety of contexts and at different scales of analysis. For example, the census has been the prime source for macro-level studies whilst for those at a more micro-scale it provides a general background as well as a sampling frame for more detailed surveys. Irrespective of the measures and data sources employed, however, any successful study of migration must employ a meaningful and rigorous conceptual framework. It is to a consideration of the several available frameworks that we must now turn.

A Typology of Migration

A major characteristic of migration studies is their diversity of purpose and perspective. Many are highly theoretical, others empirical and, more recently, a number are of a highly practical nature. This variety of purpose is further diversified by the different approaches, methodologies and scales of analysis adopted by each investigator. As a consequence there appears to be little or no unifying coherence to the study of migration and, therefore, if an overall perspective is to be achieved then there is need to bring some order to the apparent chaos. In order to simplify these complexities numerous attempts have been made to classify the movements of people into various types. A whole series of classification has been suggested based upon different criteria; very broadly these may be grouped into four categories:

Spatial

The majority of classifications based upon spatial criteria focus upon the areal units between which movements takes place. The basic distinction on this criteria is that between the movement of people within a nation, or *internal migration*, and the movement of people across political boundaries, or *international migration*. According to Kant (1962) the former type of migration can be distinguished further into intra-local or intra-regional and inter-local or inter-regional. In the United States this type of distinction is used extensively by demographers and planners when they differentiate between *local movers*, persons who move within the boundaries of a county, and *migrants*, persons who cross a county boundary while changing residential location (Roseman, 1977). Within such migratory streams and counterstreams, Goldscheider (1971) has separated first time movers and return movers, which can be described in a simple 3 $\times$ 3 matrix based places X, Y and Z. Further, Figure 2.2 illustrates the point that flows also occurs within places. Even within a small rural district, the in-migrants may be further differentiated as illustrated for the

Figure 2.2: Relationship between Different Types of Migratory Flows and Geographical Scale

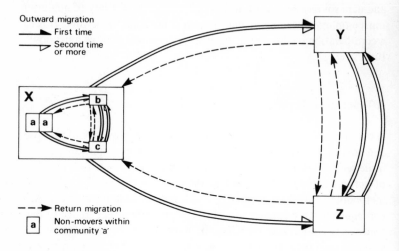

Source: After Swindell and Ford, 1975, 68–76.

Figure 2.3: A Typology of Migrants into the Colwyn District, Rural Wales

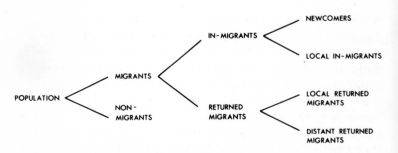

Welsh Borderland in Figure 2.3.

Since it is conceived within the overall context of human movements, one of the most meaningful typologies is the adaptation by Roseman (1971) of Cavalli-Sforza's *Morphological Classification of Human Movements* (1962). Such a classification argues that human movements may be classified into two broad categories. The first, called reciprocal movements (Figure 2.4a), begin at the home, proceed to one or more alternative locations and return to the home. The second category, migratory movements, are distinguished from the first in that

Figure 2.4: A Typology of Human Movements: a — reciprocal
movement; b — total displacement migration; c — partial displacement
migration

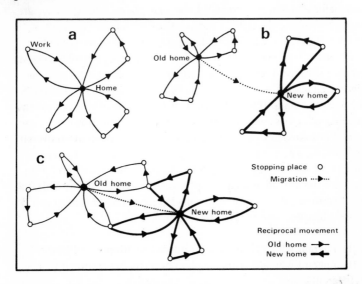

Source: After Roseman, 1971, 589–98.

they are predominantly uni-directional and permanent. Migratory
movements represent the removal of the centre of gravity of the
reciprocal movements, the home, to a new location. This, in turn, can
take two forms: firstly, total displacement migration, involving
residential changes whereby a completely new reciprocal movement
cycle is created by a movement to a new area (Figure 2.4b); and
secondly, partial displacement migration, which displaces only a part of
the reciprocal movement cycle; although the location of the home
changes, the location of some of the other activities nodes still remains
the same (Figure 2.4c). Such a distinction has a wider significance than
simply providing a more meaningful spatial perspective to migration,
since total and partial displacement migration may be conceived as
being broadly analogous to long and short distance migration
respectively.

Temporal

Essentially the focus here is on the length of residence in the host
community. With reference to Africa, Gould and Prothero (1975) have

suggested that movement may be conceived in terms of four categories: daily, periodic, seasonal and long term. Effectively, what they are doing is distinguishing between two types of mobility: the first involves daily movements and commuting and the second where overnight stays are necessary. Among the latter a further distinction has to be made between circulation which includes 'a great variety of movements usually short term repetitive or cyclical in character, but all having in common the lack of any declared intention of a permanent or long-standing change of residence' (Zelinsky, 1971, 226) and migration which, according to the United Nations (1970), involves a permanent residence of at least one year in the host community. However, these distinctions must not be overemphasized since they can often overlap; for example, a particularly interesting, yet frequently overlooked, form of permanent migration is that which involves a return of a migrant from abroad at a late stage in the life cycle or at the end of a works contract. Based upon returning Puerto Ricans, Alvarez (1967) has distinguished several types of such migrants:

1. the migrant who left from, but returned to, his place of birth;
2. the migrant who left from his place of birth, but returned to a different place;
3. the migrant who changed his residence from his place of birth prior to migrating, but returned to his place of birth;
4. the migrant who returned to his place of residence before migration, this place being different from his place of birth;
5. the migrant who changed his place of residence before emigrating, but returned to a third place.

Similarly, in a discussion of Britons returning from Canada, Richmond (1968) identified three basic types: 'permanent' returnees who had intended to settle in Canada but for diverse reasons were now more likely to remain in Britain; 'quasi-migrants' who had originally planned to return to Britain; and 'transient' migrants who migrated at frequent intervals between the two countries without settling permanently in either.

Causal

An early typology of migration based upon causal factors was that suggested by Fairchild (1925); in this classification distinctions were based on the differences in the level of culture and the presence or absence of violence (Table 2.1). Despite its shortcomings, this typology

Table 2.1: Causal Typology of Migration

Migration from	Migration to	Peaceful movement	Warlike movement
Low culture	High culture		Invasion
High culture	Low culture	Colonization	Conquest
Cultures at the same level		Immigration	

Source: Based on Fairchild (1925), 124.

has been used in an adapted form by a number of later studies, particularly those distinguishing between voluntary and forced migrations (Petersen, 1958). However, George (1970) has argued that any meaningful causal-based typology can only be effectively constructed if the distinction is made between migration resulting from economic factors and that caused by social and cultural factors.

Consequential

The most significant of the various typologies focusing upon the consequences of migration is that suggested by Petersen in his 'General typology of migration' (1958). Although his classification used a variety of criteria, its most important contribution was to distinguish between innovative and conservative migration. According to Petersen 'some persons migrate as a means of achieving the new. Let us term such a migration innovating. Others migrate in response to a change in conditions, in order to retain what they had; they move geographically in order to remain where they are in all other respects. Let us term such migration conservative' (Petersen, 1958, 256).

So far consideration has been given to a classification of migration types; however, in order for an analysis to proceed there is a need for the migration process to be conceived within some conceptual framework, thus allowing the various factors to be isolated and the more significant questions to be posed more readily identified. It is readily apparent from the literature that studies which have been concerned with the spacio-temporal and causal aspects of migration have, in general, conceived their analysis within a framework derived from Ravenstein's early generalizations whilst those concerned with the consequences of migration have adopted one based upon social change.

The 'Laws' of Migration

Following an extensive enquiry on internal migration, first in Britain and later in 20 other countries, E.G. Ravenstein published two seminal papers in the 1880s in which he postulated his 'laws' of migration (Ravenstein, 1885 and 1889). These represented his reaction to the earlier study of Farr (1876) who had remarked that migration appeared to go without any definite law. The seven 'laws' of migration suggested by Ravenstein are as follows:

1. We have already proved that the great body of our migrants only proceed a short distance and that these take place, consequently a universal shifting or displacement of the population, which produces 'currents of migration' setting in the direction of great centres of commerce and industry which absorb the migrants.
2. It is the natural outcome of this movement limited in range, but universal throughout the country, that the processes of absorption go on in the following manner: the inhabitants of a country immediately surrounding a town of rapid growth, flock to it; the gaps thus left by the rural population are filled up by the migrants from more remote districts, until the attractive force of one of our rapidly growing cities makes its influence felt, step by step, to the most remote corner of the Kingdom. Migrants enumerated in a certain centre of absorption will consequently grow less with the distance proportionately to the native population which furnishes them. . . .
3. The process of dispersion is the inverse of that of absorption and exhibits similar features.
4. Each main current of migration produces a compensating counter-current.
5. Migrants proceeding long distances generally go by preference to one of the great centres of commerce and industry.
6. The natives of towns are less migratory than those of rural parts of the country.
7. Females are more migratory than males (Ravenstein, 1885, 198–9).

Essentially, these 'laws' make five explicit and two implicit statements concerning patterns and distance of migration, migratory streams, migration motives and characteristics of migrants. This framework has been the basis of considerable geographical research on migration and nearly a century later it is surprising how many of these 'laws' are still valid (Grandstaff, 1975; Grigg, 1977).

Recently, Lee has returned to the same theme and restated Ravenstein's laws in a series of hypotheses about the volume of migration under varying conditions, the development of stream and counterstream, and the characteristic of migrants (Lee, 1966, 925-7). On the volume of migration Lee claimed that:

(1) The volume of migration within a given territory varies with the degree of diversity in area included in that territory.
(2) The volume of migration varies with the diversity of people.
(3) The volume of migration is related to the difficulty of surmounting the intervening obstacles.
(4) The volume of migration varies with fluctuations in the economy.
(5) Unless severe checks are imposed, both volume and rate of migration tend to increase with time.
(6) The volume and rate of migration vary with state of progress in a country or in an area.

On stream and counter-stream he claimed that:

(1) Migration tends to take place largely within well defined streams.
(2) For every major migration stream, a counter-stream develops.
(3) The efficiency of the stream (ratio of stream to counter-stream or the net redistribution of population affected by the opposite flows) is high if the major factors in the development of a migration stream were minus factors at origin.
(4) The efficiency of stream and counter-stream tends to be low if origin and destination are similar.
(5) The efficiency of migration streams will be high if the intervening obstacles are great.
(6) The efficiency of a migration stream varies with the economic conditions, being high in prosperous times and low in times of depression.

On the characteristics of migrants Lee claimed that:

(1) Migration is selective.
(2) Migrants responding primarily to plus factors at destination tend to be positively selective.
(3) Migrants responding primarily to minus factors at origin tend to be

Table 2.2: A Migration Framework

Places	Migrants			Organizations	
Location Function Population	Type	Social	Objective	Formal	Informal
	First time	Age	Education	Government	Kinship
	Return	Sex	Technology	Hazards	Ethnicity
	Dependent	Social status	Economic development		

Source: Swindell and Ford (1975, 71).

negatively selective; or, where the minus factors are overwhelming
to entire population groups, they may not be selected at all.

(4) Taking all migrants together, selection tends to be bi-modal.

(5) The degree of positive selection increases with the difficulty of the
intervening obstacles.

(6) The heightened propensity to migrate at certain stages in the life
cycle is important in the selection of migrants.

(7) The characteristics of migrants tend to be intermediate between the
characteristics of the population at origin and the population at
destination.

These hypotheses have been used extensively as a framework for
investigating the spatial, temporal and causal factors in migration. The
significance of Lee's work is that he has restated Ravenstein's 'laws' in
a more precise fashion and, therefore, made them more amenable to
testing. In other words, Lee has helped to shift the emphasis in
migration research from a purely descriptive to a more analytical
approach. Swindell and Ford (1975) have developed this theme a stage
further by suggesting that the migration process can be more readily
understood if conceived as a function of places and migrants moving
among those places aided by organizations, within a temporal dimension
(Table 2.2). In turn each of these three elements can be disaggregated
into their basic components. For example, places may be described as a
spatial network, with differing populations and functions, thus forming
a hierarchy of places with varying social and economic opportunities.
The migrants themselves may be distinguished in terms of, firstly, first
time, return and dependent movers; secondly, social characteristics such
as age, sex and social status; and thirdly, objectives which are primarily
determined by education, technological level and economic stage of
development. The resultant flows of migrants are also influenced

by exogeneous factors which may be termed organizations. These
include the role of governments in developing policies which
guide, and in some cases direct populations to certain places. Also in
most societies ethnic associations perform an organizational role in the
movement and assimilation of migrants whilst hazards, in the form of
natural disasters as well as wars and political partition, give rise to
extensive migrations. These organizational forces can be conceived both
formally and informally. The merit of Swindell and Ford's framework
is that it emphasizes the interrelationship of several elements in the
migration process and that any explanation must focus on these
relationships.

Migration and Social Change

In this theme migration is conceived as an independent variable acting
as an agent of social change, thus the prime focus of attention is
upon the effects of migration on the places of origin and destination
as well as the migrants themselves. Several perspectives have been
developed to analyze this relationship and in order to illustrate
its complexity, three representative frameworks, with different
purposes and at different geographical scales, will be outlined
briefly.

   At a societal level Zelinsky (1971) has provided a framework for the
interpretation of the relationship between mobility and social change
within a broad temporal dimension. In his 'Hypothesis of the mobility
transition', Zelinsky claimed that 'there are definite, patterned
regularities in the growth of personal mobility through space-time
during recent history, and these regularities comprise an essential
component of the modernization process' (Zelinsky, 1971, 221–2).
His five-stage model links the mobility and vital transitions 'as a kind of
outward diffusion of successively more advanced forms of human
activity' (Zelinsky, 1971, 231). From Figure 2.5 it can be seen that in
the pre-modern traditional society, phase I, there occurs only limited
migration and circulation, with the whole society being spatially
restricted by customary practices. The next phase, the early transitional
society, is distinguished by a rapid rise in fertility and the consequential
population growth results in the emergence of widespread migration,
particularly rural to urban, the colonization of frontier lands, the
beginnings of emigration, and an increase in circulation. By the late
transitional society, or phase III, the reduced rate of natural increase is

Figure 2.5: Comparative Time Profiles of Spatial Mobility

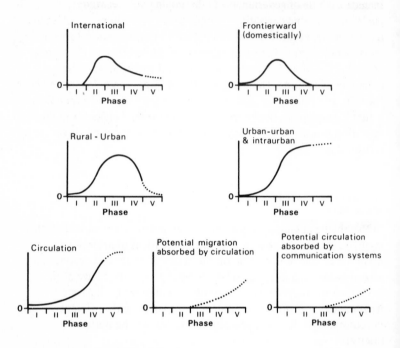

Source: After Zelinsky, 1971, 219–49.

accompanied by a slackening in the growth of the three types of
migration and an increase in the volume and complexity of the various
forms of circulation. These changes in mobility continue into the
fourth phase, the advanced society, during which natural increase is
limited as a result of a reduced fertility and mortality. This phase is
characterized by the replacement of rural to urban and settlement
migrations by those of inter-urban and intra-urban variety. Circulation
continues to increase in its intensity. The fifth phase, the future
advanced society, may be characterized by a general decline in
migration and will largely be of an inter-urban and intra-urban variety.
Some forms of circulation will decline and others increase. Since the
introduction of this hypotheses considerable discussion has taken
place as to the relationship between mobility and modernization; in
fact many have criticized this type of interpretation form, its Western
overtones and value judgements. However, Pryor (1971; 1975a) has
suggested that in the developing world it only has relevance if the

Figure 2.6: Migration and the Process of Modernization: a — the spatial structure of urbanization; b — an internal migration paradigm

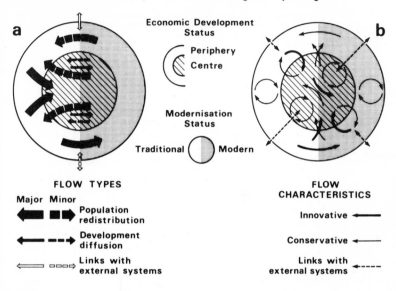

Source: After Pryor, 1975a, 23–38.

distinction between innovative and conservative migration is made. Then it may be seen that innovative and conservative migration involves differential movements between the traditional and modern sectors, and between the core and the periphery (Figure 2.6).

At the smaller scale of the community a different and more theoretical interpretation of the role of migration as an agent of social change has been suggested by Mangalam (1968) in his social organizational theory of the migration process. In this framework, a migration system within which the three elements of society of origin, society of destination and the migrants are conceived as being mutually interdependent. Each community undergoes a social change which is defined as the 'difference between social organisation of a given society at two different points in time, comprising changes in any or all the three component systems, namely the culture, social and personality systems' (Mangalam, 1968, 13). In this process migration takes place, immediately setting in motion a number of changes in the three component system of a social organization. In the scheme represented in Figure 2.7, community I has lost a number of persons and community II has gained them, thus effecting changes in the social

Figure 2.7: Migration and the Components of Community Change within a Time Perspective

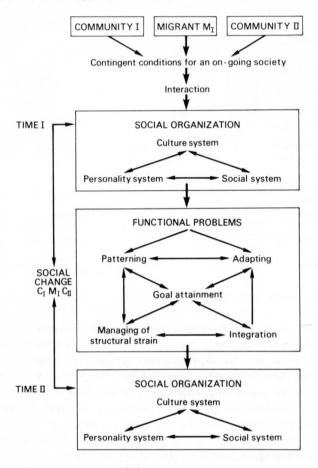

Source: Based on Mangalam, 1968.

organization and environmental conditions of both communities. At the same time the migrants (M), upon entry into community II experience a new set of environmental conditions. Therefore, within this framework migration is conceived as 'an adaptive process whose major objective is maintaining the dynamic equilibrium of a social organization with a minimum of change and at the same time providing those members ways to overcome their deprivation' (Mangalam, 1968, 15). A similar, yet a more spatial, perspective was adopted by Lewis

Figure 2.8: Migration and the Components of Social Change in the Countryside

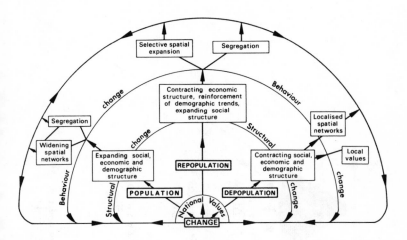

Source: After Lewis and Maund, 1976, 17–27.

and Maund (1976) in their attempt to establish a framework for
analyzing social change in the countryside. Within the past century,
the countryside of the advanced economies has undergone considerable
social change as a result of a series of distinctive population movements.
Firstly, there has been depopulation, which is effected by a net
outward migration on the population; secondly, the population of the
rural community may grow as a result of a net immigration of an
adventitious population at an early stage of the life cycle; and thirdly,
there is repopulation, which refers to the retirement to the countryside
by people at a late stage in the life cycle. The social selectivity of such
movements initiates changes within the communities involved:
structural, attitudinal and behavioural (Figure 2.8). The authors also
claim that such movements manifest themselves in a fairly clearly
identifiable space-time dimension (Figure 2.9). Within this framework,
changing residential aspirations and improvements in access to towns
and cities has brought about a re-evaluation of the countryside for
residence. As a result the three population movements occur in
different parts of the countryside at each successive time period,
although it is emphasized that they are present at all locations and it is
their relative proportions which vary with distance from an urban
centre. This simple framework has the advantage of not only

Figure 2.9: A Time-Space Perspective of Social Change in the Countryside

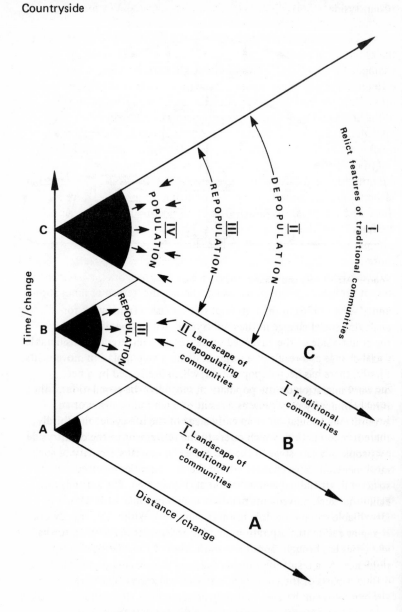

Source: After Lewis and Maund, 1976, 17–27.

identifying the relationship between different types of movement and social change but also that social change has a spatial dimension as a result of the spatial selectivity of the migration process.

At the individual level much of the focus of attention has been upon the assimilation process of the migrant into the host community. For example, Cerase (1974) has suggested that return migrants may be differentiated into three types on the basis of their level of assimilation into a host community. Firstly, there were those who failed to adjust in the host community and returned to their homeland as 'failed' migrants. It was hypothesized that these migrants are reabsorbed quickly into their home community and, therefore, their impact was a return of conservatism. The second group was composed of those who did not return until they had retired and their age precludes them from making any significant social or economic impact. Thirdly, there are those who return after some success in the host country and, therefore, are full of ambition and drive and ready to innovate within their home community. According to Cerase this is the 'return of innovation'. For those considering the impact of the returning 'foreign' workers, particularly in Europe and North Africa, this framework has some merit since it provides a means of assessing whether the 'return of innovation' is a myth or a reality.

A Systems Approach

The various approaches to the study of migration discussed so far has viewed the process as a uni-linear, cause-effect type of movement. However, such a perspective is exceedingly restrictive since it fails to emphasize that all components within the migration process are interrelated. A change in the nature of one component can have an effect upon all others (Porter, 1956). Such interrelationships can more easily be understood if migration is conceived as a system. Simply, a system is a complex of interacting elements, together with their attributes and relationships (Walmsley, 1973). Migration is then viewed as a circular, interdependent and self-modifying system in which the effects of changes in one part has a ripple effect throughout the whole system. By conceptualizing migration as a system it is therefore possible to identify the interacting elements, their attributes and their relationships.

In order to reveal the components of such a migration system a brief summary of the arguments contained in Mabogunje's paper, 'A

Figure 2.10: A Rural-Urban Migration System

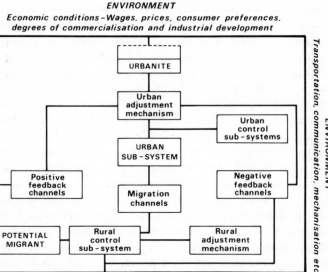

Source: After Mabogunje, 1970, 1–18.

systems approach to a theory of rural-urban migration' (1970), will be presented in the succeeding paragraphs. Although Mabogunje was concerned with rural-urban migration in Africa his conceptualization of the process in systems language has wider relevance (Figure 2.10). The *environment* of such a migration system is one where the rural communities are experiencing a break-up of their isolation and self-sufficiency. The main agent of this change is economic development which, in the majority of the African states, was initiated by the colonial administration and in recent years further reinforced by the activities of the newly independent nations. Increasingly the rural economy is being integrated into the national economy, resulting in changes in wage and price levels as well as levels of expectation and demand in the countryside. The villager becomes more aware of the greater range of opportunities the cities provide and, therefore, such an environment determines the extent and nature of the migration.

A migration system is made up of three basic *elements*. Firstly, there is the potential migrant who is encouraged to leave the rural village by stimuli from the environment. Secondly, there are the various institutions, or *control* sub-systems, which determine the level of flow within the system. In the rural-urban migration system the two most important sub-systems are the rural and urban control systems. In the rural area the nuclear and extended family, and the local community, by means of the various activities which it sponsors, can act both in a positive and negative way in determining the volume of migration. On the other hand, the urban control system determines, by means of occupational and residential opportunities, the degree of assimilation into the urban environment. Thirdly, there are the various social, economic and political forces, or *adjustment mechanisms*, which play a significant role in the process of a migrant's transformation. The act of migration sets in motion a series of adjustments both in the village and the city. Within the rural area it involves a loss of one productive unit as well as one member of family and community life, whilst in the city the migrant is incorporated to a new situation more relevant to his needs.

All systems contain a driving force, or *energy*, and in the case of the rural-urban migration system it can be likened to the stimuli acting on the rural individual to move. This involves not only a recognition of such stimuli but also the differential responses of rural dwellers to the stimuli. Mabogunje argues that, in the case of Africa, the stimulus to migrate is 'related to the degree of the integration of the rural economy into the national economy, to the degree of awareness of opportunities outside of the rural areas, and to the nature of the social and economic expectations held by the rural population' (Mabogunje, 1970, 14). In systems language, this is what is called *potential energy* and upon moving it is translated into *kinetic energy*. The actual migration raises questions of the cost and constraints of the movement since these determine the channels and patterns of the migration.

Once a rural dweller has migrated to the city his role in the system does not end because by means of a feedback of information to his original village he can modify the system's behaviour. Without the feedback through time the distribution of migrants from a village will become proportional to the size of the city in question. In other words, the system has no order or organization, and can be said to be in a state of *maximum entropy* (or disorder); that is, in the most predictable state. When the rural migrant maintains contact with his home, the feedback information can be either negative or favourable about life in the city. In the former case the migration to the city will slow down to a trickle whilst the latter will encourage a regular migration from particular villages to particular cities. Therefore, the existence of information in the system tends to encourage either a decrease in the level of entropy (or disorder) or an increase in negative entropy.

Although the migration system presented here is one designed specifically to aid an understanding of rural to urban migration in West Africa, it does, however, provide an additional insight and breadth to the migration process in general. It identifies the prime components, and their interrelatedness, involved in the process, as well as emphasizing its circular nature in that the effects of changes in one part can be traced through the whole system. In addition, such a system emphasizes the point that we should be concerned not only with why people migrate but also all the implications and ramifications of the process.

From the various interpretations of the different types of migration, in particular Mabogunje's rural-urban migration system, it is evident that a number of significant questions are raised and need answers. These questions will form the basis of the succeeding chapters.

1. What are the spatial patterns of migration? (Chapter 4)
2. How does time influence migration? (Chapter 5)
3. Who are the migrants? (Chapter 6)
4. Why do people migrate? (Chapter 7)
5. How do people decide to migrate? (Chapter 8)
6. How do organizations influence migration? (Chapter 9)
7. What are the consequences of migration? (Chapter 10)

As a backcloth to these themes the next chapter will consider some of the principal migratory flows within a time-space perspective.

3 MIGRATION IN TIME AND SPACE

The migration of people is as old as mankind; but during recorded history migration not only has increased in volume, but also the distances involved have steadily lengthened. As Haggett (1965, 42) has put so succinctly 'rapidly increasing mobility is one of the dominant features of movement this century. Mean fields for the movement of information, population, and goods have grown steadily larger as technical innovations have reduced the relative cost of distance'. Movements beyond the locality have by now become general and several moves in a lifetime is common for many people (Zelinsky, 1971). The watershed between a stable, immobile society and a highly mobile one was, of course, the onset of the Industrial Revolution, particularly from the late eighteenth century onwards. Prior to that date individuals lived in a spatially restricted world; they migrated little beyond their locality and their whole existence was circumscribed by the tyranny of distance. With the technological changes wrought by the Industrial Revolution, spatial horizons widened to include not only distant industrial growth centres but also foreign countries. These changes which, initially, involved Britain and Western Europe have now spread to encompass virtually the whole world. Some of these changing patterns of migration will now be considered in greater detail under two headings: international and internal.

International Migrations

Although today world migration is relatively insignificant in comparison to internal migration, it is still, however, worthy of consideration on at least two counts: firstly, the distribution of world population owes much to the migrations of the people in the past and, secondly, for the individual migrant it can be a dramatic experience since it can involve the abandonment of relatives and lifelong friends, national loyalties, and even cultural heritage and customs.

As far back as prehistoric times peoples and ideas spread from the cradles of civilization in Asia westward into Europe and eastwards to the Americas, as well as infiltrating Africa and the Mediterranean basin. However, since *circa* 1600 a bewildering series of migratory flows has

33

Figure 3.1: Major World Migrations since 1600

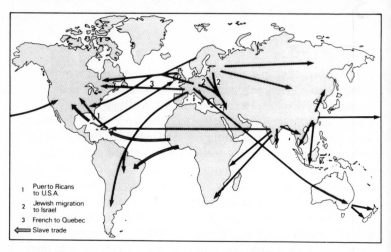

1 Puerto Ricans
   to U.S.A.
2 Jewish migration
   to Israel
3 French to Quebec
⇐ Slave trade

developed which involves the whole world (Figure 3.1). Several of these
streams involved peoples from Europe, which has been the source of
migrants for the opening up of the Americas, Australia and New
Zealand. In fact, Europe has generated more migratory movements in
the last 200 years than any other part of the world. It has been
estimated that between 1846 and 1935 an annual total of three per
thousand of the European population emigrated, which amounts to
something in the region of 60 million people, with over a half having
settled in North America (Figure 3.2).

Since 1935 the world migration of peoples has changed its character
quite markedly (OECD, 1975). The introduction of quota restrictions
on migrants by the majority of the world's nations has reduced to a
trickle the number of international migrants, although those countries
in need of labour have allowed some immigration of workers on a
temporary basis. Paralleling this decline in voluntary migration has been
an increase in the numbers of those forced to migrate because of wars
and political persecution (George, 1976). These changes will now be
considered briefly.

Since the early years of this century the majority of nations have
progressively restricted immigration by introducing legal restrictions
on movement. The most severe of these are those introduced by the
developed countries as a means of reducing the immigration of peoples
from the third world (George, 1976). For example, the United States
in 1921 introduced the first of the quota laws which fixed the

Figure 3.2: European Emigration to the United States of America, 1820–1914

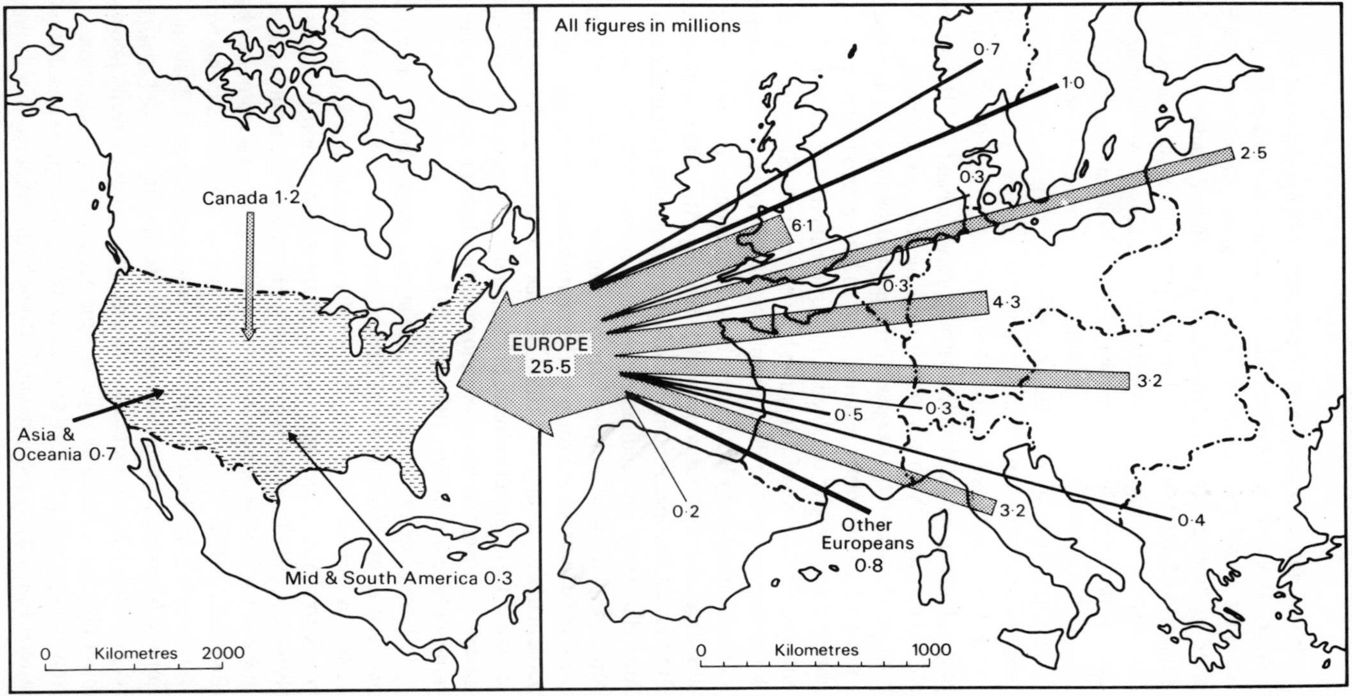

All figures in millions

2·5

1·0

0·7

0·3

6·1

0·3

4·3

3·2

0·3

0·5

0·4

3·2

0·2

Other Europeans 0·8

EUROPE 25·5

Canada 1·2

Mid & South America 0·3

Asia & Oceania 0·7

0   1000
Kilometres

0   2000
Kilometres

permitted annual admissions at 3 per cent of the population of each
country as represented in the United States at the 1910 census.
Australia is even more selective of its immigrants since preference is
given to Anglo-Saxons who are relatively young, skilled and with the
physical and intellectual qualities to adjust to a new environment. So
dramatic has been the effect of these restrictions on world migration
that 'almost everywhere in the world, since 1960 international
migration is a comparatively insignificant component in population
growth or change in population composition' (Bogue, 1969, 801). As a
result of this decline in world migration certain new trends have, by
today, begun to emerge (United Nations, 1978). Only the United
States, Canada, Israel, Brazil, Australia, New Zealand and Hong Kong
still admit migrants for permanent settlement in any numbers. In
contrast those countries experiencing population pressure, as well as
those with communistic regimes, tend to have a zero or near zero
immigration. Despite the decline in world migration Europe still
remains the fulcrum of migration between nations. Since the Second
World War nearly 10 million people have left Western Europe, about a
half originating from Britain and Italy. Interestingly language affinities
still affect the direction movements: the majority of the Anglo-Saxons
and Central Europeans continue to emigrate to North America and
Australia, whilst the Mediterranean emigrants go mainly to Latin
America. A smaller counterstream of immigrants can also be identified:
these include those returning to their native lands, those admitted,
particularly in the case of Britain, France and the Netherlands, by
reason of their former colonial origins, and those encouraged to enter
Europe by governments and employers, on a temporary basis, as a
result of labour shortages (Böhning, 1972).

In Europe labour migration is a relatively recent phenomenon, yet it
has been an established part of African society for generations (Board,
1976). In West and East Africa it involves a circular movement from
village to city and back again to the village within a short time-span
(Prothero, 1957), whilst in southern Africa there have been massive
flows to the centres of mining and manufacturing on a temporary basis
(Swindell, 1979). What is of particular interest since the Second World
War, however, has been the growth in labour migration in Western
Europe. Migrants were encouraged to fill temporary labour gaps, by
staying for a few years and then leaving again. Nobody really knows the
exact number involved at any one time because labour migration
statistics are only produced nationally and each country uses different
criteria to define a labour migrant. It has been estimated that during the

early seventies there were some 15 million labour migrants in Western
Europe, the majority of whom stayed a short period since they
returned home when their contracts expired (Böhning, 1979). To many
of these migrants such contracts are a means of aiding their families at
home, or to earn money to buy land or businesses (Rhoades, 1978).
The majority of the West European migrants come from the outlying
parts of Europe — southern Italy, Greece, Turkey and Yugoslavia — and
Algeria and Tunisia in North Africa (*Sunday Times*, 1973). It is
generally agreed that 1973 was a watershed in labour migration in
Western Europe because the oil crisis and the ensuing depression led to
a sharp decline in the demand for labour. As a result only a few new
migrants have arrived, and many have returned to their native lands.
This can be exemplified from the Italian Federation of Migrant Workers
estimate that in the first half of 1975 over 250,000 migrants had
returned home from West Germany and Switzerland alone (Power and
Hardman, 1976, 10).

  Within the international context, since 1935 the voluntary
movement described so far has been overshadowed by a vast amount
of involuntary migration. These people have been forced to migrate
out of necessity for fear of their lives, or because of loss of opportunity
of earning a living. Such migrations have been a consequence of war or
of internal political upheavals in which particular groups of citizens
were declared unwelcome and were ordered to leave or in which
individuals with divergent political beliefs or ethnic backgrounds fled
to escape living under a new regime. Of course, 'population transfer' or
'repatriation' is not a new phenomenon; probably the most notorious
being the African slave trade, it having been estimated that some 20
million Africans were deported to North America and another 10 to 15
million to the east as part of the Arab and Hindu slave trade (Figure
3.1). For the period 1935 to 1955, Cook (1957) has estimated that
something like 55 million people were forced to leave their homelands
in search of political or economic stability. To comprehend the
magnitude of this movement, it might be noted that the total number
of immigrants to the United States from all nations of the world during
the 145 years from 1820 to 1965 was about 43 million. Among those
involved in forced migrations since the thirties include millions of Jews
who fled Hitler's Germany for other countries in Europe as well as
North America. After the end of the Second World War in the Pacific
about 3 million Japanese were returned by decree to Japan from
Manchuria, Korea, Taiwan and the islands in the western Pacific. In
1947 the independence of India and the partition of Pakistan provoked

Figure 3.3: The Flows of Vietnamese Refugees in Southeast Asia, 1975–79. The figures exclude approximately 300,000 refugees resettled elsewhere

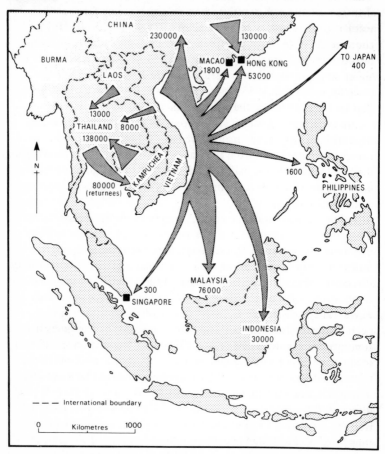

7 million Muslims to flee from India to Pakistan and more than 8½ million Hindus fled from Pakistan to India. Even in more recent times the process of forced migration still continues, for example, the expulsion of Asians from Uganda in 1974 and the Vietnamese 'boat-people' (Figure 3.3). There are still many tense situations that could break out into new expulsions.

Internal Migrations

Whilst international migration has, in general, attenuated in its significance, internal migration has continued to increase in both volume and distance. High mobility rates characterize most developed countries. For the United States it has been estimated that at least one-fifth of its population moves in any one year, whereas for Australia about 40 per cent of people aged over 5 years changed their usual place of residence between 1966 and 1971, a rate slightly lower than that for England and Wales.

Prior to industrialization migrations took place when individuals were compelled to increase the extent of the lands which they occupied, either because of increasing numbers or increasing needs. If the best lands were already occupied migrants tended to settle in more inhospitable locales, as for example in thirteenth-century Europe migrants were forced to occupy higher and higher slopes of the western Alps. By late medieval times in Britain certain new migratory trends were evident; for example, there was an increasing shift of the population to the better agricultural lands of the midlands and south as well as the growing market towns and regional centres (Patten, 1976). The emergence of a highly mobile society, however, came when Europe was transformed into a modern technical society by the Industrial Revolution from the late eighteenth century onwards. Briefly, the exploitation of the coalfields and the development of machines which concentrated into factories the work formerly done by dozens of scattered craftsmen, caused people to begin leaving the countryside for the growing urban and industrial centres (Redford, 1926; Lawton, 1967). This process began in Britain during the first half of the nineteenth century and then spread rapidly to other countries in Western Europe and North America (Friedlander, 1970). At the same time local migrations were also increasing in volume and diversity (Perry, 1969); for example, from birthplace evidence it has been shown that in a part of rural Wales during the mid-nineteenth century several migratory streams were developing (Lewis, 1979a): namely moves to a local lead and zinc mining industry, agricultural migrations, and movements generated by marriage and housing (Figure 3.4).

In the 'new lands' the process of settlement was still taking place during the nineteenth century. From decade to decade there were continuous waves of immigrants who overcame considerable obstacles in their occupation of new territory (Hudson, 1970). In North America the picture of the pioneer fringe moving progressively

Figure 3.4: Migrations to a Group of Rural Parishes in Wales, 1851 and 1871. The data source is the birthplaces of the head of household

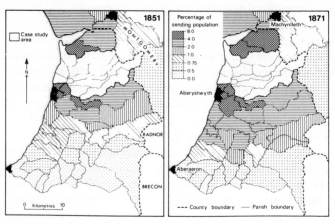

Source: After Lewis, 1979, 347–61.

westward across the vast expanse of the Middle West is an impressive one, '. . . stand at the Cumberland Gap and watch the procession of civilization, marching single file — the buffalo following the trail to the salt springs, the Indian, the fur trader and hunter, the cattle raiser, the pioneer farmer — and the frontier has passed by. Stand at the South Pass in the Rockies a century later and see the same procession with wider intervals between' (Turner, 1920, 12).

In general, rural to urban migration in Western Europe and North America has continued until recent times, no doubt reflecting the accelerating decline in the agricultural labour force since 1945 (Salt and Clout, 1976; Roseman, 1977). However, by the late fifties this rural exodus had been numerically balanced by an influx of town dwellers, thereby initiating a whole series of changes in the migratory movements of people in Western countries. In Britain rural decline began to show signs of attenuating during the fifties (Saville, 1957, 41). Although predominantly agricultural districts still suffered a fall in population as a result of a continuation in the contraction of the agricultural labour force, the decline was, however, beginning to exhibit signs of levelling off because of the reduction in the size of the population from which migrants came. By the mid-sixties those rural districts adjacent to major cities and conurbations experienced a population growth whilst the central cities themselves suffered a net outflow of migrants (Champion, 1976; Lind, 1969; Fielding, 1971).

According to Friedlander and Roshier (1966) small towns also
gained heavily through migration from larger centres during the
1960s. These trends reflected not only an increasing divorce between
place of work and residence, but also residential mobility consequent
upon the stages of family formation and retirement as well as the
decentralization of industrial and office employment (Hollingsworth,
1970, 39). Interestingly, in the United States the 1950s was the
first decade in its history when there occurred an absolute decline
in rural numbers (Morrison and Wheeler, 1976), but this trend
has been considered only a temporary reversal because 'of the
expansion of the rural non-farm population and the impending
reduction of the farm population to its absolute lower limit' (Zelinsky,
1962, 497). In Canada, on the other hand, migration from overseas has
been of major significance in maintaining a positive balance of net
migration to metropolitan areas (Kalbach, 1970, 100). Generally,
however, migration has been of declining significance in the growth of
cities in developed countries (United Nations, 1973, 159) because of
the reduction in international migration, the relatively small volume of
rural-urban migrants, and the spread of urbanization beyond
metropolitan boundaries. These trends were most striking in Australia
between 1966 and 1976 (Rowland, 1979). Of all migrations during this
period 95 per cent were over short distances, including movements
within cities and between cities and their surrounding rural areas. For
example, the cities of New South Wales and Victoria lost population to
their adjacent rural districts, whilst at the same time the rural districts
themselves were experiencing a net loss to the smaller urban centres
(Jarvie and Browett, 1980). But the most striking feature of migration
trends in Australia between 1966 and 1976 was the role played by the
state capitals as origins and destinations of inter-state migrants (McKay
and Whitelaw, 1978). Even these movements, however, were
constrained by the 'frictional effect' of distance; for example, there was
a higher exchange of migrants between New South Wales and
Queensland than between Queensland and Victoria. The only other
migratory flows of significance involved the mineral exploitation in the
north and west, the development of coastal resorts, and the growth of
the Australian Capital Territory.

On the basis of such evidence Bogue (1969) has concluded that
since the Second World War the majority of the developed countries
were experiencing two major migratory movements:

1. A massive exodus of persons from low income rural and

economically depressed areas towards the great metropolises where new employment opportunities and new economic growth are concentrated.

2. A massive exodus of persons from the core of the metropolitan centre to the periphery. Modern metropolises all over the world seem to be suburbanizing rapidly while population densities at their centre are declining (Bogue, 1969, 773).

So far the discussion has been restricted to that of the developed world; henceforth the emphasis will be on developing countries. Until recently migration in these countries has not been the subject of rigorous and sustained research and, therefore, generalizations have to be exceedingly tentative (Elizaga, 1965; Prothero, 1968). Despite a certain degree of industrialization and a rapid population growth, migration still only involves a small proportion of their population. For example, in India the overwhelming majority of its population still spend their entire life in or near their place of birth. In 1921 only 10 per cent of its population were enumerated outside the district of their birth, a figure which rose to nearly 14 per cent by 1971 (Zachariah, 1964; Gosal and Krishan, 1975). However, it must be emphasized that these are relative figures; in absolute terms the number of migrants beyond their district of birth was in excess of 70 million. Inter-state and inter-district migration formed only 16 per cent of India's migrants, thus emphasizing the relative insignificance of long-distance movements. Where these migrations have occurred it usually involved some form of major economic development, such as newly developed agricultural lands, the growth of mining activity and associated industries, and, of course, major cities. Yet, surprisingly, only about 15 per cent of all migrants moved from the countryside to the major cities, and those involved in urban to urban migration amounted to only 7 per cent. Local moves, that is intra-district migration, are by far the most significant in contemporary India and, interestingly, it has been suggested that over three-quarters of these moves were the result of marriage (Connell *et al.*, 1976). In fact, 73 per cent of all migrants moved within rural areas, thus illustrating the continuing agricultural and village base of Indian society. Similar migratory trends can be identified elsewhere in the developing world. It has been estimated that between 1955 and 1960 only 4 per cent of Thailand's population changed their place of residence (Ng, 1969, 710–30). Urbanward migration, mainly to the capital, Bangkok, and rural-rural migration, particularly involving the agriculturally rich Upper Chao Phyo Plain, are

Figure 3.5: Migration in Thailand, 1955–60: a — percentage population change by net internal migration; b — major migration outflow from each province

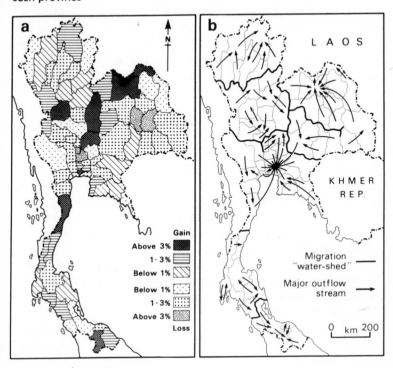

Source: After Ng, 1969, 710–30.

of equal significance (Figure 3.5). However, recent rural to urban migration has involved a greater share of the migrants, both permanent and seasonal; the latter often representing a circular movement from village to city and back to village. Similarly, in Ghana the annual rate of migration has been increasing, and now stands at about 5 per cent of the total population per annum (Caldwell, 1969). Although the principal stream in 1970 was still directed to the cocoa farms and gold mines, the rural to urban movement was involving an increasing share of the population. Such migrations tend to take two forms: temporary movements, which are particularly characteristic of the immigrants from adjacent countries, and seasonal movements, which are favoured by the internal migrants. The growing significance of net rural to urban migration has led Caldwell (1969) to predict an increase in long-term internal migration, greater family movements and a general decline in seasonal migration. The available evidence suggests that modernization has generated tremendous pressures for urbanward migration. Only the lack of industry and the initiation of rural development programmes is preventing an even more sweeping rural-urban migration in the majority of developing countries (Amin, 1974).

Bearing in mind the limited available evidence, Bogue has, however, tentatively suggested that internal migration in developing countries is of three basic types:

> 1. In most of the developing nations, the largest principal political, commercial and industrial centres are enjoying moderate to rapid growth, both as a result of high fertility and of net in-migration. However, wholesale exodus from rural areas to principal urban centres has not materialized.
> 2. An amazingly high proportion of the rapidly accumulating 'surplus population' in the developing nations appears to be staying in the rural village areas and is struggling to exist through more intensive cultivation of the land.
> 3. Whenever significant industrial and commercial expansion does take place, an immediate stream of migration ensues. Much of this migration results in failure and in return to the place of origin. (Bogue, 1969, 775)

Spatial Patterns

In his analysis of migration trends in Britain and other European countries during the late nineteenth century, Ravenstein (1885; 1889) identified several spatial biases in the pattern of migratory flows. In particular, he emphasized the predominance of short-distance moves, as well as directional biases towards the major centres of employment. More often than not these moves involved individuals in a series of short-distance moves in the direction of the employment centres, thus producing over time a wave-like pattern. Any short-circuiting of distance usually involved major cities and metropolitan centres. From our review of contemporary internal migration in both the developed and developing world many of these spatial biases are still apparent today. In other words, the spatial structure of migratory flows persist in both time and space, irrespective of levels of economic development and the mobility of the population. These spatial biases have been

Figure 3.6: Hypothetical Migration Fields

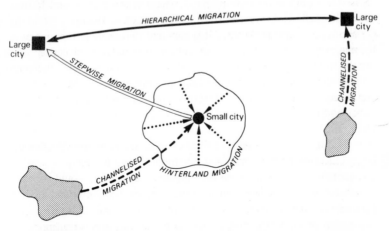

summarized and represented diagrammatically in Figure 3.6, where
moves to and from cities of different sizes are depicted. Essentially
what is shown is what Hägerstrand (1957) has called a migration field,
i.e. 'the geographic area that sends major migration flows to a given
place (e.g. a city, metropolitan area or country), or that area that
receives major flows from a place' (Jakle, Roseman and Brunn, 1976,
165). Let us now consider in greater detail some of the principal spatial
biases depicted in Figure 3.6.
(1) Despite variations in their economic background the people of both
the developed and developing world still migrate only short distances.
In other words, the level of migration between any two places will be
greater the closer they are located one to another. This concentration
of local moves means that any city, village or suburb has a surrounding
locality, or hinterland, from which it receives as well as sends the
majority of its migrants. Such short-distance moves result from the
'frictional' effect of distance upon knowledge of available opportunities
as well as movement costs. The flow of this information is related to
the structure of the lower levels of the urban system since local and
regional media sources provide information about potential migration
destinations within the immediate region. For example, during the
mid-nineteenth century it was estimated that in a series of small
parishes in rural Wales migration was largely circumscribed within a
radius of about eight miles (Lewis, 1979a). Similarly today, the most
widespread form of migration in the developed countries involves
residential changes within cities and between cities and their peripheries.

Even within the countryside local moves still predominate, as
illustrated from the Welsh Borderland, where between 1966 and 1976
over half of all moves were of short distance (Lewis, 1981a).
(2) From the available evidence it is apparent that there is a tendency
for migrants to move progressively from smaller to larger places: a
feature similar to Ravenstein's conclusion that during the late nineteenth
century there was 'a universal shifting or displacement of the
population, which produces currents of migration settling in the
direction of the great centres of commerce and industry' (Ravenstein,
1885, 198). This progressive series of moves to larger places is known as
stepwise migration. Evidence of the existence of moves from smaller to
larger places in the developed and developing world is largely
contradictory. Compared with the nineteenth century it would appear
today that in the developed world moves beyond the hinterland have
become ones over long or medium distances. Once again this reflects
the impact of the burgeoning of mass communication and transport
technology, which widen the horizons of the individual and make
stepwise moves less significant. For example, in Australia the only form
of stepwise movement is one down the urban hierarchy. Support for
this form of migratory flow was evident in Britain between 1961 and
1971, when large cities lost population at the expense of smaller ones.
This evidence gives some support, albeit indirect, that there is a
universal shifting of people out of the city centre, and down the urban
hierarchy. On a micro-scale a similar pattern of migration has occurred
within and without the city of Leicester (Lewis, 1981b). Between 1966
and 1971, the major migratory flows have been out of the inner city to
the suburbs and beyond; in fact, the greatest in-migration taking place
in the adjacent villages and hamlets. In this instance the process
involved is very different to that envisaged in Ravenstein's conception
of stepwise migration since the theme here is that of a decanting of
employment and peoples from the metropolitan areas and major cities.
With the improvements in transport people are able to live at greater
distances from their place of work. This reverses the process initiated
during the nineteenth century (Conway, 1980). These trends must not
be overemphasized, however, since in the developing world stepwise
migration is still evident. A case study from Sierra Leone neatly
illustrates the nature of this movement (Riddell and Harvey, 1972).
From a comparison of the idealized and actual stepwise migration flow
pattern it was concluded that the two agree for only a limited number
of regions in the country. A number of reasons accounted for these
differences. Some of the centres were so close to the capital, Freetown,

that migrants were able to bypass the intermediate-sized centres. In other regions the urban system was so weakly developed that the movements became almost random and the effect of the diamond fields in Kono was to distort some of the flow toward that area. Finally, in some regions poor accessibility detracted from the attractiveness of centres in those regions. Clearly this type of evidence emphasizes the fact that a number of influences can distort stepwise migration, even in countries with a poor transport system and a weakly developed media network. Yet, beneath the distortions identified in Sierra Leone there did exist a definite shift of population in the direction of larger places.

(3) In both developed and developing countries certain migrations short-circuited the distance bias by involving more distant major cities and metropolitan centres. Also there were moves between major cities and between distant regions. Numerous terms have been coined to describe this form of migration, including inter-regional and hierarchical migration. The importance of other cities in the migration fields of all cities was clearly identifiable in the migratory flows within Australia between 1966 and 1976. Similar evidence is to be found in such countries as Britain where between 1961 and 1971 urban to urban migration was by far the most significant migratory stream (Lind, 1969). Essentially, this type of migration involves moves between major cities as well as those up and down the urban hierarchy. Like that of hinterland migration, many of these movements are related to the flow of information. In this instance the urban hierarchy structures the flow of information through the media and, therefore, the knowledge individuals have about places and opportunities. In general, the larger the place the greater the likelihood of an individual having knowledge about it and of coming into contact or communicating with another individual with experience of that city.

(4) Plenty of evidence exists to suggest that distance is often short-circuited by what has become known as channelized or chain migration (MacDonald and MacDonald, 1964). Large numbers of people through time migrate from, say, a small rural area to the same city, often bypassing opportunities nearby. The basis of this type of migration is inter-personal influence among relatives and friends. Once an individual has moved to a city he will be in contact with those still back home, thus increasing their information about the opportunities in that city. Also the city is more attractive because the early migrant can provide assistance with gaining employment and, generally, assist in the adjustment process. Numerous examples of this form of migration exist

from different parts of the world. Hillery and Brown (1965, 47) have shown that the

> southern Appalachians is not a region in the sense of its parts belonging to the same migration system. Rather it is a collection of fringes, or, as it has often been put, of backyards which are connected to non-Appalachian areas, often distant cities, as a result of migration. The kinship structure provides a highly persuasive line of communication between kinsfolk in the home and the new community which channels information about available job opportunities, and living standards directly . . . [to rural] families. Thus, kinship linkage tends to direct migrants to those areas where their groups are already established.

Even movements across international boundaries often reveal similar lines of channelization; for example, the Asian immigrants in Leicester originate from specific districts within the Indian states of Punjab and Gujarat (Lewis, 1981b). Closely allied to chain migration is the tendency for migrants to return to their home areas. Again at an international scale, temporary foreign workers in France and West Germany return home when their contracts expire and, even among the more permanent migrants, there is a tendency to return home either at retirement or when sufficient capital has been accumulated.

This chapter has outlined, albeit briefly, some of the world's migratory trends, both in the past and present. Essentially, it has emphasized that through time migration has increased and the distances involved lengthened. More and more people move in search of jobs and housing and many move several times during their lives. Yet, throughout these changing migratory trends the spatial component of the flows have remained relatively constant. It is, therefore, to a consideration of the role of space and time in the migration process that we must now turn in the succeeding two chapters.

4   SPATIAL ASPECTS

In the preceding chapter a wide variety of empirical evidence illustrated the tendency, suggested by Zelinsky (1971) in his theory of 'Mobility Transition', for migration to increase in a regular fashion both in time and space. As far back as Ravenstein's (1885, 1889) seminal work geographers have been interested in the spatial aspects of the migration process (Gale, 1973; Brummell, 1979). Until recently considerable effort has been expended in modelling the migration process, particularly in the form of an analogy with physical interaction, which uses some derivation of distance and the other indices of the relative attractiveness of origin and destination (Weeden, 1973). Although the forces prompting migration are based upon individual circumstances and individual responses to change in the milieu, these gravity and spatial interaction models are concerned with an aggregate of people, rather than individuals (see Chapters 6, 7, 8). The purpose of spatial modelling has been to describe and explain patterns of migration as 'functions of structural parameters such as distance, size and interconnectiveness of places and intervening opportunities between alternative destinations' (Shaw, 1975, 41).

Distance

Traditionally, distance has been viewed as a barrier to migratory movements and, therefore, it would be expected that the probability of migration between two places diminishes as distance increases. The evidence provided in the previous chapter in the form of hinterland migration from both the past and present emphasizes the significance of distance in determining migration flows. Over the past three decades a plethora of studies have attempted to describe more precisely this distance component in the migration process (Morrill, 1960). At a simple level, the migration-distance relationship may be expressed as:

$$M = PD$$

where: M = migration interaction D = distance

Figure 4.1: The Relationship between Migration and Distance for
(a) 1860-69 and (b) 1930-39 in Asby parish, Sweden. The distance
exponent for the earlier time period was 3.0 and for the latter 2.4

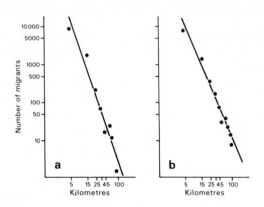

Source: After Hägerstrand, 1957, 27-158.

Upon closer inspection it is evident, however, that spatially migration
can be viewed in two ways; firstly, as movement between a point and a
group of surrounding points; and secondly, as movement between a
whole group of points within a defined area. In order to measure the
migration-distance relationship it is, of course, necessary to determine
the distances migrated and to sum them in a frequency distribution.
However, the analysis is complicated by the fact that distance can be
measured in a number of ways. The conventional measure is simply that
of a straight line between two points. But Huff (1960) has stressed that
the migrant's view of remoteness and distance may not be so simple;
in fact, he argues that a migrant tends to regard nearby areas as strongly
differentiated and remote areas as uniform. Similarly, Hägerstrand
(1957) has suggested that the economic and psychological view of
distance may be generalized within a logarithmitic transformation of
distance, whilst Gould and White (1968) have shown how perceived
distance differs markedly from Euclidean distance. Despite these
differing interpretations of the distance component, the inverse
distance rule is by now a well established generalization within
migration studies. For example, Figure 4.1 illustrates the relationship
between migration and distance for two periods, 1860-69 and 1930-39,
in the small community of Asby in Sweden (Hägerstrand, 1957). This
evidence reveals the operation of the inverse distance rule at two

different historical time periods as well as the tendency for migration fields to become larger as more people move over longer distances. It has also been established that the migration-distance relationship differs for various social groups. For example, Ravenstein (1885) stated that men moved longer distances than females; Rose (1958) found that higher-status people moved longer average distances; Friedlander and Roshier (1966) observed that skilled persons were inclined to move farther than unskilled; and Tarver (1964) identified significant differences in moves over three distance zones, among various occupational groups. The selectivity of migration will be considered in greater detail in Chapter 6.

Having established a relationship between migration levels and distance there still remains the problem as to how it can be adequately explained. Certainly a part of the explanation lies in the fact that movement costs increase with the distance migrated, whilst barriers such as mountains, rivers, etc, can add to this cost. Some researchers have also suggested the operation of a drag-like effect of social ties. For example, Tolley (1963) distinguished between short-distance moves (below 100 miles) where social ties can be maintained, inter-regional moves (between 100 and 1,000 miles) where ties are broken but since it is often a similar environment new social ties can easily be developed, and long-distance moves (over 1,000 miles), which involves moves to a different environment. Many researchers have also argued that migration distances are strongly influenced by biases in information levels. Most individuals' information tends to be locally biased since it is closely related to individual day-to-day activities, thus providing the basis for a link between information and migration. Hägerstrand (1957) conceptualized the tendency to communicate over distance by the introduction of a mean information field. Thus if an information field can be established independently of migration it can presumably be used to predict migration just as readily as the migration field can be used to predict information flow.

Direction

In the previous chapter it was observed that migration flows not only declined with distance but also contained a directional bias. In other words any migration field or channel was oriented towards some specific destination or node. In view of the geographical significance of this tendency a battery of techniques have been developed by geographers and regional scientists to measure its intensity and extent.

In view of the profusion of the literature on this theme only a limited range of the methodologies will be mentioned here; for a more detailed consideration see Bachi (1963) and Willis (1974).

Using a simple measure of centre of gravity, Bachi (1965) traced, in the United States, the shift caused by inter-state migration between the centre of birth and centre of place of residence of migrants at different dates. The average birthplace-current residence move in 1870 was 582 km, rising to 641 km in 1890, falling to 442 km in 1940 but rising again to 482 km in 1950. The main direction of the shift had constantly been to the west. Similarly, Johnston (1966) measured the changing centre of gravity of high-status residence in Melbourne over several decades, the results of which confirmed their localization to a particular part of the urban area. For the period 1955–60, Wolpert (1967) computed the median centres of in-migration, out-migration and net-migration for 506 State Economic Areas in the United States. By use of measures of central tendency it was revealed that specific nodes in migration fields operated as principal receivers. In two separate studies Tarver and his associates (1967 and 1970) calculated in- and out-migration vectors using polar co-ordinates which show the average distance of movements per migration and the direction and magnitude of movement.

At an intra-urban scale an interesting recent development has been the use of standard ellipses to compute the shape and size of migration fields. Following the lead of Clark (1971) and Whitelaw and Robinson (1972), Balderson (1981) has computed the migration fields of inner city and suburban residents of Leicester. By comparing the present with the former residence it was possible by means of the size and shape of the ellipsoid to determine the directional bias of the two sample groups. The small and circular form of the inner city residents ellipse, emphasized the local nature of their movements; on the other hand, the surburbanites had a larger and more elongated shaped ellipse, illustrating a wider spread of movements which was sectorally biased.

The great majority of the attempts to interpret these biases have, like the distance decay one, emphasized a relationship with knowledge and information. For example, at an intra-urban scale, it has been argued by Adams (1969) that this directional bias is dependent to a large extent on the migrant household's image of the urban area. On the basis of an analysis of migration within Minneapolis over the periods 1890–95, 1920–25 and 1946–51, Adams claims that the individual builds up and retains a relatively narrow image of the city which is sharply in focus for the area within which he carries out his daily and weekly activities. On a regional and national scale the directional bias would be related to more indirect contacts, particularly relatives, friends and the mass media (Gold, 1980).

Gravity Concept

The isolation of the distance and directional biases in migration flows is in some ways unreal, in the sense that the two are related and, in turn, cannot be divorced from the distribution of opportunities. Therefore, it is little wonder that the greater part of the geographical analysis of migration has been involved with attempts to interrelate distance and gravity factors (ter Heide, 1963; Taylor, 1975). Much of this approach is summarized in Zipf's 'least effort principle' which postulates that 'inter-community movement between any two communities P_1 and P_2 that are separated by an easiest transport distance D will be directly proportionate to the product P_1 and P_2 and inversely proportionate to the distance D' (Zipf, 1946, 685). According to Carrothers (1956), the first attempt to operationalize the gravity concept was Ravenstein's (1885) study of migration flows between English cities. Destinations were treated as centres of absorption, and volumes of migratory movement were shown to decrease with increasing distance between a given origin and destination. The concept has subsequently been formulated in several ways, although basically it can be summarised as follows:

$$M_{ij} = K \frac{P_i P_j}{d_{ij}} b$$

where

    M = migration from place i to j
    P = population at places i and j
    d = distance between places i and j
    K and b = a constant relating volume of migration at any specific time

According to Olsson (1965) a significant advantage of the gravity concept over that of distance alone is the implicit incorporation into the equation of the distribution of available opportunities. Since the number of employment opportunities is often correlated with the size of the place, population is used as an operational substitute for alternative destinations. A vast literature, beginning with Young's (1924) study of family population migration in the United States, exists on the testing of the gravity hypothesis but, unfortunately, it fails to reach a satisfactory conclusion as to its adequacy. A few examples will suffice to illustrate the basis of this impasse. For migration data obtained from the 1961 and 1966 censuses for the six conurbations of England and Wales, Masser (1970) achieved encouraging results when applying the gravity model. He not only obtained good fits but also found that models calibrated with 1961 data gave excellent predictions of the flows recorded five years later. Another important contribution to the analysis of the gravity model was Olsson's (1965) study of migratory movements between urban centres of different sizes in Sweden. Interestingly it was concluded that migrants from large urban centres moved longer distances than those from small centres, and each migratory stream was strongly correlated with its own counterstream. On the other hand, a study of inter-provincial migration flows in Chile by Shaw (1975), indicated little support for the gravity formulation, possibly due to the existence of powerful directional biases. A similar conclusion was reached by Schwind (1971) in a study of migration in the United States between 1955 and 1960. The data were aggregated into 225 regions as well as a coarser mesh of 133 areal units; the analysis concluded that only 55 per cent in the case of the former areal basis and 57 per cent of the latter of the gross migration flows could be accounted for by the gravity formulation. The model adopted was highly simplified since the only variables employed were the populations of the areas of origin and destinations, and the intervening distance.

As a result of these 'failures' there has been considerable discussion concerning the adeqency of the gravity model as an explanation of the spatial patterning of migration. Both Olsson (1965) and Claeson (1969) have suggested that the basic weakness of the model is its lack of an adequate theoretical basis. Like distance, population (or mass) can be measured in a number of ways. The assumption that all places are populated by standard people with identical needs, tastes and contacts is questionable. Also it is apparent that not all migrants seek advantages that are a function of population size: a fact that can be demonstrated by return migration, compulsory moves and migrations of the highly specialized. It is little wonder, therefore, that Olsson (1965, 25) has gone as far as to suggest that an analysis by means of the gravity formulation is nothing more than a highly simplified regression analysis.

Intervening Opportunity

In contrast to the Zipf-type formulation, Stouffer (1940, 1960) argued that migration is not a mere function of distance and population size but also of the existence of what he called intervening opportunities (e.g. housing vacancies, employment opportunities, etc). Stouffer assumed that:

> there is no necessary relationship between mobility and distance . . . the number of persons going a given distance is directly proportional to the number of opportunities at that distance and inversely proportional to the number of intervening opportunities. The relation between mobility and distance may be said to depend on an auxiliary relationship, which express the cumulated (intervening) opportunities as a function of distance. (Stouffer, 1940, 846)

Underlying this concept is the premise that migration is expensive and that the potential migrant will cease searching as soon as he finds an appropriate opportunity. The major handicap with testing this theory is that of defining 'opportunity'. In a study of migration in Cleveland, Stouffer (1940) used the number of vacant houses within a given census-defined area as being opportunities. Any vacancies between two areas were regarded as 'intervening opportunities'. The analysis revealed considerable agreement between expected and observed values. In their study of net inter-state migration in the United States in 1930, Bright and Thomas concluded that such migration 'has in general followed the pattern of opportunities very closely . . . but . . . only if we allow for the major disturbances in the pattern attributable to qualitative differences in the opportunities sought in California and elsewhere and if allowance is made for the directional factor in the movement from the Middle West' (Bright and Thomas, 1941, 783). Isbell (1944) carried out a similar test of Stouffer's hypotheses on inter-county migration in Sweden in 1921–30, and again the results tended to substantiate the hypotheses (Figure 4.2). However, as a result of certain discrepancies in the expected and observed relationships between migration and intervening opportunities, Stouffer (1960) refined his theory by introducing an additional variable which he called 'competing migrants'. This revised model postulated that the total number of individuals migrating from place A to place B was a function of the number of opportunities at place B and an inverse function of the number of opportunities intervening between place A and place B, as well as the

Figure 4.2: Migration and Intervening Opportunities in Sweden, 1921–30

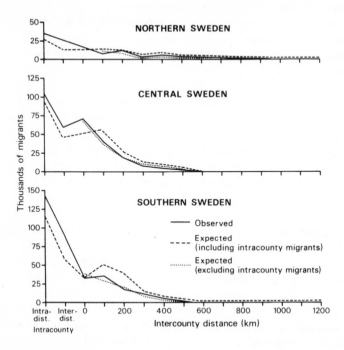

Source: After Isbell, 1944, 627–39.

number of other individuals competing for opportunities at place B. This revised model can be expressed as:

$$M_{ij} = K \cdot \frac{(P_i P_j)^{b_1}}{(O_{ij})^{b_2} (C_{ij})^{b_3}}$$

where:

M = migration from place i and j
P = population at places i and j
O = the number of intervening opportunities, measured by the total number of out-migrants in the circle centred midway between i and j and passing through i and j
C = the number of competing migrants, measured by the total number of in-migrants in the circle centred on j and passing through i

An important study by Galle and Taeuber (1966) applied this new model to both the 1940 and 1960 migration data of the United States. They found that the 1940 data fitted more closely than the 1960 and thus emphasize the increasing complexity of the migration process. Another interesting application of the intervening opportunity model was Jansen and King's (1968) study of inter-county migration in Belgium in 1965. Since Belgium is a bilingual nation the migration streams were split into three: (i) migrations between counties speaking a different language; (ii) migrations between the bilingual area around Brussels and either French or Flemish speaking counties; and (iii) migrations between counties speaking the same language. In the latter case the flows fitted the model formulation fairly closely, whilst the fit for the first two groups was much weaker, thus illustrating the barrier-like effect of linguistic divisions upon migratory flows.

While the intervening opportunity theory has been supported by a number of additional studies, especially in connection with inter-urban migration, there are several criticisms and qualifications which have to be made. Bogue (1969) has commented that migration allows a siphoning of excess population into areas of greater opportunity, thereby becoming now only a mechanism of personal adjustment but also a process of maintaining equilibrium within a system. This, however, assures a degree of rational behaviour and the 'opportunities' hypothesis as a general theory only seems to work when applied to migrants of homogeneous status and motives (Gibson, 1975). For example, a study of Negro migration in the United States in 1935–40 and 1955–60 found that the intervening opportunity variable did not play a statistically significant role in the model (Shaw, 1975). Obviously in this case links between the South and cities in the North led to many nearby opportunities being overlooked. Similarly, the migration to California is determined as much by climate as economic opportunities (Wadycki, 1975). In other words, as ter Heide (1963, 65) has remarked, 'these opportunities cannot all be represented by one indicator'.

One further consideration relevant to the discussion is the over-representation of capital cities and large cities in offering opportunities, for they have a distinctive character in attracting migrants regardless of the number of intervening opportunities. The excess of migrants to such places suggests a qualitative difference in the opportunities of such cities not adequately allowed for in Stouffer's theory when applied to total migration. Thus Stewart's (1960) suggestion that migration is a function of city ranking rather than a function of absolute population may be appropriate, and this analogy between migration and central place theory has also been taken up by other investigators. 'Since potential migrants could be viewed as analogous to consumers trying to satisfy their needs in a spatially given system, central place theory and migration might be connected via the concept of range . . . the potential migrant first decides in which type of place his intentions can be best fulfilled and then, by minimising costs and efforts, moves to the nearest of these alternatives. This implies that a migrant would never move from place A to place B if there is a larger place C at a shorter distance from A' (Olsson, 1967, 35–6). Such a model, however, could only be applied to migrants seeking opportunities and advantages which were a positive function of population size. Stub (1962) expressed a similar principle when he observed that the geographic position of a city has different 'opportunity' significance for migrants from different segments of the population. Olsson (1967, 36) concluded that 'it seems quite possible that the individual behaviour that generates the central place system also generates the spatial distribution of migrations', and it would seem that the two factors of 'opportunity' and 'distance' are satisfactorily linked by such a concept (Smith and Goodchild, 1980).

Maximum Entropy

From an epistemological point of view a major criticism of the distance and gravity concepts is their determinative nature and, as a result, a number of researchers have agreed the need for rooting the gravity model in a more probabilitive framework (Olsson, 1967). A major contribution to this end has been that by Wilson (1970) who has sought a statistical process to generate the distribution observed in the real world. The basis of Wilson's work is the concept of entropy, which in the case of population movements may be regarded as the spatial distribution of flows which is the most probable of all possible configurations. If, attempting to determine the likely distribution of urban residents in relation to their place of work, say, in the city centre, then the following expression can be used:

$$W = \frac{n!}{\prod_i n_i!}$$

where:

Figure 4.3: The Configuration of Urban Residents' Location with Respect to City Centre According to Principles of Maximum Entropy

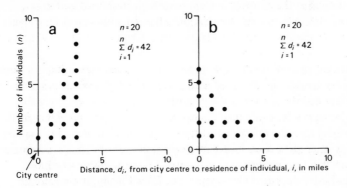

Source: After Gould, 1972, 689-700.

n = total number of individuals

ni = number of individuals who live at a given distance, i, from their place of work

W = number of ways that a specified allocation of individuals to distance bands can occur

The operation of the model can be illustrated if we assume a simple situation of where 5 individuals are constrained in such a way that two must live seven miles from their workplace, and the other three, two miles from work. Thus $W = 5!/(3! \, 2!) = 10$. In other words, there are 10 ways in which our 5 individuals could be arranged according to the stipulated constraints. These arrangements are:

Individual Identity Numbers

Miles from work	TWO	123;124;125;135;145;134;234;245;235; 345.
	SEVEN	45;35;34;24;23;25;15;13;14;12.

The likely occurrence of a particular arrangement can be illustrated from Figure 4.3 (Gould, 1972). In a situation with 20 individuals and constrains of 42 miles, (a) has a probability of occurrence which is only 1/7560 of that likely descending situation shown in (b). Clearly, the whole operation becomes more complex to handle as the matrix becomes larger, yet, the basic idea remains relatively simple. The matrix derives the most likely distribution to occur and, interestingly, a distance-decay distribution is the end result. So far the majority of studies using the entropy concept have been concerned with transport flows, its use in studies of migration is limited, although as illustrated above it does have considerable potential (Clark and Avery, 1978).

It is evident that recent work on the spatial modelling of the migration process have been concerned with developing explanation, as against merely describing empirical regularities. This has involved not only adopting greater mathematical sophistication but also providing greater meaning to such concepts as distance and opportunities. At the same time other researchers have considered it necessary to achieve a greater understanding of migration regularities by the adoption of a more behavioural approach (see Chapters 6, 7, 8). Finally, it must not be overlooked that migration exists not only in space but also in time, which is the prime focus of the next chapter.

5 TEMPORAL ASPECTS

It is an often repeated truism that the migration of people has increased in volume and lengthened in distance with the passage of time. Yet, surprisingly, the time element has been largely neglected in migration study, despite the fact that time, as well as space, is implicit in all forms of spatial interaction (Roseman, 1971). Although an arbitrary time-span has been employed in most studies of migration the emphasis has been upon migration 'in time', as in Chapter 4, rather than migration 'through time' (Parkes and Thrift, 1980). The importance of the 'through time' element to any migration analysis is the fact that the susceptibility of individuals to migrate changes through their life history.

Much of the reason for the paucity of studies of migration 'through time' lies in a dearth of suitable data (Douglas and Blomfield, 1956; Walter, 1980). Shryock and Larmon (1965) have rightly pointed out that most of what is known about migration is derived from cross-sectional data which, of course, refers to a cross-section of a population at a specific date. This type of data does not, therefore, permit the delineation of specific individual acts of migration or relate the successive moves of individual migrants. Only when information is provided on present and past places of residence does the census become a source of longitudinal data and, yet, when this information is tabulated its usefulness is weakened by the absence of a complete record of residences. According to Bogue an ideal census would be one which enumerated for each individual 'a complete migration history, obtaining dates of arrival and departure from each community in which the person had lived' (Bogue, 1959, 488). Such information is not readily available except in those countries which maintain population registers, such as the Netherlands and Norway, or which occasionally carry out special surveys such as the famous American survey of residence and smoking in 1958 (Taeuber, Chiazze and Haenszel, 1968).

In their conceptualization of the longitudinal approach Shryock and Larmon (1965) argue that it provides a valuable insight into the migration process because, unlike a cross-sectional approach, it has the potentiality to determine:

(a) how migration develops over an individual's life and its relationship with chronological age and changes in occupation, social status or key events in the life cycle;

(b) the extent to which migration is between specific types of areas, for example, similar areas or different areas in a step-like fashion;

(c) the extent of circular and return migration to the same address or locality;

(d) the proportion of the population to have spent their lives in the same residence or locality; and

(e) the frequency of moves by individuals during their life history or a specified time period.

As a result of the difficulties in obtaining longitudinal data, social scientists, including geographers, have adopted two contrasting approaches to the study of migration through time. The first, residence history analysis, which is empirical and individualistic, relies upon information collected by social surveys and national registers to derive information about previous residences; on the other hand, the second approach is more aggregative and predictive, since it relies upon stochastic processes within a probabalistic framework to simulate, from cross-sectional data, the time process in migration. Although these two approaches differ quite markedly in their perspective and methodology they are, however, not as mutually independent as might at first glance appear. Increasingly the empirical evidence provided by residence history analysis forms a significant input into the attempts to improve the predictive powers of the stochastic models (Ginsberg, 1978; Shaw, 1975). However, in order to assess the contribution of a temporal perspective to our understanding of the migration process, these two procedures will now be considered separately, using the conceptualization of the longitudinal approach made by Shryock and Larmon as a guiding framework.

Residence History Analysis

Residence history analysis may be described as the study of the migration behaviour of individuals through time (Pryor, 1979a). It records the place of residence of an individual or a group during their life and the timing of the migration between places (Rowland, 1976). By explicitly focusing upon individual behaviour through time 'migration is thus conceived not only as a function of a person's current characteristics but also as a function of his preceding behaviour and of concomitant changes in other characteristics' (Taeuber, 1966, 417). In other words, migration is viewed as part of an individual's life history and, therefore, linked to other key life sequences such as the family life cycle, educational history, career cycle, etc. The sources of data used for such a study are diverse and include population registers, directories and surveys at both local and national scales. Unfortunately, the quality of the information collected varies widely: those at a national scale often lack the detail required by migration research whilst those conducted by individual researchers usually involve sample sizes which are too small to allow a meaningful tabulation of the figures. Both of these weaknesses impose limitations on the nature of the investigation and the methods of statistical analysis employed (Karweit, 1973; Carr Hill and MacDonald, 1973).

Life History

Recently residence analysis has provided considerable insights into the ways the migratory behaviour of an individual develops over a lifetime. The tracing of such migration histories is both complex and time-consuming. A major contribution to the analysis of individual migration histories has been that of Price (1963) among several immigrant groups in Australia. For example, using data derived from naturalization papers, he has painstakingly traced the settlement history of a group of Ithacan Greeks in Western Australia. In the group's early settlement, chain migration was a significant factor as well as in their subsequent moves to the gold-mining areas of Kalgoorlie-Collgardie, whereas the major outflows from the mining districts in 1916 were due to antagonism towards this immigrant group as a result of Greece's favouring of the Kaiser. Throughout his detailed research Price emphasized that any interpretation of migratory behaviour must begin with reference to an individual's life history. Figure 5.1 illustrates this point with reference to the residence history of three Dalmation immigrants at the turn of the century. Certainly at a micro-scale, research has confirmed the existence of a relationship between migration and the life cycle, educational history and career cycle of an individual (Pryor, 1979a) whilst at the macro-scale the evidence is much more fragmentary. One of the few large-scale life history analyses of residence was that carried out by Taeuber, Haenszel and Sirken (1961) in the United States, which concluded that relatively few change their residence between birth and adolescence, whereas by their late twenties, over two-thirds leave their place of birth and, thereafter, an individual's potential to migrate declines. As a result of a dearth of

Figure 5.1: The Migration and Residence History of three Dalmation Immigrants in Australia

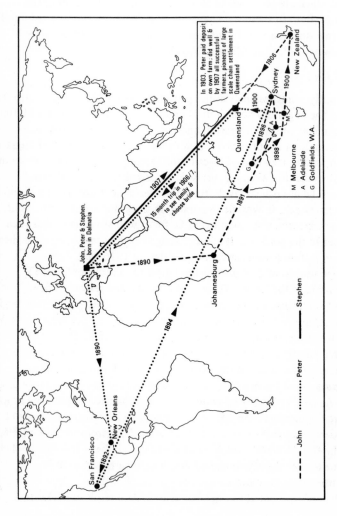

In 1903, Peter paid deposit
on own farm. did well &
by 1907 all successful
farmers. pioneers of large
scale chain settlement in
Queensland

John, Peter & Stephen,
born in Dalmatia

15 month trip in 1906/7.
to see family &
choose bride

M Melbourne
A Adelaide
G Goldfields, W.A.

New Zealand

Queensland   Sydney

Johannesburg

San Francisco
New Orleans

John   Peter   Stephen

Source: Based on Price, 1963, 280–1

sufficient data on life history much of the research on these structural
factors in the migration process has, therefore, been based upon cross-
sectional evidence. For example, researches by Rossi (1955) and
Michelson (1977) have found significant links between movers and life
cycle changes, a relationship which will form a major part of the
discussion in the next chapter.

Type of Migration

A longitudinal approach to migration also has potentiality to unravel
the different types of movement that an individual might be involved
in during a particular time period. According to M.L. Young (1979)
residence histories are a particularly valuable source for the analysis of
step and return migrations, circular and seasonal movements, since they
provide a simultaneous source of data on the spatial and temporal
aspects of migration. Some of these movements are illustrated in Figure
5.2 within the life history of several individuals.

Figure 5.2: Types of Movement and Life History of Eight Individuals

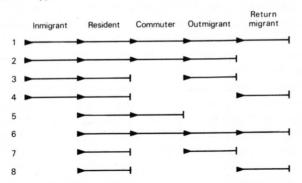

Despite the apparent potential of residence history analysis to
distinguish different types of migration and the areas involved only a
handful of worthwhile studies have been carried out so far (Pryor,
1979a). One of the earliest and the most significant was that by Shryock
and Larmon (1965), who attempted to distinguish the types of places
people had resided within in the United States. Broadly, these could be
summarized into:

   (a) always lived in the same type of residence;
   (b) circular movement terminating in the original residence;
   (c) net shift from farm to non-farm or from non-metropolitan to

metropolitan ('urbanward'); and
(d) net shift in the opposite direction ('ruralward').

From the sample it was found that a half of the adult population had always resided in the same type of residence, 22 per cent had moved 'urbanward', whilst only 7 per cent had engaged in circular mobility and 7 per cent in 'ruralward' movement. More recently similar studies have been carried out among small communities in the third world, which surprisingly have emphasized the complexity of lifetime migrations. For example, even within the simple economies of a series of small Pacific islands, Chapman (1976) conceived the mobility experience of the islanders within the context of three types of population movements: shifts in village locations; moves by young adult males for educational and wage labour purposes; and short-term mainly familial moves of a highly spontaneous nature. On the basis of such evidence Chapman concluded that the components of the islanders' mobility systems are not simple and linear but highly complex and curvilinear.

The significance of circular migration, involving as it does movements of a cyclic and seasonal nature, has been demonstrated in many parts of the third world. For example, seasonal migrations have long been recognized as important features of life in Africa (Gould and Prothero, 1975; Swindell, 1979), whilst only recently have they been established as significant in Latin America (Conaway, 1977), Southeast Asia (Goldstein, 1978), and the Pacific (Hugo, 1975; Chapman, 1976). The intricacies of such movements at a micro-level have been revealed by Bedford (1973) in a study in the New Hebrides (Figure 5.3). Using a modified version of Shimbel's (1953) graph-theoretic measure of accessibility within a network, a circulation index was computed on the basis of the migratory experience of the islanders. Where the index does not exceed 1, then the out-migrants have returned to their place of origin, either directly or via one other alternative place of residence. On the other hand, movements between different places without returning to the place of origin, result in indices exceeding 1, which indicate stepwise rather than circular migration at certain stages in an individual's life history. On the other hand, within the developed world such migrations tend to be more of a direct return movement to former places of residence. From the available evidence for the United States, however, considerable controversy exists as to the significance of such movements. For 1958 Shryock and Larman (1965) estimated that only 7 per cent of the actual population had returned to the places where

Figure 5.3: The Migration Networks of two New Hebridean Islanders

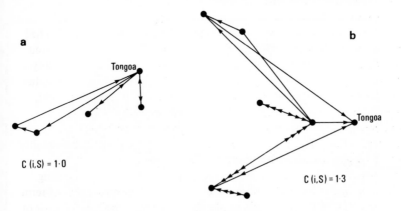

Source: After Bedford, 1973, 213.

they formerly lived, whilst in a later national survey Da Vanzo and Morrison (1978) mentioned that approximately a quarter of all migrants were return migrants. The latter study was of particular significance in that it differentiated for the first time between 'failed' migrants, those who returned home after only a short interval of time, and 'adjusted' migrants, those who only returned after a lengthy period away.

The suggestion that individuals tend to move progressively from small to larger places in a step or stage-like fashion with the passage of time has been a source of intensive research. In the third world there exists considerable evidence to support this suggestion. According to Harvey and Riddell (1975), recent movements in Sierra Leone exhibit a strong tendency to involve successively larger places in the direction of the capital Freetown (Figure 5.4). The sparsely populated and poorly connected interior regions exhibited a perfect stepwise pattern (1, 2, 3, 4), whilst a certain degree of short-circuiting in the direction of the larger interior cities characterized the pattern of the arboriculture and diamond mining areas (1, 3, 2, 4). Preference for migration to the capital, Freetown, was restricted to its hinterland, thus reflecting the attenuating effect of distance and the presence of localized employment and regional capitals. On the other hand, in the developed world evidence suggests that lifetime migrations fail to conform to such a pattern. In fact, Taeuber, Haenszel and Sirken (1961, 833) concluded from the US statistics (1958) that 'the adult

Figure 5.4: Migration Preferences in Sierra Leone; numbers indicate urban (1) → rural (4) continuum

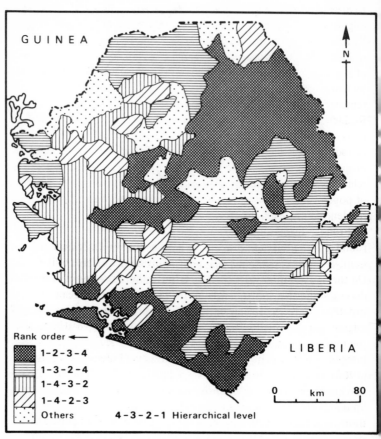

Source: After Harvey and Riddell, 1975, 51–65.

population has extensive residential experience (ten or more years) in only one or two different sizes of place. This indicates a marked stability in the sizes of places in which people live, despite high rates of residential mobility'. As a means of summarizing lifetime residential experience the authors then put forward the concept of 'exposure residence', defined as the size of place category lived in for a specified period. The significance of the conclusions reached by Taeuber and his colleagues has still to be validated elsewhere.

Movers and Stayers

From the evidence provided by cross-sectional analysis it is difficult
to discern whether high migration rates are the product of repeated
migration of the same people from place to place or to single moves
by many people to specific places where they become continuous
residents (Hollingsworth and El Rouby, 1976). Such a distinction is
of significance in any study of community change since single moves
by many tend to create demographic and social instability whilst
repeated migration by a few, provides continuity and stability.
Residence history data allows such a distinction to be made and on the
basis of such evidence the concept of a mover-stayer has been
introduced into migration study. Simply, this implies that a large
proportion of the migration from a community can be attributed to a
relatively constant number of people and, therefore the redistribution
of population is largely a function of habitual movers changing
residence repeatedly and frequently.

From statistics derived from directories, Goldstein (1954; 1958)
found that in Norristown, Pennsylvania, the out-migration rate of
in-migrants was over twice that of the continuous residents of the city.
On the basis of this evidence he concluded that high rates of migration
do not necessarily mean a high degree of population change or
instability; rather that the turnover of the population involved only the
migrant segment. According to Goldstein the short-term residence of
the repeat migrants meant that they found it difficult to become fully
integrated into the life of the city. A subsequent study by Goldstein
(1964), using data from Copenhagen, Denmark, for the period 1950–61,
also concluded that the majority of the population were highly
immobile. Those involved in moves into and out of the city over a
short time period, tended to be from the 24–44 age group, whilst the
stayers were more likely to be the old and young residents. Similar
mobility patterns characterized the population of a small commuter
village in Leicestershire. Between 1965 and 1978 the rate of migration
of the in-migrants was five times that of the long-term residents and
despite a high turnover of the population less than 25 per cent of the
residents were actually involved in moving. This evidence clearly
illustrates the operation of the 'newcomer-established' concept within
a migratory framework. Clearly all this empirical evidence suggests that
in any migration analysis it is necessary to differentiate between the
mobile and sedentary portions of the population.

Duration of Residence

The evidence illustrating the mover-stayer concept has also revealed that 'the probability of moving within a specified time . . . decreases as the length of maintaining the same residence increases' (Rider and Badger, 1943, 124). This tendency towards stability within a population has been termed the duration of residence effect, or the axiom of cumulative inertia, which according to McGinnis (1968, 710) may be defined as 'the probability of remaining in any state of nature increases as a strict monotone function of prior residence in that state'. The principal reasoning underlying this concept is that residence in the same locality fosters ever increasing ties which can operate as inertia factors to migration: in other words, accumulated residence appears to generate inertia.

Initial support for the relevance of the duration of residence effect upon migration potential was provided by Myers, McGinnis and Masnick (1967) in a study of the migration of the families of 1,700 high school students between school catchment areas in Seattle. In Britain, a similar pattern of movement was discovered by Rowntree (1957) using data from the National Register kept during and immediately after the Second World War. Of the migrants who moved for a second time within three years, 43 per cent did so again less than six months after the first, the proportion falling to 26 per cent within six to eleven months, and 9 per cent in 24 to 35 months. Additional supporting evidence for this hypothesis is provided again from a Leicestershire commuter village where between 1965 and 1978, 51 per cent of all the migrants moving within a three-year period made their second move less than 9 months after the first, which then fell to 23 per cent for the period 9 to 15 months. In a study using statistics from the population registers of Amsterdam and Zeist, Netherlands, Morrison (1967) not only provided similar evidence but also suggested the likely effects of age upon the propensity to move. Later, using data from the Rand Social Security Continuous Work History Sample and the United States Survey of Economic Opportunities, Morrison (1970, 24) concluded that the most significant predictor of migration was 'last year's residence in a different house'. For example, only 4.2 per cent of those individuals who had not moved in the previous eight years did so in the ninth, whilst of those who had moved eight times in the last eight years, about 70 per cent migrated in the ninth. These findings were held consistent when controlling for age. Further supporting evidence has been provided by Land (1969) from a sample of males aged 21–64 years in Monterey, where it was found that the correlation of duration of residence and age accounted for 70–90 per cent of the variation in the probabilities to migrate.

From the evidence provided here residence history analysis appears to provide a means of disentangling the complexities of the time dimension in the migration process. By focusing on the individual, valuable insights into migratory behaviour has been achieved because, as Hägerstrand (1975, 200) has pointed out, 'a great deal can be learnt in regards to macro aspects if familiarity has first been attained with some elementary microscopic features'. It is to the macro approaches to migration and time that we must now turn.

Stochastic Approach

In parallel to residence history analysis a growing number of geographers during the past two decades have become increasingly involved in a more aggregate and predictive approach to the study of time and migration (Olsson, 1965; Shaw, 1975). This approach is primarily concerned with the flows of migration through a whole region over time within a stochastic and probabilistic framework (T.W. Rogers, 1968). A stochastic approach is one in which there is uncertainty about the outcome of events, and consequently predictions can be made only in terms of probabilities. According to Willis (1974, 143) the usefulness of conceiving migration in probabilistic terms 'results from both a failure to fully specify the system (because its full limits are not yet known) and the unpredictable character of such human behaviour'. Although the stochastic approach to migration behaviour is essentially predictive it is, however, lacking in theory, since it bases its prediction on empirically derived probabilities and, therefore, tends to focus on observable inputs and outputs, rather than causal explanations. By conceptualizing the flow of migration through time as a stochastic process, it is possible to use the powerful mathematics of probabilities, such as Markov chain analysis and simulation techniques.

To many researchers the attractiveness of the stochastic model in the study of migration is the simple, yet efficient, manner in which it derives migratory flows from readily available empirical data. It provides a broad-brush picture on a wide time-space canvas which is of considerable value as a basis for more detailed investigation and for public policy decision-making at both local and national levels. As a result of the model's increasing usefulness numerous attempts have been made to improve its efficiency, in particular by the inclusion of such concepts as mover-stayer and duration of residence as structural factors in the migration process. These recent developments emphasize a growing interrelationship between the stochastic and residence history approaches in the study of migration through time.

Markov Chain Analysis

In the formulation of stochastic models of migration considerable use has been made of Markov chain analysis. Essentially, a Markov chain process is one which develops over time, and where events at time 2 are not independent of events at time 1. In a study of residential mobility within the countryside, for example, events may be defined as residence in a high-, medium- or low-status village and that the most likely moves would be from low to medium status and from medium-to high-status villages. In other words, the probability of a move from a low to a high-status village or vice versa is exceedingly low. Although this model was introduced as long ago as 1912 by A.A. Markov, its widespread use in the social sciences has only taken place in the last two decades. The application of Markov chain analysis in geography was initiated by Tarver and Gurley (1965) and A. Rogers (1968), and its potentiality discussed extensively by Brown (1970), Willis (1974) and Collins (1976).

The basic Markovian model may be represented in matrix form. If we have knowledge of the initial state, S_1, for example, the number of residents within different types of villages who have moved to other villages, it is possible to derive the probability of making a transition from one state to another, i.e. a transition probability matrix. Given two states, say low- and high-status villages, S_1 and S_2 respectively, then matrix P may be represented as:

To village:

		S_1	S_2
From	S_1	P_{11}	P_{12}
village:	S_2	P_{21}	P_{22}

P_{11} is the probability of staying in the same village S_1, which is likely to be high compared to moving from S_1, a low-status village, to S_2, a high-status village. The operation of such a matrix can be illustrated from data on the number of people who had migrated between three villages in rural Wales, or remained within the same village during the period 1971-6. By dividing the numbers in each row of the matrix by the row total, the probability of moving from village to village, or of staying in the same village can be derived:

		To village:			
		X	Y	Z	Σ
From	X	.6	.3	.1	1.00
village:	Y	.2	.5	.3	1.00
	Z	.3	.3	.4	1.00

These values can be used to compute the probability of a person remaining in village Y or migrating to villages X or Z, after one or more time periods. Such probabilities can be represented in terms of possible migration paths, and the probability of each path is termed a 'Markov chain'. For example, the probability of the residents of village Y remaining at Y, moving to X, or moving to Z, are 0.5, 0.2 and 0.3 respectively. Then the probability of remaining at Y after two time periods would involve (1) moving to X and then back to Y (0.2 × 0.3); (2) remaining at Y (0.5 × 0.5); and (3) moving to Z and then back to Y (0.3 × 0.3). Summing the products of these paths yields the probability of remaining at B after two time periods of 0.4. This procedure has to be repeated for A and C. The repetitive operations can be substantially eliminated by recourse to matrix multiplication by successively powering the transition probability matrix, which yields the probability of moving to any location after n number of time periods. Thus:

P_1 shows the population redistribution after one time interval;
P_2 shows the population redistribution after two time intervals,
    i.e. $(P_2 = P_1 \times P_1)$

After a number of time periods there is a convergence towards some average of 'equilibrium state' in which movement between states would serve to maintain the system at the same level. This can be represented by:

$$S_1 + n = S_1 \times P_n$$

where:

S_1 = the initial population distribution

$S_1 + n$ = population distribution after n intervals of time

Figure 5.5: The Relative Stability of Population in Australia, 1971.
Based on an extrapolation of 1966–71 internal migration trends as a
Markov process

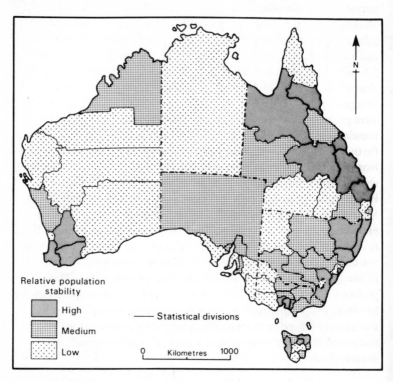

Source: After Rowland, 1979, 167.

One of the major strengths of Markov chain analysis is that in the
study of migratory trends it can be employed at different geographical
scales. For example, Compton (1969) and Brown, Odland and Golledge
(1970) used standard statistical divisions in their studies of internal
migration in Hungary and the United States, respectively, whilst Brown
and Longbrake (1970), in a study of residential mobility in Cedar
Rapids, employed small neighbourhoods classified by means of a
factorial analysis into such types as late life cycle and upper middle
class; middle life cycle and middle class, etc. However, despite this
potential, studies adopting a Markovian approach have still, in general,

been primarily concerned with migratory flows at a macro-scale, particularly the likely future redistribution of population.

Following the lead of Rogers (1968), in his study of internal migration in Australia, Rowland (1979) identified by means of a Markov chain analysis those statistical divisions experiencing the most substantial population changes as a result of migration between 1971 and a theoretical equilibrium. The results are summarized in Figure 5.5, where high stability refers to population growth or decline of less than 10 per cent between 1971 and equilibrium, medium stability to changes ranging from 10 to 19 per cent and instability to changes that were greater. Briefly, the analysis revealed that the main areas of likely population gain were the fringes of Sydney and Brisbane, the cities of Perth and Canberra, and the mining districts of Western Australia and Northern Territory, whilst population losses through internal migration, was most likely in the outback of New South Wales, the Yorke Peninsula in South Australia, southern Tasmania, and parts of Western Victoria. However, as Rowland rightly pointed out, all changes apparent during one inter-censal period need not persist; for example, in Australia post-war developments such as the growth of Canberra and the mining districts such as the Pilbarra should eventually become part of the prevalent equilibrium, with little population growth being derived from internal migration. In an earlier paper Hirst (1976) derived the likely population redistribution in Uganda from a Markov chain analysis of inter-regional migration between 1959 and 1969. This analysis was geographically interesting in that it was based on the degree of hierarchical migration as well as migration between regions. By the use of a multivariate hierarchical programme, four groupings of districts were identified (Figure 5.6a), which suggests the existence of functional regions in which inter-district migration and the flows of information, and goods and services are intertwined. Yet at the same time it was evident that there was considerable variation in the nearness or accessibility of individual districts within the overall system, which was confirmed by the application of the same grouping algorithm (Figure 5.6b). Essentially, the hierarchical structure displays a concentric geographical pattern centred on the capital, Kampala, with group 1 forming a core region around which the others are located at increasing distance from the coast. Such a pattern provides further confirmation of the persistence of a step-wise migration in the third world.

Despite the widespread use of the Markov chain model in the analysis of migration through time, a good deal of criticism has been

Figure 5.6: Inter-district Redistribution of Population in Uganda, 1959–69, as a Markov Process: (a) migration flows which form four distinct functional regions; (b) flows which form a hierarchy of regions based on accessibility to the core region (1)

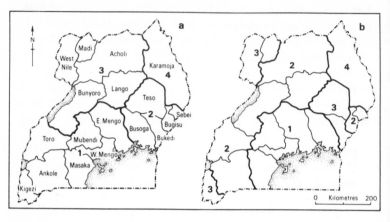

Source: After Hirst, 1976, 79–94.

levelled at its assumptions and limitations. To many the model is too simplistic since it effectively only extrapolates migration trends without reference to changes in births and deaths. Further, recent evidence provided by residence history analysis has led to the questioning of two of the model's basic tenets: that the probability of moving from one place to another being solely dependent upon the last place occupied and that the pattern of migration, as represented by the transition matrix, remains constant through time. In addition, the assumption that the total population of the area under investigation remains unchanged through time has also been attacked severely for its lack of realism. Although Joseph (1975) agreed with these critical points, he suggests, however, that the model's purpose is not to interpret reality but rather to let reality change along predetermined lines.

As a result of these limitations numerous attempts have been made to incorporate such structural factors as duration-of-residence effects and the mover-stayer concept into the Markovian model (Spilerman, 1972). In order to accommodate these factors it has been necessary to relax some of the Markovian assumptions, in particular, (a) that the system be closed and therefore undisturbed by outside forces, and (b) that the probability of a migration between two areas be dependent only upon location at time t–1. According to McGinnis (1968) in such a revised model each probability, p, for migrating to another area is a weighted average of the ps for the various duration of residence sub-groups within the areas. Those individuals who have stayed in the same area for one time unit (d = 1) have one set of migration probabilities, those who have stayed for two time units (d = 2) have another, and so on. Therefore the conditional probability that an individual will be found within the jth area (j = 1, 2, 3 ... r) at time t if he is within the ith area at time t-1 can be expressed as:

$$P_{ij}^{(t)} = \sum_{d = 1}^{M} pr_i \left[d_i^{(t-1)}\right] pdij$$

where:

pri $\left[d_i^{(t-1)}\right]$ = the probability at time t-1 of having remained in the ith area for d time units, and pdij = the conditional probability of being in the ith area for d time units at time t-1.
m = the last duration of stay category.

The same procedure may be adopted with respect to other factors, such as age and income, when relevant as determinants of differential rates of migration. Despite this provision of greater realism into the model, Ginsberg (1972) has argued that such a formulation contains a number of difficulties, in particular its two-dimensional nature makes the number of states so large that it is difficult to manipulate and, in order to estimate the number of duration-specific probabilies, an immense amount of data is required. Also it has been suggested that realism can only be achieved if several structural factors are incorporated simultaneously into the model.

As a result of these strictures Ginsberg has developed a more generalized, semi-Markovaian and more easily operational mobility-type model. In this model 'non-Markovian duration-of-residence effects are specifically included; age effects and secular changes are controlled and estimated with the device of operational time; the semi-Markov model is defined in continuous time, thus, enabling us to estimate the effects of fixed observation intervals on our predictions; and properties of the destination (pulls) as well as those of the origin (pushes) may determine the probability of a move' (Ginsberg, 1972, 69). Later papers by Ginsberg (1973; 1978) focus on the incorporation of more parameters into his model which relate to the causal structure underlying the migration process.

More recently studies have attempted to test certain aspects of the semi-Markovian model by means of actual residence history data. For example, Huff and Clark (1978) argued in a study of intra-urban migration that the transition matrix was non-stationary through time because of the redistribution of opportunities, the heterogeneity of the residents and their changing preferences. The object of their study was to devise a means for separating the effects of changing housing opportunities upon the transition probabilities from the combined effects of heterogeneity and changing preferences. By sub-dividing the population into groups it is then possible to imply that the changes in the transition probabilities are the result of change in either housing opportunities or individual preferences. Data for the period 1960–70 for Amsterdam was derived and an algorithm known as the bi-proportional operation method was used to transform an initial matrix $P(t-1)$ into a new matrix $P(t)$ which generated the expected distribution $D(t-1)$ from the previous population distribution, $D(t)$. Even though the expected matrices of the model, when compared with the actual, were rejected on a chi-square test, it was, however, significant that the model was a better predictor than the assumption of stationarity. In other words, any prediction of residential mobility must take account of changing preferences and changing house opportunities within the city. On the other hand, Ginsberg (1978) has been concerned with the time intervals between moves in residence histories as revealed in the Population Register of Norway, 1965–71. From the application of his semi-Markovian model Ginsberg questioned the validity of the duration of stay effect as a structural factor in the migration process. It was evident that the duration-of-stay effect was only significant when considered in conjunction with age and other variables, thus indicating that each age group should be analyzed separately (Smith, 1979). These examples illustrate a recent trend towards the incorporation of causal as well as structural factors into the semi-Markovian model.

Simulation

From a geographical viewpoint one of the major deficiencies in the Markov chain model is its essentially aspatial perspective. Therefore, as an alternative means of migration analysis some geographers have developed simulation techniques that explicitly incorporate distance within a time perspective. A major contribution to this approach has been Morrill's (1965a; 1965b; 1965c) simulation of the development of towns in Sweden, the growth of the Negro ghetto and the extension of the urban fringe in American cities. In order to illustrate the manner in which migration through time may be simulated, we will restrict our attention to Morrill's (1965a) study of the growth of towns in Småland in southern Sweden between 1950 and 1960. The model adopted was of a Monte Carlo variety in that locational decisions were conceived as being subject to both errors and uncertainties that could not be specified or ignored. Such random-type processes were considered to operate within the context of the model's three basic components: central place activities, non-central place activities (e.g. manufacturing and transport), and the migration of the residents. The migration itself was viewed as a function of (a) distance between origin and all possible destinations, (b) the relative attractiveness between an origin and potential destinations, and (c) the availability of information about destinations which, in turn, is largely a function of destinations of prior migrants from a certain origin. Thus the probability of migrating varied directly with the relative attractiveness of the possible destinations and inversely with distance, which was expressed as:

$$M_{ij} = \frac{A_j}{d_{ij}^b}$$

where

M_{ij} = migration between origin i and destination j
A_j = attractiveness of destination j
d_{ij} = distance between i and j
b = an empirically derived exponent

The model was made operative by initially assigning each of the 155 sub-areas of Småland a probability index of attraction (A_j), which reflected their accessibility to the transport system, level of urban growth and population density. Also since the probability of migrating from one sub-area to all possible destinations varies inversely with distance, those close to an origin were assigned greater weighting than ones at greater distance. Of course the probability weightings again sum to 1.00. Next each origin was allocated a set of numbers (say, 0–99 or 0–9999, etc) according to their relative attractiveness and pairwise distances. Finally, the model was made to run by the use of random numbers as a means of determining specific destinations, for example, if 10 potential migrants wished to leave an origin then random numbers were drawn in sequence, their destinations being selected by matching a random number with a numbered destination. From this the gain or losses due to migration were calculated as well as modifying the

Figure 5.7: Population Change in Småland, Southern Sweden: (a) actual population development 1940–60; (b) prediction simulation, 1960–80

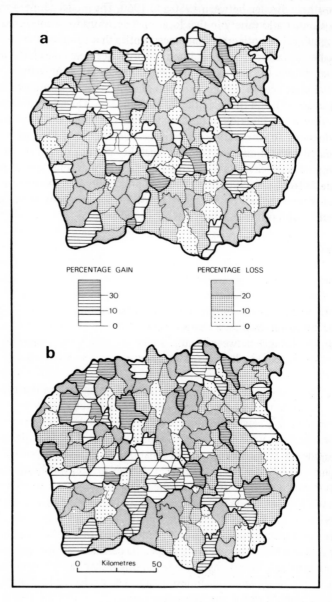

Source: After Morrill, 1965a, 137 and 148.

index of relative attractiveness for the next generation. The results of such an operation are illustrated in Figure 5.7, where the actual population between 1940–60 forms the basis for the simulation of change between 1960–80.

Despite the valuable insights they provide about spatial processes, simulation models suffer from a number of inherent weaknesses which have made them less attractive than the Markov chain approach in recent years. One of the major difficulties concerns the weighting given to the index of attraction, which unfortunately has to be empirically determined and statistically tested. Recently, Lindsay and Barr (1972) compared the Markov chain and Monte Carlo simulation model in a study of migration in the Peace River area of Alberta, Canada. On the basis of their analysis, they concluded that although the Markov chain models were less successful in reducing the gap between 'predicted' and 'actual' as compared to the Monte Carlo models, they were, however, less computationally cumbersome to operate and, therefore, better at providing a 'quick-scan' appreciation of migration trends.

It is evident from the empirical evidence referred to in this chapter that the students of migration have, in general, overlooked the significance of time in the migration process. Because census data afford only a glimpse of the links between migration histories and life histories, researchers have been forced to adopt either an exceedingly detailed and empirical type of study, such as residence history analyses, or a highly stochastic and probabilistic framework, such as Markov chain analysis or simulation techniques. What is of significance is that many of the findings of residence history analyses are increasingly being incorporated into the probabilistic assumptions of the stochastic models, thus making them more realistic and valuable. In both residential history analysis and in the stochastic models of migration there has been a steady shift towards the consideration of structural factors as determinants of the likelihood of movement at different times and in different places. This emphasizes the need to consider the selectivity of migration, which forms the main theme of the next chapters.

6 SELECTION OF MIGRANTS

It was established in the previous chapter that some persons migrate, often frequently, to new places of residence whilst others remain behind. In other words, 'migration tends to characterize a limited segment of a population who make frequent and repeated moves rather than the entire population' (Lind, 1969, 76). Essentially, this mover-stayer dichotomy suggests that the inducements to migrate do not exert their force equally and, hence, the tendency for some individuals to be more prone to migrate than others. Even as long ago as 1889 E.G. Ravenstein (1889) identified the existence of a certain degree of differential migration by postulating that females were more migratory than males and the natives of towns were less migratory than those of rural parts of a country. In other words, the personal attributes of migrants differ significantly from those of the sedentary population.

Since the publication of Ravenstein's 'laws', a wide variety of studies have been carried out on the self-selection by which migrants differentiate themselves from the sedentary population. The prime purpose of such studies has been to establish migration differentials which apply in all countries at all times. If such universal differentials were established it would not only aid our understanding of the migration process but also provide a sounder basis for predicting future migrations. In addition, the selectivity of migrants is a crucial factor in generating social change, both in the areas of origin and the areas of destination (Chapter 10). However, apart from age selectivity which Dorothy Thomas (1938) identified in her wide-ranging analysis to be the only differential which has been consistently significant in several contexts, little progress has been made towards establishing a general theory of migration selectivity. In fact, Thomas (1938, 85) concluded that 'our examination of researches bearing on these differentials led us to almost no acceptable generalizations about the strength and direction of selective migration'. More recently a similar comment was made by Illsley, Finlayson and Thompson (1963, 237): 'the voluminous literature on migration differentials make depressing reading for those who seek generalizations about the characteristics of migrants'. A more realistic view was taken, however, by Lee in his preliminary revision of Thomas's 1938 paper, 'many gaps have been noted in the existing knowledge of mobility differentials, but it has been possible to arrive at a few generalizations which may have more than temporary validity' (Lee, 1970, 438). An attempt to derive such basic generalizations about migration differentials has been made by Beshers and Nishuira (1961). Initially, a framework of migration types was set up derived from two scales of future-orientation: firstly, purposive/rational to short-run/hedonistic, and secondly, localized to non-localized. On the basis of this typology a series of hypotheses were proposed, which may be summarized as follows:

(1) Young adults are the most mobile segment of the population.
(2) Males tend to be more migratory than females.
(3) Unemployed persons are more likely to move than employed persons.
(4) Professionals are among the most mobile elements of the population.
(5) Whites move more than non-whites.

A good deal of controversy exists over such generalizations, with one author going as far as to assert that, apart from age, 'further differentials do not exist and should not be expected to exist' (Bogue, 1961, 5). Bearing in mind such comments, let us now briefly consider the extent to which Beshers and Nishiura's generalizations are valid in contemporary settings. For the ease of discussion the factors involved in migration selectivity have been grouped into three: demographic, socio-economic and ethnic-cultural.

Demographic Selectivity

In general, there is plenty of evidence to support the hypothesis that persons in their twenties and early thirties are the most mobile (Figure 6.1). The reasons often advanced as to why young adults are the most mobile of all age groups revolve around the fact that they are often beginning their working life and, therefore, are prepared to take advantage of new opportunities as they arise without the economic and social ties which constrains older groups to their place of residence. Even in the third world similar patterns of age selectivity have been identified by a number of studies (e.g. Connell, *et al.*, 1976; Browning and Fendt, 1968). However, the evidence contained in Figure 6.1 suggests that age-specific rates do not taper off uniformly with movement along the age continuum, since between the ages of 60 and

Figure 6.1: Proportions Migrating within England and Wales, and Australia, 1966–71, by Age

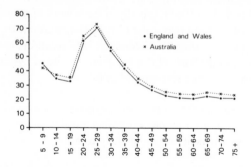

70 years there is a slight increase in the rate of migration. According to Allon-Smith (1978) this includes moves upon retirement as well as those related to widowhood and institutionalization, the latter involving short-distance moves, and the former longer distances, often to new locations at or near the coast (Figure 6.2). This movement to the coast upon retirement has during the past two decades become an increasingly significant element in the migration process of advanced economies such as the United States (Wiseman, 1978; Chevan and Fischer, 1979), France (Cribier, 1975), Britain (Law and Warnes, 1976) and Australia (Murphy, 1979). Not surprisingly, however, there is little retirement migration in the countries of the third world.

Contrary to Ravenstein's (1889) claim, contemporary evidence in the Western world indicates that males are more migratory than females, although compared to age, sex is less selective than age (House and Knight, 1965). However, Richmond (1969) has claimed that as economies develop females take a more active part in the labour force and, therefore, sex selectivity becomes less significant. An interesting confirmation of this proposition was provided by George (1970) in a study of inter-provincial migration in Canada using historical data. On the other hand, the evidence from the less developed societies is less clear and, therefore, raises a crucial question mark over Richmond's proposition. For example, rural to urban migrations in Ghana (Caldwell, 1969) and Sierra Leone (Swindell, 1970) is certainly dominated by males, yet in Chile the opposite is true due to the availability of female-dominated employment in the urban areas (Shaw, 1975).

Figure 6.2: Migration and the Elderly in England and Wales: (a) Inter-regional net migration flows of the elderly, 1966–71; (b) Administrative areas with significant proportion of elderly, 1971

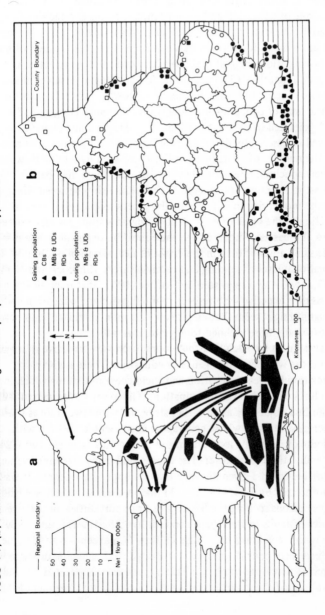

Source: After Allon-Smith, 1978.

Socio-economic Selectivity

The dominant variables with regard to socio-economic selectivity
include, of course, education, social class and occupation, yet the
exact role of education and socio-economic status as a factor of
selectivity remains in debate (McInnis, 1971). One of the major early
studies on migration differentials concluded that 'the findings of most
. . . investigations suggest that the better educated are selected in
cityward migration' (Thomas, 1938, 38) and Bogue observed that
'the rate of migration from an area tends to vary inversely with the
general level of educational attainment in that area' (Bogue, 1959, 504).
Data examined in Britain for 1935–50 by Shryock and Nam (1965)
showed an essentially direct association between the migration rate
and the number of years of schooling completed by adults. However,
in their concluding remarks they suggest that 'there may be less
interest in selection in the sense of the relationship between education
and the propensity to migrate for the general population, than in
selection in the sense of education of migrants from particular areas or
types of areas as compared with the education of the non-migrants in
these same areas or than in the effect of net migration upon the
educational level of sending and receiving areas' (Shryock and Nam,
1965, 299). It was suggested by Hofstee (1952) that migration is not
necessarily selective with respect to intelligence and education and,
though it might seem that empirically the more intelligent and better
educated are more inclined to migrate, it is rather that the
circumstances are such that they more often have a motive to migrate
than those with less intelligence or education. There is also a
correlation between education and socio-economic status which in
turn links education with occupation. 'The lower status migrant achieves
his limited objectives at an earlier stage and with fewer moves than the
upper class migrant whose geographic movement keeps step with
periodic changes in a long drawn out career' (Illsley *et al.*, 1963, 218).
Generally, therefore, lower-class people find many more intervening
opportunities in a given distance than do upper-class people. It was
hypothesized by Rose (1958, 421) that in the United States 'higher
status persons seeking the better jobs or opportunities must move a
greater distance to find them', and his hypothesis was found to be
true within the limits of a single culture. (An exception to his general
findings were poor Negroes who migrated a considerable distance in
search of new opportunities.) This hypothesis was retested by Stub who
corroborated the major findings and concluded that 'median distance

of migration generally declines as one proceeds from those occupied as professionals to foremen and labourers' (Stub, 1962, 89). A further study of occupational differentials in the USA by Tarver (1964) also rejected any hypothesis that proposed equal migration rates among twelve occupational groups and concluded that in nearly every case-study professionals were more mobile than all other occupations. Income and occupation, too, are closely related factors and Olsson (1965) has hypothesized that the length of a migration is positively related to the level of income in both the place of origin and the place of destination, and found this to be a significant relationship. From this evidence it appears that occupational selectivity operates within specific socio-economic contexts, which depend heavily on the operating constraints between the sending and receiving areas (Long, 1973). As a result of this interstream occupational selectivity Stone (1969) has attempted to hypothesize the context for these differences. Briefly they may be summarized as:

(1) The structure of a region's economic activity and the composition of its population are related to the composition of the migration flows into the region.

(2) The greater the specialization of certain occupations within a region, the greater the migration among those persons involved in those occupations.

(3) The composition of in-migration to a region is related to the composition of its out-migration and both are systematically correlated to the structures of employed populations in the region.

Cultural and Ethnic Selectivity

Evidence of cultural and ethnic differentials in migration can best be illustrated from North America, where it has been extensively studied. For example, Stone (1969) found in Canada that the inter-provincial migration rate of English-speaking Canadians was much greater than for the French speakers. On the other hand, there was little difference in the intra-provisional migration rates of the two groups. Such evidence suggests the continued significance of cultural cohesion within French Quebec as well as the lack of inter-provincial ethnic and cultural assimilation. However, the differential which has been most extensively studied is the migration rates of white and non-white populations in the United States (Deskins, 1972). Broadly, these studies conclude that the mobility of the Negro population is less than that of the white population unless '(1) the demand for unskilled labour is more insistent than it was during the 1950s and early 1960s, (2) racial discrimination is reduced, and (3) the education and skill level of the Negro population becomes more comparable to that of the white population' (Lansing and Mueller, 1967, 288).

Another important factor which contributes towards migration selectivity is the nature and form of family attachments (Miller, 1970). It has been argued that an extended family structure hinders migration because the potential disruption of a move may deter a migration decision or even avert its consideration in the first instance (Crawford, 1966; Brandes, 1975). For example, Johnston (1971) has detailed the extent to which extended family attachment constrained the level of migration out of a series of village communities in the Yorkshire Dales. On the other hand, studies of migratory flows from Appalachia have emphasized that kin connection in neighbouring cities is not only a stimulus to migration but also provides the basis for the selection of a destination by the ruralite (Brown, Schwarzweller and Mangalam, 1963). Despite this conflicting evidence on the role of kinship on migration potential it is true, however, that while geographic mobility may modify kin structures, it is not necessarily disruptive of kin relationships (Litwak, 1960). It may be that family obligations require a potential migrant to remain at home despite beliefs that aspirations cannot be satisfied there (Hannan, 1970). In contrast, migration does not necessarily break the bonds of family attachment (Tilly and Brown, 1967), and, because there is no regular contact, it does not mean that there is no affective tie. A study of the middle classes in London suggested that 'geographic proximity in itself does not imply, or socially necessitate, intense contact between kin' (Hubert, 1965).

From the foregoing discussion it is readily apparent that a variety of factors contribute to the selectivity of migrants; yet their significance is far from uniform in both time and space. Despite this lack of uniformity, however, when the factors of differentiation are considered in relation to each other, fundamental implications for a theory of migration selectivity emerge. From the evidence provided by the case-studies quoted in the preceding paragraphs it may be put forward as a working hypothesis that differential migration varies in character according to the nature of the population and the environment involved. Of the differentials discussed, age, education and occupation appear to operate as the more powerful discriminators of migrants, thus making Bogue's (1969, 793) comment of considerable significance:

Only one migration differential seems to have systematically withstood the test — that for age. The following generalization has been found to be valid in many places and for long periods of time. Persons in their late teens, twenties and early thirties are much more mobile than younger or older persons. Migration is highly associated with the first commitment and acts of adjustment of adulthood that are made by adolescents as they mature (e.g. entrance in the labour force, marriage, family foundation).

This suggests not only that many of the differentials are not independent of each other, but are highly interrelated within a life cycle and career pattern. Further, it is evident that this form of selectivity itself is not uniform in all places at all times; in other words, certain principles of selectivity can be identified under specified combinations of environmental and population conditions at places of origin and destination. Therefore, 'in any particular sub-region and at any particular moment in time, internal migration is selective of persons with particular combinations of traits' (Bogue, 1969, 794). In an effort to interrelate the significance of various factors in explaining the propensity of an individual to migrate, let us now consider the role of life cycle and differential environmental conditions as predictors of migration selectivity.

Life Cycle and Career Pattern

In their study of individual migration histories Van Arsdol, Jnr., Sabagh and Butler (1968) noted that an individual's migratory potential changed with his or her position in the family life cycle. From the formation to the dissolution of the cycle, critical events can be identified which increase or decrease the propensity to migrate (Table 6.1), which, at an intra-urban scale, involves outward shifts of families towards the suburbs until old age is reached when a reversal in direction begins (Figure 6.3). Among the critical events which commonly increase the probability to migrate are marriage and child-bearing; by the time the last child has been born a phase of reduced mobility is reached since suitable housing has usually been found to accommodate the family at its maximum size (Michelson, 1977; 1980). In support of this suggestion Long (1972, 380-1) has revealed that in the United States the largest families have the lowest rate of inter-county movements. This stability continues until the

Table 6.1: Life Cycle and Migration Potential

Age	Family Membership	Migration
0	Family of origin	← All moves are tied to the family
12		
18	Single person	← Decision to leave home
25	Married couple	← Move on marriage
30		← Moves as a result of the expansion of the family and the need for more dwelling space
	Member of a rearing family	Long period of stability because of desire for educational continuity
	Decreasing family	← Children begin to leave home
50	Older couple	← Moves adjusting dwelling space to reduced needs
60		← Retirement migration
70	Single older person	← Widowhood

Note: Each arrow (←) represents a possible move.

phase of family dissolution is reached when the probability to migrate increases again. As the children leave home the parents begin to reconsider their residential needs, and retirement provides a further opportunity to re-evaluate not only their housing but also their environmental circumstances. Finally, infirmity caused by age and the death of the spouse can also precipitate moves as the home becomes more difficult to manage. According to Golant (1972) and Wiseman and Virden (1977), in their studies in Toronto and Kansas City respectively, the major movement of the elderly was away from the central city into suburban areas with only a small counter-flow toward the city centre. Therefore, demographic factors such as an individual's age, sex and marital status in combination with such conditions as family size, home ownership, status, etc., are usually conceived as indicators of the family life cycle.

The first, and most significant, interpretation of migration by means of the life cycle approach was Rossi's (1955) classic study of residential mobility in Philadelphia, which concluded that the 'major function of mobility is the process by which families adjust their housing to the housing needs that are generated by the shifts in family composition that accompany life cycle changes' (Rossi, 1955, 4). Despite several later researchers, for example Simmons (1974) in Toronto and Herbert (1973a) in Swansea, reaching similar conclusions, many others, however, have revealed that life cycle changes are never perfectly correlated with mobility levels and, therefore, raise a question mark

Figure 6.3: Life Cycle Changes and Likely Residential Mobility Within a City

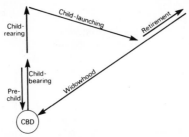

over the universality of the cycle as a differentiator in migration potential. Even among intra-urban migrants, Morgan (1976) has argued that in Exeter the life cycle dimension only partly explained the selectivity of migrants; in fact he suggests that constraints of housing availability, access to mortgages and council housing, etc., provided significant additional predictors of migratory potential (Speare, 1970; Pickvance, 1974). In another context, Nalson's (1968) study of farmer mobility in Staffordshire suggests that the nature of the occupation and the opportunities within it were crucial differentiating factors. Clearly the evidence provided by these studies suggests the necessity to consider the selectivity of the life cycle dimension within the broader context of social mobility and career patterns (Musgrave, 1963). Even Rossi (1955, 179) recognized this when he argued that 'families moving up the occupational "ladder" are particularly sensitive to the social aspects of location and use residential mobility to bring their residences into line with their prestige needs'. At a regional scale Keowan (1971) has revealed that in New Zealand career advancement was reflected in a stepwise migration process (Figure 6.4). With reference to Western Sutherland three groups of career transients were identified: those leaving for the regional capital early in their career, those leaving either for other country areas or for the regional capital, consequent upon a promotion, and those arriving from either the regional capital or other country areas to take up intermediate positions of responsibility. Despite this evidence, however, a number of other studies suggest that the role of social mobility in generating migration should not be overemphasized. For example, Lipset and Bendix (1952) using two class categories, found that only 30 per cent of North Americans leave the social class in which they were raised and hence residential relocation is required only once in the lifetime of a third of the population. Goldstein and Mayer (1963) also revealed that in

Figure 6.4: Migration and Distance According to Career Group

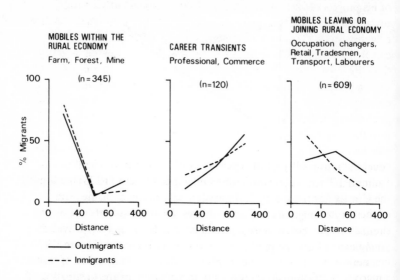

Source: After Keowan, 1971, 175–84.

Rhode Island over 60 per cent of all moves adjust housing within a neighbourhood of similar characteristics. Such movement patterns suggest the need to distinguish between two types of careerists – the spiralists and the locals.

> The ideal-type of the spiralist is to be found in William H. Whyte's American 'Organisation Man', a manager in a large corporation who moves around the country either at the corporation's bidding or while changing corporations. He is prepared to go anywhere to further his career. If, on the other hand, the middle-class man achieves his career progression while staying within one particular locality, he is termed a local. (Mann, 1973)

A notable attempt to assess the relative significance of life cycle and career factors in determining differential propensity to migrate was Leslie and Richardson's (1961) pioneering study of residential mobility in Lafayette. For the purpose of analysis the life cycle dimension was identified by three variables: age of household head, household size and tenure status, and the career dimension by five: years of formal education completed by head of household, the respondent's estimate of his social class compared with his neighbours, respondent's estimate of his prospects for upward social mobility, respondent's attitude towards present housing, and respondent's attitude towards his present neighbourhood. The results obtained suggested that, in general, the career variables were more highly correlated with residential mobility than life cycle ones. Of the individual variables, it was found that the respondent's estimation of his prospects for upward social mobility in combination with years of formal education were the most significant predictors of migration. A similar study carried out by Jansen (1968) into the future migratory intentions of the residents of Bristol also concluded that migratory behaviour was highly associated with higher educational and occupational status. Even at the regional scale Ladinsky's (1966) study of inter-county migration of professionals in the United States between 1955 and 1966 confirmed the significance of social mobility as the prime predictor of differential migration. In summary what these studies suggest is that whereas a combination of young married professional with a higher educational level but a low income would stimulate migration, a change in status from a single to a married professional (especially if a family were involved) would tend to dampen migration. Although the life cycle and career pattern framework provides some useful insights into the differential susceptibility of individuals to migrate, according to Shaw (1975, 36), however, the processes involved 'are little more than loose interrelations of various factors believed to influence the selectivity of migrants'. Also more recent evidence suggests that migration differentials are more time and place specific than generalizable.

Environmental Conditions

According to Bogue, much of the difficulty encountered in any attempt to derive a theory of migration selectivity is that 'migration can be highly selective with respect to a given characteristic in one area and be selective to a mild degree, or not at all, in another area' (Bogue, 1969, 795). This suggests that if the principles of selectivity are to be built into general models of migration, then the selective components may have to be weighted according to the setting and composition of the population sub-groups.

In order to illustrate Bogue's point, reference will be made to three case-studies, each emphasizing different scales and contexts of migration. The first, Lewis's (1981a) study of mobility in a part of the

Welsh Borderland between 1966 and 1976, emphasized the complexity
of migration selectivity even at a local scale. Two likely factors of
selectivity, occupational and life cycle, were investigated within the
context of parochial, in- and out-migrations. Of the five
occupational types used in the analysis the out-migrants were
predominantly of professional and intermediate occupations,
particularly over long distances, with the skilled and semi-skilled of
greater significance at short and medium distances. The in-migrants
were less selective, with only a slight emphasis on intermediate
occupations, and little difference according to distance. On the
other hand, inter-parochial migrants, in general, were of the semi-skilled
and unskilled types of occupations. Clearly this pattern of occupational
selectivity indicates that anyone with skills and education if they desire
advancement were forced to migrate beyond the study area. Also the
manual nature of the local migrants' occupations suggests the operation
of a local employment and housing market whilst the lack of any clear-cut
differences in the occupations of the in-migrants indicates the
growing significance of retirement and even commuting in the
migration process. In terms of selectivity by sex, females were most
predominant among the short- and medium-distance out-migrants and
only marginally so among inter-parochial and long-distance movers. On
the other hand, in-migrants, irrespective of distance, were not
particularly differentiated by sex. Clearly this pattern of selectivity
emphasizes the lack of tertiary employment in and around the district.
As would be expected the young age groups were by far the most
mobile, although the older groups revealed higher rates than the mature
categories. Yet the inter-parochial migrants tended to be those of
the middle age groups, no doubt indicating the influence of
housing needs as marriage takes place and families are formed. Over
long distances the out-migrants were predominantly from the younger
age groups, whilst the in-migrants over similar distances were of the
older groups. From this brief summary it is clear, however, that the
life cycle factor did play a significant role in the migratory behaviour
of these rural residents. Since the young residents were aspiring towards
career advancement and better housing, the limited economic and social
opportunities of not only the local area but also the region as a whole
were reflected in the greater distances they were prepared to migrate.
In contrast, the in-migration of the elderly was over both long and short
distances: the former in search of rural residence upon retirement and
the latter upon widowhood or senility, often to reside with their
children or in some cases entry into an old people's home. The stability

Figure 6.5: Classification of the Age Structure of Mover and Stayer
Populations in Australia, 1966–71

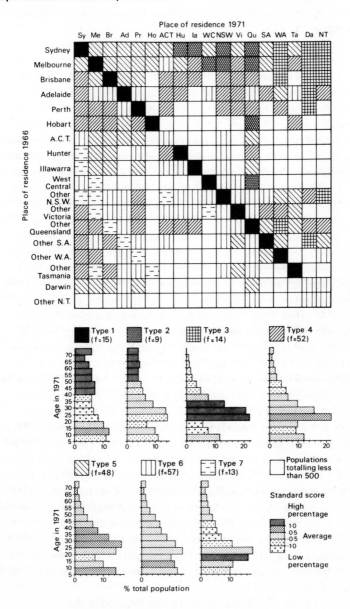

Source: After Rowland, 1979, 105.

of the middle age group was particularly evident; only a few moved out and even less entered the district. Evidently this group had reached a *modus vivendi* with the limited social and economic opportunities of the region.

Similar differences in the pattern of migration selectivity has been identified by studies in other contexts. For example, between 1955 and 1960, 14 per cent of United States migrants were return migrants, and Deaton and Anschel (1974) attempted to delineate their characteristics with reference to those returning to eastern Kentucky from Cincinnati. By means of discriminant analysis it was found that return migrants differed from those migrants remaining in the city in that they were older, less educated, received lower incomes, had lower expectations of remaining in the city, and had lower rates of home ownership. Even at the regional scale the selectivity within migratory flows is evident. For example, Rowland (1979), in his analysis of movement between the 18 major statistical divisions of Australia, has revealed significant age-selectivity between origins and destinations. From a cluster analysis seven major types of mover-stayer populations were recognized (Figure 6.5). Briefly, Type 1 identified the stayer population, the majority of whom were aged 40 years or over, and clearly reflected the tendency towards stability with the advancement in age. Although Type 2 also involved middle aged and older people, these were movers, principally from capital cities to 'select' locations like the coast or metropolitan fringes. Type 3 populations, which were distinguished by involving only frontier destinations, included family migrations and movements of industrial workers. Many of these moves involved young men seeking employment in the northern mining areas which include much of Australia's development frontier. Although Types 4, 5 and 6 moves were characterized by a family-dominated age structure, they, however, involved a variety of origins and destinations, including inter-state streams and counter-streams between capital cities and other non-metropolitan cities, between non-metropolitan areas, and between capital cities as well as intra-state migrants from capital cities to their hinterland. It is evident from Figure 6.5 that among the inter-state moves there was a high degree of population change. Finally, Type 7 was distinguished by intra-state moves from non-metropolitan hinterlands to capital cities, thus identifying in an Australian context the well-known exodus of young people from the countryside to the major cities.

On the basis of evidence similar to that outlined in the preceding paragraphs, Bogue has suggested that certain principles of migration selectivity can be identified under specified combinations of environmental and population conditions at places of origin and destination. These principles were summarized by Jansen (1970, 15-16) as follows:

(1) There is a series of stages in the development of any major migration stream. From initial invasion it develops into a phase of settlement which at its peak becomes routine, institutionalized. In the initial stages, men outnumber the women, but with the settlement phase sex selectivity tends to disappear or even favour women. During initial stages, migration is highly selective of young but mature adults, persons who are single, divorced or widowed.

(2) Migration stimulated by economic growth, technological improvements, etc., attracts the better educated. Conversely, areas tending to stagnation lose their better educated and skilled persons first.

(3) If between two population points streams of equal size tend to flow, neither making net gains, then the composition of migration streams in each direction tends to be of minimum selectivity. If the stream flowing in one direction is greater than that flowing in the other direction, there is a greater selectivity in both streams. But the place showing a net gain would have a greater proportion of males, young adults, single, divorced and widowed, while the place having a net loss would have high proportions of 'migration failures' (returnees), employees of new establishments, local migrants 'passing through' on their way to bigger centres and retired migrants returning to their place of origin.

(4) Where the 'push' factor is very strong (famine, drought, etc.), origin selectivity is at a minimum; where 'pull' stimulus is greater, there will be an appreciable selectivity.

(5) In modern technological societies, major streams which flow between metropolitan centres tend to have very little selectivity of migrants.

Although this summary provides a broad generalization about the selectivity of migration in differing environmental conditions, it still, however, fails to develop a meaningful socio-economic profile of each migratory stream. An interesting attempt to derive such profiles was Wolpert's (1969) identification, based on a one in a thousand sample from the 1960 United States census, of the socio-economic and demographic characteristics of migrants moving to or from rural, town, city and metropolitan residences. These profiles were achieved by means of an interactive analysis of variance classification scheme known as the Automatic Interaction Detector (AID), which essentially provides a classification of a population into relatively homogeneous groups on a continuum from least to most mobile. In the analysis household migration was the dependent variable and ten independent variables such as age, sex, education, social status, etc., were employed as predictors of migration. Although the results obtained confirmed Bogue's suggestions that migration selectivity varies in time and space, they, however, cannot be taken as universals since there is still a dearth of similar analytical studies elsewhere.

Despite the quest for universals of differential migration being so far largely unsuccessful, it is, however, evident that there does appear to exist a small number of variables which are highly associated with an individual's propensity to migrate. Such variables do provide a useful insight into the migration process, particularly when considered within an individual's position in the life cycle and career pattern and the broader context of time and space. Evidently, individuals differently located in space and social structure have different degrees of knowledge about, and are able to benefit to differing extents from, opportunities at places other than those in which they currently reside. Therefore, the succeeding two chapters will be concerned with that knowledge; firstly, with the underlying motives for migrating, and secondly, with how people decide to migrate.

7 CAUSES OF MIGRATION

Unlike birth and death, migration has no physiological component; rather it is a response by humans to a series of economic, social and political stimuli within the environment. Such stimuli take the form of attractiveness of a location which can be generated by changes within the environment or in a person's value system. If, as a result of these changes, the person becomes dissatisfied with his home location, then a desire to migrate will be generated. The strength of the desire to migrate, and whether it is fulfilled or not, will vary according to the needs of the individual, the constraints upon him and the strength of the dissatisfaction (Pryor, 1975b). For example, according to Lord Eversley the vast exodus of labourers from the rural districts into the towns of England and Wales during the nineteenth century was due not only to 'greater prosperity and the general rise of wages in the manufacturing and mining districts', but also 'to a growing disinclination to farm work among labourers in rural districts, to the absence of opportunities to them of rising in their vocation, and to a desire for the greater independence and freedom of life in towns' (Eversley, 1907, 280). Within this listing of the factors explaining migration, two undifferentiated sets of forces appear to exist: on the one hand, there are stimuli to migrate created by changes within the environment and, on the other, changes in the personal motives of the individual.

The analysis of migration causes has attracted considerable attention, in particular the decision to migrate, the decision where to migrate to, and the criteria involved in such decisions. Most of the emphasis of the research, however, has been on the latter aspect of the causal nexus (Cebula, 1980); the decision-making context having only recently become a focus of attention (see Chapter 8). Yet despite the diversity and volume of these causal studies, Lee (1966, 49) emphasized the need for caution when interpreting their results, 'since we can never specify the exact set of factors which impels or prohibits migration for a given person, we can in general, only set forth a few which seem of special importance and note the general or average reaction of a given group'.

99

A Simple Causal Model

PUSH + PULL

As long ago as 1938 Herberle (1938) argued that migration is caused by a series of forces which encourage an individual to leave one place (push) and attract him to another (pull). In other words, if an individual's needs cannot be satisfied at his present location, then a move elsewhere may be considered. On the other hand, despite being satisfied with his present situation, information about greater opportunities elsewhere may persuade the individual to move. For each migration, however, several push and pull forces may be operating and interacting, so that the move cannot be attributed wholly to either force. However, by examining large migration flows, the common stimulants to movement may be established. Bogue has succinctly summarized these 'push-pull' forces as follows:

Push factors
(1) Decline in a national resource or in the prices paid for it; decreased demand for a particular product or the services of a particular industry; exhaustion of mines, timber or agricultural resources.
(2) Loss of employment resulting from being discharged for incompetence, for a decline in need for a particular activity, or from mechanization or automation of tasks previously performed by more labour-intensive procedures.
(3) Oppressive or repressive discriminatory treatment because of political, religious or ethnic origins or membership.
(4) Alienation from a community because one no longer subscribes to prevailing beliefs, actions or mode of behaviour – either within one's family or within the community.
(5) Retreat from a community because it offers few or no opportunities for personal development employment or marriage.
(6) Retreat from a community because of catastrophe – floods, fire, drought, earthquake or epidemic.
Pull factors
(1) Superior opportunities for employment in one's occupation or opportunities to enter a preferred occupation.
(2) Opportunities to earn a larger income.
(3) Opportunities to obtain desired specialized education or training such as a college education.
(4) Preferable environment and living conditions – climate, housing, schools, other community facilities.

Figure 7.1: Origin and Destination Factors and Intervening Obstacles in Migration

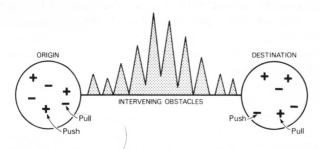

Source: Adapted from Lee, 1966, 47–57.

(5) Dependency — movement of other persons to whom one is related or betrothed, such as the movement of dependents with a bread-winner or migration of a bride to join her husband.
(6) Line of new or different activities, environment or people, such as the cultural, intellectual or recreational activities of a large metropolis for rural and small-town residence (Bogue, 1969, 753–4).

Despite the push-pull theory's elegant abstraction of the specific forces generating migration, a number of researchers have criticized it as an oversimplification of a highly complex process. For example, Brinley Thomas (1954, 26) has cogently argued that

all sorts of promptings may lie behind the decision of an individual or family to leave one country in order to live in another . . . It is not by making a catalogue of such 'reasons' that one can hope to understand the phenomenon of migration any more than an attempt to describe the manifold motives leading people to want to buy a commodity would constitute analysis of demand. Nothing is easier than to draw up a list of factors labelled 'push' and 'pull' and then write a descriptive account in terms of these two sets of influences.

In response to such comments, Lee (1966) has suggested that migration causation needs to be viewed within a framework of factors associated with area of origin, area of destination, intervening obstacles, and the migrants themselves. What is suggested in Figure 7.1 is that each individual is exposed to a set of positive and negative factors at both the place of origin and different potential destinations. The decision whether to move will depend, therefore, upon an evaluation of all these forces within the context of various group and societal norms or biases. Such decisions may be modified by a set of intervening obstacles, such as legal restrictions, family attachments, personal anxiety, costs of the move, etc. Many of these obstacles may be slight in some instances and insurmountable in others and what may be trivial to some people may be prohibitive to others.

Levels of Analysis

In order to aid our interpretation, the causal analysis of migration may usefully be conceived, as suggested by Germani (1965), in terms of three levels of analysis. Each of the three approaches, though overlapping, focuses on a different perspective and, to a certain extent, involves a different spatial scale.

Objective

This level of analysis is concerned with the broad pattern of migration flows, the causes of which are derived from the attributes of the environment as well as those of the migration streams. Essentially, the approach has been to infer the influence of these determinants in terms of assumptions concerning the migrant's orientation to his environment and impute motives to the migrant. Within such a procedure, according to Speare, Goldstein and Frey (1974), a clear distinction must be made between what they term the 'areal determinants of residential mobility' (for example, locational, physical and social characteristics of areas), and 'individual and household determinants of mobility' (such as life cycle, socio-economic and ethnic factors, mobility potential and social and economic bonds). Most of this research has been involved with inter-regional and inter-urban migration, though of late there have been several attempts to consider migratory flows within cities (Simmons, 1968; Moore, 1972).

Normative

According to Germani (1965), objective conditions do not operate in a vacuum since institutional roles, expectations, beliefs and values of a society, provide a framework within which an individual makes a decision whether to migrate or not. For example, to an outsider what might appear to be bad economic conditions, might not generate a desire to migrate 'if they correspond to a traditional pattern which is not only institutionalized in the norms, values and beliefs of the society but, also, continues to operate as an internalized expectation in the mind of the people' (Germani, 1965, 162). Much of the research in this field has been based on interview or questionnaire response to a limited number of questions such as 'Why did you move?', 'Why did you choose your present residence?' etc. Usually such questions have been asked of individuals and groups within recognizably defined small areas such as cities, residential districts, villages, etc.; on the other hand, large-scale surveys, although increasing in number, have been more limited due to the time, cost and sampling problems involved.

Psycho-social

Many researchers have argued that a knowledge of ideal norms and values provide an insufficient basis for an adequate understanding of the migration process, thus leading Germani (1965, 162) to suggest that 'the attitudes and expectations of concrete individuals must also be taken into account'. Essentially this level of analysis is concerned with the decision-making processes of individuals, it being more holistic and individually based than the first two approaches. All the factors involved in the act of migration are considered, with the emphasis being placed upon how individuals decide to migrate, the forces generating the desire to move and the resistances hampering the achievement of such desires.

   Although these three levels of analysis may be conceived as lying on a continuum of increasing ability to specify the reasons for migrating, it must be stressed, however, that the elements involved do not operate independently: on the contrary they are closely interdependent. Effectively, what is being highlighted by Germani is that migration is a highly complex system, which can only be unravelled by the adoption of several alternative approaches. Therefore, in order to achieve a greater understanding of the complexity of migration causation, the three suggested approaches will now be considered in greater detail; the first two levels will be considered in this chapter whilst the third, often referred to as the behavioural approach, forms the basis of the succeeding chapter.

The Objective Level

This approach to migration causation interprets the amount and direction of migratory flows as being the results of prolonged disequilibria of particular kinds between areas. At the national and regional scales it has been claimed that economic differentials are the prime causes of migration whilst social and cultural forces have only tentatively been acknowledged. Such an analysis 'explains' the migratory streams in terms of the attributes of the environment and of the population of the areas involved and, therefore, relies heavily on the use of secondary data, aggregative predictive models, and sophisticated statistical techniques for the estimation of general parameters (ter Heide, 1963; Cebula, 1980). Even within this approach several different procedures have been adopted by researchers; for illustrative purposes only three will be considered here: economic growth models, cost-benefit analysis and *ad hoc* regression models.

Economic Growth

Economic growth models view migration as a cause and consequence of the modernization and growth of an economy, and, therefore, existing and potential employment opportunities are basically a function of its level and rate of development (Gober-Meyers, 1978a). Within the growth of an economy there are cycles of 'booms' and 'depressions' and it has been posited that there is a relationship between these cyclical economic fluctuations and the volume of migration. Undoubtedly, one of the most significant contributions on this theme is the three-volume study *Population Redistribution and Economic Growth, United States: 1870–1950* (D.S. Thomas and S. Kuznets, 1957–64). It was demonstrated that between 1870 and 1950 population redistribution was the result of differential economic development in different regions and states at different periods. In a similar vein a United Nations study (1953, 16) concluded that 'migration to and from cities is related to fluctuations in the business cycle. During periods of prosperity the increasing demand for labour in industrial areas is satisfied partly by an increased inflow of migrants . . . during periods of depression and unemployment in industrial areas the city-ward migration is checked, and . . . may even be turned in the direction of rural areas'. However, evidence from several third world countries fails to confirm this hypothesis (Herrick, 1965), yet at the international scale a number of studies, for example, Jerome (1926) for the United States and Dorothy Thomas (1941) for Sweden, have shown how immigration fluctuated with the phase of the business cycle in a country. However, Brinley Thomas (1954, 34) has suggested that this is too limited a perspective arguing that 'what is needed is a concept of economic development which stresses the ordering of markets, the dynamic of increasing returns, and the international mobility of labour and capital as a medium through which an international economy grows and changes its character'. He then proceeds to view the nations on both sides of the Atlantic as a single evolving economy, in which there is a flow of labour, capital and commodities from one to the other. Clearly, any changes in the relationship between the two economies affects not only international migration but also migratory movement within each country.

Cost-benefit Analysis

Another economic interpretation of migration is provided by those who adopt a cost-benefit procedure. Essentially, in such a procedure migration is regarded as an investment activity which requires a cost to be incurred and a return to be produced (Okun and Richardson, 1961). Such costs include both financial costs, such as 'opportunities foregone', and costs incurred in moving the family and its effects, and social costs, which involve an estimate of the loss in leaving the home environment, friends and relatives. In other words, cost is 'perceived more concretely and positively than most other indices of general economic development as far as the individual migrant is concerned' (Todaro, 1969, 137). A pioneering work along these lines was that of Sjastaad (1962) who developed a migration model in the form:

$$\text{Mij} = \frac{(\text{Ydj} - \text{Yi}) - \text{T}}{\text{N}(1 + \text{r})^j}$$

where:

Mij	=	migration from area i to j
Ydj	=	earnings in qth year at destination
Yi	=	earnings in qth year at the origin
T	=	cost of moving
N	=	number of years in which earnings are expected
r	=	discount rate on future earnings

This formulation has been tested in a variety of different situations (Shaw, 1974). An interesting early application was that by Diehl (1966) in a study of rural out-migration in the United States. Although the variables used in the study were only indirectly related to the theoretical constructs, the results obtained, however, did largely confirm the predictive capacity of the model. Since then, several

promising attempts have been made to elaborate Sjastaad's model
by the inclusion of additional parameters known to influence the costs
and returns in the equation, including risk of unemployment,
proximity to friends, psychological costs of moving, etc. For example,
Todaro and associates (Harris and Todaro, 1970; Rempel and Todaro,
1972; Todaro, 1976), in their attempts to explain the increasing rural
to urban migration rates in third world countries, developed a model
which incorporated not only expected rather than observed incomes
but also the probability of urban employment. Speare (1971), in his
analysis of rural-urban migration in Taiwan, went as far as to include an
information factor as well as a non-pecuniary one in the form of the
location of the migrant's parents relative to the path of migration. By
transforming the cost-benefit equation into a multiple regression form
and using data derived from a personal migration survey, Speare
attempted to estimate the significance of the components involved. His
results indicated the ordering of the factors to be: cost of moving,
parents of respondent living at place of destination, information on job
opportunities, expected income to be higher at destination than at
origin, wife's parents living at destination, unemployment level in place
of origin, and home ownership at place of origin. However, despite the
success of the study, Speare (1971, 129) concluded that 'it should not
be interpreted to mean that the costs and benefits of migration are
actually calculated. In fact, our limited data suggests that people have
only vague concepts of costs and benefits'.

Regression Models

A more rigorous approach to the interpretation of migratory movement
as a function of man's response to economic stress and opportunities
has been the application of regression-based models. Essentially, such
models involve the investigation of the dependency of some measure of
migration on one or more explanatory variables, such as changes in
employment or total population over a period of time, wage rates,
unemployment rates, social structure, and even distance. Since the
causes of migration cannot be reduced to a single factor a variety of
influences have to be considered, which the model ranks according to
their predictive power. For example, in a study of net-migration
between counties in the United States, Kariel (1963) employed four
independent variables: median family income, size of labour force,
changes in the number employed in manufacturing, and the proportion
of professional employees. Of these variables it was found that the size
of labour force was the main predictor. On the other hand, population

size and distance between areas were the most influential of 21 variables in determining inter-metropolitan migration in the United States (R.B. Adams, 1969). By the inclusion not only of 'push-pull' factors but also measures of distance and intervening opportunities, it has been argued that regression models provide a more holistic 'explanation' of the migration process.

Despite the widespread use of regression procedures in migration analysis, many of the early attempts failed to recognize the high degree of interrelatedness among the independent variables (Bogue, Shryock and Hoermann, 1953), thus reducing the validity of their conclusions and making comparisons more difficult. For example, when population size and, to a lesser extent, the distance factor are major predictors of migration, it is no doubt due to the fact that both include a wide variety of other related factors. A number of suggestions have been put forward to overcome these problems of multicollinearity (Willis, 1975; Hauser, 1974; Taylor, 1980). Several researchers, including Olsson (1965), have employed a stepwise regression technique in order to reduce the multicollinearity within their data sets. Unfortunately, such a procedure is weakened by the tendency for highly intercorrelated variables to eliminate each other. Only when there are prior guidelines and the number of variables is small can the stepwise procedure be used effectively. On the other hand, an alternative solution was proposed by Riddell (1970) in a study of migration to Freetown, Sierra Leone, when he reduced the correlated explanatory variables by means of a principal component analysis, which produced a new set of independent dimensions which expressed the underlying similarities of the original variables. Similarly, in an analysis of migration in southern Italy, Allan Rodgers (1970) also subjected a set of socio-economic variables to a principal component analysis and produced a first component (levels of socio-economic health) which accounted for 37 per cent of the variance identified (Figure 7.2). A stepwise multiple regression between net migration ratios for 1952–68 and the scores on this first component revealed that two-thirds of the spatial variations in migration levels in southern Italy was accounted for by differences in socio-economic health. Even though socio-economic health was twice as important as component II (variables measuring the origins of previous migrants, termed migrant stock), Rodgers (1970, 128) rightly pointed out that 'migrant stock as measured in this analysis, is not independent of the variables in principal component I, so that the problems of multicollinearity, which are not resolved by the stepwise regression format, may weaken our "explanation".'

Figure 7.2: Migration from southern Italy: a — net out-migration, 1952–68, as a percentage of 1960 population; b — socio-economic health (principal component I)

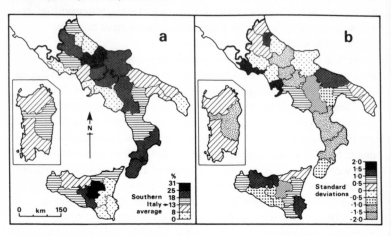

Source: After Rodgers, 1977, 111–35.

In view of these continuing difficulties with regression analysis, Hocking (1976) has argued that if prior guidelines exist, as they certainly do in the case of migration causation, then a few specifically chosen regressors should be applied directly within a full multiple-regression. 'It is very important, therefore, to have a sound theoretical model of the process being studied before any analysis is undertaken as this can lead to inconsistent and nonsensical results' (Willis, 1975, 45). This point can be illustrated at two geographical scales: intra-urban and inter-regional migrations.

Residential mobility within the city has, in general, been interpreted within the economists' residential trade-off model. Briefly, this assumes that householders trade off accessibility and space in order to maximize utility, which results in the poor living close to their work in order to reduce transport costs whilst the wealthy are located on the urban periphery because of their high income elasticity of demand for space. Such a model has been used as a guideline for the incorporation of life cycle, housing and neighbourhood variables into a regression analysis of the causes of residential mobility. For example, Moore (1971) selected six variables (age, single females, family dwellings, owner-occupation, Australian-born and accessibility) as likely determinants of population turnover in southern Brisbane in 1961. Yet, despite the general applicability of the assumptions, it was found that meaningful relationships between the variables over and above some association with accessibility was not achieved. According to Clark (1972), such inconclusive relationships result from a failure to consider the economic constraints of income and housing costs. He argued that given the initial location of a household and a statement of the income distribution characteristics of a city's sub-areas, it is possible to determine those sub-areas to which a household is most likely to move. In a study of Milwaukee residents, he found that income and housing costs were the prime determinants of moves and, therefore, argued that 'it is only within these constraints that the perturbations of preferences can be examined and measured' (Clark, 1976, 59). Thus if these can be linked to the already established notions of distance decay (Chapter 4), then we may be a little closer to an understanding of movements within the city (Weinberg, 1979).

In contrast, attempts to *a priori* specify causes of inter-regional migrations in regression terms have, in general, emphasized the role of employment opportunities as the major factor in determining the size and direction of movement. Of the several models suggested, conceptually, the Lowry model appears to be the most satisfactory. This model can be represented by the equation (Lowry, 1966):

$$ \text{Mij} = K \ \frac{\text{Ui}}{\text{uj}} \ \frac{\text{Wj}}{\text{Wi}} \ \frac{\text{LiLj}}{\text{Dij}} \ \text{Eij} $$

where

Mij	=	number of migrants from i to j
LiLj	=	numbers of persons in non-agricultural employment at i and j respectively
Ui,Uj	=	unemployment as a percentage of the number in non-agricultural employment at i and j respectively
Wi,Wj	=	hourly manufacturing wage at i and j respectively
Dij	=	straight line distance separating i and j
Eij	=	error term
K	=	constant

Andrei Rogers (1967; 1968) in a study of inter-county migration in California, had to make some modification to the variables. Such changes reflect the significant role of agriculture in a number of the counties in California. The modifications were:

Li,Lj = number of persons in the civilian labour force at i and j respectively

Ui,Uj = unemployment as a percentage of the civilian labour force at i and j respectively

Dij   = road mileage separating the major county seats at i and j

Based upon a regression analysis Rogers was able to claim that over 90 per cent of the variation in the migration pattern in California was accounted for by the seven variables, of which four were significantly different from zero at the 5 per cent confidence level. Five of the seven variables had the signs which one would have expected. The coefficient of unemployment rates at i and j should, on *a priori* grounds, be positive and negative respectively, but surprisingly the analysis revealed a reversal of these signs and neither were statistically significant. Rogers found such a finding difficult to explain and, therefore, argued that it should be left out of the model. Similar adaptations of the Lowry model have been applied extensively to explain inter-regional flows of migration in different parts of the world, for example, United States (Greenwood, 1968; Alperovich, Bergsman and Eheman, 1977), Latin America (Jones and Zannaras, 1976), and southern Asia (Greenwood, 1971). In order to assess the validity of its basic component parts, some illustrative examples from two contrasting environments, Britain and Africa, will now be discussed briefly.

Until recently any explanation of inter-regional migration in Britain has been dominated by the view of labour economists that its prime determinant is spatial differences in unemployment. For example, in a study of inter-regional movements in England and Wales between 1951 and 1961, Oliver (1964) argued that the most striking feature was the loss of people through migration from regions with high unemployment and the gains by regions with high employment opportunities. But, however, there was also contradictory evidence.

There is a large measure of disparity in the response to changes in unemployment conditions in the various regions. The models are useful for male migration and for total migration. They work best for the Midlands and Scotland and quite well for London, the North West and Northern Region. The remaining four regions show no evidence that unemployment influences the volume of their net migration. (Oliver, 1964, 63).

During the past decade these doubts over the efficacy of

unemployment as a prime predictor of migration between regions has been confirmed mainly as a result of a series of significant papers by Hart. Using a gravity formulation combined with variables selected on the basis of residuals from the migration/gravity relationship, Hart (1970) found that unemployment and indices of relative earnings contributed little to the explanation of gross inter-regional migration in England and Wales between 1960 and 1961. Once the size and proximity of regions had been taken into account, the highest propensity to move was between regions with similarly high long-term rates of industrial building, while low migration took place between regions of slow growth. 'It is clear that the migration pattern in England and Wales is different from the one which is popularly emphasized. While there is certainly a fair degree of movement from underemployed to prosperous regions, by far the most significant degree of movement is taking place between prosperous and prosperous regions' (Hart, 1970, 272). This conclusion suggests that the employment structure of a region is of particular importance since many moves were in fact within the same employment sector, thus emphasizing the need to consider migration within the context of different socio-economic groups. Later Hart (1973) produced evidence for the different migratory behaviour and causation of professional, intermediate and manual workers by Standard Regions of Britain in 1966. At the more detailed county scale, the pattern of migration in 1965–6 bore little relation with unemployment and differential wage rates (Hart, 1972). Interestingly the most significant predictor of inter-county movements was changing employment opportunities in the previous period, 1961–6, thus raising the question as to the degree to which short-term employment growth and migration are independent. At this scale it must be pointed out that residential mobility must form a significant proportion of total migration. From this evidence it would appear that in order to achieve a fuller understanding there is a need to consider migration explanation in terms of the disaggregation of socio-economic groups as well as upon gross migration between areas smaller than regions (Bonnar, 1979).

The application of a Lowry-type regression model to explain migration in third world countries has been limited largely due to the dearth of suitable data. However, as a result of the inclusion of birthplace data in the recent censuses of several African countries, there has been a proliferation in the use of regression analysis in the study of migration in that continent (for example, Beals, Levy and Moses, 1967; Riddell, 1970; Claeson and Egero, 1972; Masser and Gould, 1975). One of the most significant of these contributions was that by Masser

112   *Causes of Migration*

Figure 7.3: Inter-regional Migration in Uganda, 1969. Positive (a) and negative (b) residuals in excess of 1.5 standard deviations from the mean

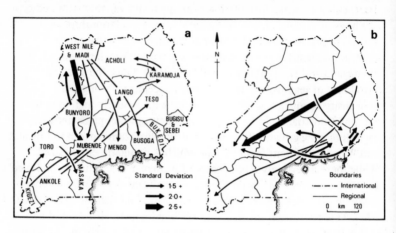

Source: After Masser and Gould, 1975, 86-7.

and Gould (1975) who developed a regression model to account for inter-regional migration in Uganda for 1969. Briefly, in the model migration between district i and j is related to the distances between district centres; population born in districts i and j; mean income per head of population; the proportion of males of working age employed in the urban wage sector; and the proportion of males who had received some education. The distribution of the residuals, in general, confirmed the model, although short-distance moves between rural areas had been slightly underestimated (Figure 7.3a) while long-distance rural migration was overestimated (Figure 7.3b). For example, the large positive residuals associated with West Nile and Kigezi suggest an underestimation of the outflows from these densely populated and depressed peripheral regions. The tendency for the model to underestimate moves into Mubende and to overestimate those into Toro reflect, respectively, changes in administrative boundaries and the omission from the census of one of the main foci. The significance of this study, apart from drawing attention to weaknesses in the data base, is that it emphasized the complexity of inter-rural migration as well as demonstrating the need for studies of African migration to consider all forms of mobility, rather than concentrating on rural to urban movements.

From the widespread application of regression techniques it would appear that inter-regional out-migration depends more on the size and structure of the population of the origin area than on levels of economic opportunity, and that in-migration is related to the size and condition of the labour market of the destination areas (D.W. Jones, 1975; Flowerdew and Salt, 1979; Kennett, 1980). On the other hand, many inconsistencies and contradictions have arisen, many of which can be attributed to the assumptions made in the model itself, at least three of which are worth mentioning here. Firstly, the push-pull hypothesis is an oversimplification of the migration process, since the nature of the areas involved and the migrants themselves need to be considered; secondly, the assumption that migration flows are independent random variables is not true since they are all interrelated in that destinations are competing with one another for migrants and migrants are competing against each other for destinations; and thirdly, despite attempts to provide the gravity hypothesis with a theoretical base (see Chapter 4), it is likely that more can be learnt about migration from a consideration of deviations from the model rather than from the regularities themselves. As a result of these deficiences several researchers have attempted to overcome them by the application of regression techniques within a highly specific context. Three of these studies will now be considered briefly.

The first was the attempt by Da Vanzo (1975) to show that push-pull factors operate differently for return and non-return migrants within inter-regional flows. From a multiple regression analysis of migration data from the United States census of 1960, it was concluded that: (1) economic factors explained a greater proportion of variance in non-return migration; (2) unemployment prompted return migration; (3) return migrants were less sensitive to higher earnings opportunities than non-return migrants; (4) financing was a less significant consideration in return migration; (5) information and psychic costs of return moves were lower and so distance was not a deterrent; and (6) black migrants were less likely to return south than their white counterparts. Clearly this study has revealed that return and non-return migrants respond differently and, therefore, should be treated separately (Bell and Kirwan, 1979). On the other hand, in the second study, Todd (1980) limited his 'explanation' of rural out-migration in Manitoba over the period 1966–71 to a series of 'push' factors. By so doing it was possible to isolate not only the major factors generating out-migration — average family income and high farm sales — but also the interdependence of migration levels, agricultural wellbeing and the state of the rural economy, which can promote further rural decline. In the

Figure 7.4: Inter-regional Migration in the United States, 1955–60:
a — destination regions and origin state attributes; b — origin regions
and destination state attributes

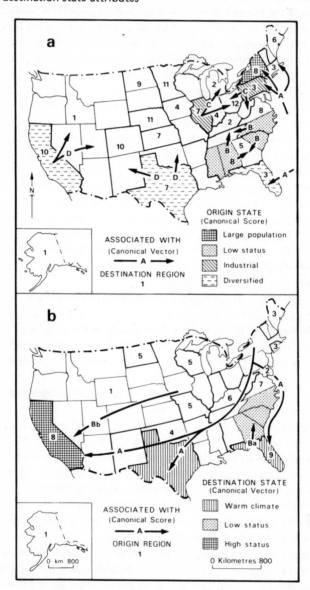

Source: After Schwind, 1975, 1–16.

third study, Schwind (1975) attempted to reduce the complexity of inter-regional migration flows in the United States by grouping them into a small number of origin and destination regions (or migration fields), and then estimating the relationship between migration and the socio-economic characteristics of each field. Following an earlier study (Schwind, 1971), a factorial procedure was adopted to identify both the groups of states with similar socio-economic characteristics and migration levels between 1955–60. The degree to which levels of migration were determined by the socio-economic character of each field was determined, using factor scores as input data, by means of a canonical analysis. Although the results obtained suggested that migration behaviour is not always determined by the attributes of the area involved, it is evident from Figure 7.4, however, that a number of interesting spatial relationships were found. Briefly, these may be summarized as follows:

(1) Certain migration and destination patterns were structured by large origin state populations and by amenable climate and high socio-economic status at the destination states, for example, New York to Florida, North east to Florida, Texas and California, and Midwest to California.
(2) A pronounced internal circulation among southern states of low socio-economic status.
(3) A tendency towards internal circulation among the states of the manufacturing belt, with the expected moves from the Appalachian states of unemployment to those of the manufacturing belt not being particularly significant.
(4) The association between migration and the diversified labour force of the southwestern states was only weakly significant and, therefore, difficult to interpret.
(5) The migration to and from the Mid Atlantic and New England fields had no attributes associated with it.

Despite the development of more elegant and sophisticated methodologies and approaches to the objective analysis of migration causation, little that is new has really emerged. The conclusions reached by Bogue, Shryock and Hoermann (1953) in the late forties in a study of *Subregional Migration in the United States, 1935–40*, are still valid today. Briefly, it was concluded that the direction and flow of migration was determined by:

(1) 'differences in employment between the place of origin and possible destinations . . .';
(2) 'basic shifts in the regional and territorial balance of the economy';
(3) 'above average educational attainment and employment in white collar occupations'; and
(4) 'a great variety of conditions, of which the economic may or may not comprise an important set of considerations, can lead to migration, and cause persons to join the particular migration streams they do' (quoted in Bogue, 1969, 792–3).

If the objective approach to migration analysis is to contribute towards a greater understanding of the process in the future, at least three problems will have to be overcome. Firstly, the recognition that the decision to migrate tends to lag behind the factors that originally stimulated the move (Greenwood, 1970); secondly, there has been a failure to recognize that there is a two-way interaction between socio-economic variables and the level of migration, often referred to as a simultaneous equation bias (Gober-Mayers, 1978b); and thirdly, there has been an overemphasis on purposively rational behaviour, thus denying the existence of differential motives and behaviour. As a result of these shortcomings there have over the past few years been attempts to utilize a more normative approach to the determination of migratory causation.

The Normative Level

The needs and desires which urge people to move from one place to another are notoriously difficult to identify because of their wide variety, even for an individual. Basically, we are dealing with what Davis (1945, 248) calls 'the motives that migrants carry in their heads', that is the most proximate factors directly taken into consideration by migrants in deciding whether to move from, or to remain in, their community of origin. Their personal beliefs, aspirations and obligations are the only variables of importance, social structural factors such as class, education or sex being significant only in so far as their effects are mediated through the more proximate personal motives.

In any consideration of the value of the normative level to the study of migration, some reference must be made to the problems involved in asking questions. Often the reasons for moving may be the result of several causes, which may not be mutually exclusive, and sometimes those which appear trivial might be the basis for finally triggering off the desire to move. Care must also be taken when framing the questions that the respondent clearly understand that reference is being made to a general area, or a neighbourhood, or a dwelling, etc. When comparing the results of several studies cognizance must be taken of whether the questions asked were pre-coded, open-ended or simply hypothetical, referring to future rather than past moves, since these procedures can provide a different ordering in the importance of the reasons elicited. Due to the cost and time involved in mounting a social survey, normative studies of migration causation tend to focus on a small locality or a specific social group. Where they are available, however, they are of considerable use in the evaluation of the objectively derived determinants of migration, although the linking of causes derived at a micro-scale to broad patterns of migration still remains a methodological difficulty. A part of this difficulty may be overcome if the results of the micro-studies are considered within the context of different migratory flows.

Inter-regional Migrations

Due to the problems of acquiring a representative sample, the number of normative studies of migration causation at an inter-regional level has been exceedingly limited. Of the few that are available they do provide support for the thesis that inter-regional migration is generated by employment and other economic factors (Morgan, 1977; Long and Hansen, 1979). Table 7.1 illustrates this point since all the three studies listed conclude that approximately 50 per cent of migrants in the United States stated that the reasons for moving were 'to take a job' and 'to look for work'. Similar reasons have been obtained by surveys in Britain (e.g. Harris and Clausen, 1963; North Regional Planning Committee, 1967; Department of the Environment, 1972), whilst an important survey undertaken by Girard, Bastide and Pourcher (1970) in France, not only emphasized the role of economic motives in regional migration but also suggested that they differ in their significance according to the destinations involved. For example, it was found that among those who had moved into cities employment and career advancement were the prime reasons; on the other hand, social reasons were the principal motives for moving into small towns and rural destinations. In third world countries large-scale migration surveys are much more limited. One of the earliest and most

Table 7.1: Reasons for Migrating in USA

a	%	b	%	c	%
Take a job	49.9	Take a job	29.5	Economic	58
Look for work	13.2	Look for work	11.9	Economic and	
Housing	15.0	Job transfer	8.1	non-economic	14
Change in marital		Marriage and		Non-economic	23
status	3.5	family	14.6	No reason	5
Health	2.7	Others	35.3		
Others	15.2				

Source: a: Current Population Survey, 1945–46.
b: Bureau of Labour Statistics, 1963.
c: Lansing and Mueller, 1967.

comprehensive was Caldwell's (1969) national study of Ghana, which
revealed that nearly three-quarters of both urban and rural migrants
 had <u>moved because of employment and income</u>. Among those who
had moved to the cities, the availability of educational and
entertainment facilities were additional motivating factors whilst lack
of water supplies, medical facilities and shortage of consumer goods
were frequently mentioned disadvantages of rural life.

Even though the purpose of these surveys may have differed, the
preeminence of the economic motive in migration is markedly similar
in both the developed and developing world. However, this similarity
should not be overemphasized since it would appear that in the third
world inter-regional migration is undertaken mainly by the
unemployed and the underpriviledged whilst in Western Europe and
North America migration is rapidly becoming an integral part of a
prosperous life-style. Inevitably any attempt to determine personal
reasons for migrating at a macro-scale conceals major differences
between various streams and between various social groups. In order
to overcome this difficulty most normative studies have tended to focus
upon place of origin or destination, whether it be rural or urban, and
even when the concern is a specific social group, it usually has been
considered within a particular environmental context.

Urban Migrations

Migratory flows involving an urban environment include movements
into, out of, and within towns and cities. Those surveys concerned with

the causes of movements into cities have, in general, confirmed many of the conclusions reached by inter-regional studies. For example, Pourcher's (1970) survey in 1961 of the residents of Greater Paris, aged 21–60 and born in the provinces, suggested that factors related to a prosperous life-style were the prime motives for moving into the capital city. Only 14 per cent of the respondents gave a lack of work or means of subsistence in the provinces as the reason for moving. In fact, career advancement (45 per cent), marriage and motives independent of owner (14 per cent) and family and housing reasons (12 per cent) were the predominant motives. A similar set of conclusions were reached in a study of migration involving four contrasting British cities (Johnson, Salt and Wood, 1974). The operation of non-economic motives in generating migration in developed societies is most evident among elderly movements to coastal resorts. According to Law and Warnes (1980), those migrating to Cornwall and Devon upon retirement were motivated by environmental, leisure and housing factors. This suggests that in any discussion of migration causation it is necessary to consider the social groups involved as well as the type of city. In fact, many would go further and argue that the location of the cities involved can also be a differentiating factor, for example, the reasons given by residents for moves into new and expanded towns in Britain vary considerably. According to Jones (1976), migrants to the growth centre of Newtown, Mid-Wales, were attracted by available employment (56 per cent of sample), whilst on the other hand, migrants into those new towns located close to major centres of population had been primarily motivated by better housing (Karn, 1970). On the other hand, moves to third world cities were overwhelmingly dominated by work reasons. For example, Elizaga's (1966) study of migration into Santiago and that of Zachariah's (1966) of moves to Bombay found that over 65 per cent of their respective samples of movers had been motivated by employment needs, this proportion being even higher among those from rural areas, whilst those from urban settings being inclined towards career improvements, educational and other social reasons.

In recent years a major focus among those interested in urban migration has been upon residential mobility within cities (Adams and Gilder, 1976; Michelson, 1977). Much of this work stems from Rossi's (1955; 1980) now classic study of residential mobility in Baltimore in the early 1950s. After distinguishing between voluntary (e.g. housing space, better neighbourhoods, cheaper rents) and involuntary (e.g. divorce, marriage, eviction, dwelling demolition, employment) causes, Rossi concluded that the dominant proportion of all intra-urban moves were stimulated by changing neighbourhood and household requirements. Many later studies have confirmed these findings (Butler *et al*., 1969; Sabagh and Van Arsdol, 1969). For example, Balderson (1981) has found in Leicester that of a sample of 400 households which moved in the late 1970s, 41 per cent indicated that their previous house was too small, another 31 per cent wanted to own their own home, and only 13 per cent indicated dissatisfaction with their previous neighbourhood. Although broadly confirming these results, Barrett's (1973) study in Toronto, however, emphasized that changes in the respondents' attitudes towards housing and neighbourhoods were the major cause of residential change. Rossi (1955) also argued that changing space requirements can only fully be understood within the context of changes in the life cycle. For example, Simmons (1968) found that within Toronto over 50 per cent of the intra-urban moves were tied to changes in the life cycle. Among the middle- and high-income residents of Leicester moves were most likely upon marriage and as children arrived, and again late in life, when children had left home and retirement age reached; on the other hand, there was greater stability among those with children at school as well as those whose career patterns had reached a ceiling (Balderson, 1981). Although Rossi (1955) mentioned dissatisfaction with the former neigbourhood as a factor stimulating residential mobility, it has, however, been found to be relatively insignificant. According to Troy (1973) and Balderson (1981), the quality and size of housing produced greater dissatisfaction than did access to work, schools, friends, etc. However, Simmons (1968) did show that for those living more than 40 minutes from work in Toronto accessibility did contribute significantly to the decision to change residence. The emphasis in all these studies of residential mobility has been upon 'push' factors, yet Balderson (1981) has identified a certain set of 'pull' factors being also operative, in fact about 18 per cent of his responses could be categorized as such. Among these factors are included (i) a move to a more expensive house as a form of long-term investment, (ii) a move for social prestige in order to achieve a house and neighbourhood commensurate with one's job, and (iii) a move in order to become more involved in community life. It also has been suggested that some of these factors might be the 'real' reasons for moving even when space requirements are mentioned as the prime motivator (Bell, 1958).

Despite the consistency of these findings on residential mobility it must be admitted that they are only relevant when considering middle-

and high-income migrants. Since the focus of the majority of studies has been upon those residents with high mobility rates, such a bias is readily understandable (Clark, 1972). However, many have argued that the factors which generate the wealthy to move do not operate to the same extent among low-income migrants (Jansen, 1968; Simmie, 1972). For example, Short (1978a), in his study of residential mobility in Bristol, illustrated this point with reference to four contrasting neighbourhoods. Among the recent migrants into the 'poor' inner city district of St Paul's, over 21 per cent of the movers had left their previous residence because they were forced to move and another 12 per cent were driven out by high rents or the poor physical condition of the dwelling. A further 20 per cent moved largely into owner occupation as space requirements increased with growing families and 21 per cent new households were set up, largely students renting accommodation. Since the district contains a large proportion of private renters, two movements predominated: from private renting sector into owner occupation and movement within the private renting sector. In contrast the main reason for movement in the wealthy suburb of Westbury was change in household size, especially at the child rearing and child launching stages in the life cycle. Among the younger households the desire to own a house was the prime cause of movement. Further contrasts were provided by the low-income non-manual and high-income manual districts of Bedminster and St George, respectively. In these cases marriage and the desire to own a house were the most important reasons that stimulated movements. The departure of children or the death of a spouse contributed also to a small number of moves. Essentially, this study emphasizes that when determining intra-urban migration causation there is a need also to consider the socio-economic background of the migrants and the age, tenure and cost of housing. In other words, the operation of the housing market provides a structure within which individuals make decisions about whether to migrate or not (see Chapter 9).

Rural Migrations

Much of the focus of rural-based causal surveys of migration has been upon out-migration, which, in general, have provided further support to the hypothesis that economic considerations are the major determinants of migration. Hannan (1970), for example, stressed the significance of limited local employment in the intentions of young adults to migrate from western Ireland. Overwhelmingly, these intentions were determined by 'beliefs about one's ability to fulfil economic type aspirations locally' (Hannan, 1970, 202). Similarly, House and Knight's (1965) survey of rural northeast England revealed that 72 per cent of those who left the area did so for employment reasons, whilst another 25 per cent migrated upon marriage and 3 per cent moved for educational purposes. Cowie and Giles (1957), in a study of farm labourers' mobility in Gloucestershire in 1950, revealed that 40 per cent of the respondents listed 'long hours' and 'low pay' as their prime reason for leaving agriculture, and this figure rose to 60 per cent among those aged between 16 and 25 years. This, of course, is the age when marriage is being contemplated, which heightens the consideration of long-term prospects in agriculture. In the developing countries the role of the economic motive in rural migration has also been shown to be significant (Todaro, 1976; Van Binsbergen and Meilink, 1978; Swindell, 1979). For example, according to Prothero (1959), 52 per cent of the seasonal migrants leaving Sokota province in Nigeria migrated to 'seek money', and another 24 per cent to carry out trade. Among the Mossi from the Upper Volta, Skinner (1964) has claimed that so much emphasis is placed upon the economic motive in labour migration that no other reason was mentioned in a major survey.

Despite considerable evidence from both developed and developing countries of the economic factor in determining rural migration, other studies have warned against overstressing it (Mitchell, 1969; Connell *et al.*, 1976). In less isolated rural communities, where the outlook and activities of the people have been affected by urbanization, the motives for migration are increasingly related to psycho-social factors. An investigation carried out by Imogene (1967) in the new town of Sapele, in mid-western Nigeria, and in a nearby but isolated village of Jesse, tends to support this hypothesis.

As in the case of urban migration, that involving rural locations is not uni-directional since it includes not only out-migration but also inward and intra-rural movements. The latter two types of migrations have not claimed much attention, although Lewis (1981a), in a survey of the sparsely populated Colwyn district on the Welsh Borderlands, revealed that different reasons prompted these three different types of rural movements. By collapsing the reasons given by the migrants for moving into five broad categories and then considering only the first two ranked motives together in a simple 5 × 5 matrix whose total came to a 100 per cent, comparison was made of the three migratory flows. Among the out-migrants the pairing of occupational and income aspirations was by far the most significant, thus emphasizing that the search was not only for better employment than that available locally but also for additional income to 'improve one's way of life'. An interesting secondary group of pairings included income-personal, occupational-personal and community-personal aspirations. These social motives manifested themselves not only among the elderly and widowed but also the young, particularly those aged between 16 and 24 years. Many of these young adults had left the district simply because it was the 'done thing'. So prevalent had out-migration become during the past half century that it was now a part of family life for the young to leave home, irrespective of their educational attainment or desired occupation. Even when occupational or income aspirations could be met locally, many still left because if they remained they would be judged by the community as 'failures'. Also, for some, community dissatisfaction along with personal motives caused them to leave, no doubt reflecting the lack of social facilities in the district's small towns and villages. Essentially, these features illustrate the indirect effects of long-term depopulation — a small and declining population which fails to maintain an adequate level of services and employment — a set of weaknesses which have become so imbedded in the subconscious of the population that the young are 'expected' to leave, whether there is any economic necessity for them to do so or not. In contrast social motives were the prime reasons for moving into the district. The first of the three significant paired motives, personal and community aspiration, involved elderly people who had moved into the district upon retirement, and had been attracted by its remoteness, beautiful scenery and community feeling. On the other hand, those who had been motivated to move into the district for residential and community reasons included those seeking 'better housing' and 'village life' as well as those moving into the private housing market for the first time whether from council renting or the private renting sector. The pairing of occupational-residence motives involved those who had moved to work in one of the Borderlands' small towns and had chosen the district for residence. Similarly, inter-parochial migration had been generated by a series of social motives, in particular residence, with personal and occupational motives forming only secondary reasons. The residential motive included those achieving a council house as well as those entering the private housing market for the first time, whilst those moving for occupational reasons were largely restricted to the agricultural sector, no doubt reflecting the regular seasonal changes undertaken by farm workers. Essentially this study

Figure 7.5: An Estimate of the Motivational Composition of Migrants in England and Wales, 1960–61. Percentages of migrants with short-range motivation

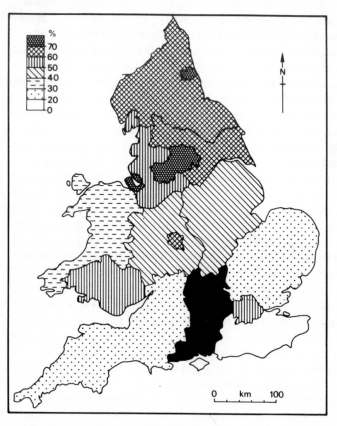

Source: After Hyman and Gleave, 1978, 179–201.

has emphasized the tendency for individuals to perceive environments differently, thus leading towards considerable differential migration.

From the empirical evidence provided by both the objective and normative levels of migration analysis it would appear that economic motives, so beloved by labour economists, are not as significant as many would like us to believe. Rather, economic factors, such as employment and wages, tend to be of greater significance in determining long-distance (or total displacement) migration, whereas social motives, such as family, housing, slum clearance, etc., are of greater relevance in explaining short-distance (or partial displacement) migration. In a recent analysis of migration causation and distance on the Italio-Yugoslav border, Thomas (1979) has provided detailed confirmation of this conclusion. Similar patterns were also obtained by Harris and Clausen (1963) in their national survey of migration causation in England and Wales, the results of which have been used by Hyman and Gleave (1978) to estimate the motivational composition of migration between regions and conurbations in 1960-61. From Figure 7.5 it is apparent that migrants in the north are more likely to have shorter-distance motivations than those in the south as do migrants within conurbations compared to those outside. The importance of this study is that it attempts to employ normative-type data within an objective analysis, yet its full significance is weakened by a failure to incorporate directions of flows and population composition into the analysis. Such factors are of utmost significance in any understanding of migration motivation because people differently located in space and social structure have different degrees of knowledge about, and are able to benefit to different extents from, opportunities at places other than at which they currently reside. 'Clearly, insofar as people have different goals, different information, and different opportunities, their choices will vary' (McFarland, 1970, 474). The next chapter will therefore be concerned with how people decide to migrate in the light of such knowledge.

8 MIGRATION DECISION-MAKING

Despite the plethora of studies which have attempted to explain the migration process, a number of researchers have not been entirely content with the generalizations made about how migration events occur (Clark, 1972; Short, 1978b). For example, the push-pull model when conceived in economic terms and measured by correlating variables characterizing socio-economic factors, only possessed relatively low degrees of prediction. Hägerstrand (1970, 8) even went as far as to claim that 'nothing truly general can be said about aggregate regularities until it has been made clear how far they remain invariant with organizational differences at the micro-level'. In response to such comments some progress has been made by a shift towards the determination of the push-pull forces by means of asking questions, yet this procedure itself suffers from a failure to determine by what evaluative process individuals arrived at decisions whether to migrate and whether there are systematic influences that condition migration decisions (Pryor, 1975b). People differently located in space and social structure have different degrees of knowledge about, different perceptions of, and are able to benefit to different extents from opportunities at places other than those in which they currently reside (Jones, 1980). If this is so, then simply asking questions about motives tells us little about how individuals decide whether to migrate and where to migrate to (Taylor, 1969). Only by conceiving the migration process in a sequential decision-making framework can this be achieved.

During the last decade or so this behavioural approach to migration has become the focus of considerable research activity, in particular the urban residential decision (Adams and Gilder, 1976; Michelson, 1977). Although this research bias colours the discussion that follows, it is, however, readily apparent that many of the concepts introduced and procedures adopted have wider application. Certainly Petersen's (1958, 258) stricture that there have been 'few attempts to distinguish among underlying causes, facilitative environment, precipitants and motives of migration', is less relevant today, yet the decisions of individuals are still far from clear; only when they are clear enough will it be efficient to use them in a model based on aggregate data (Hudson, 1976).

Migration Decisions

Only with the adoption of a more behavioural approach to migration analysis have geographers begun to give some attention to decision-making theory (Golledge and Rushton, 1976; Gold, 1980). According to Herbst (1964), the conscious decision to leave a place of origin involves transposing indecision into a resolution of commitment to the organization (or social and economic environment) of which the migrant is a part. Usually, in such a situation the decision-making unit is the household, which may be defined as one or two or more persons living together. Within this unit some of its members are more directly involved in the decision-making process than others; for example, young children do not participate in the decision although their interest may be taken into account. Obviously there are a number of variants to this situation, for example, the most common being when a single individual leaves a family and creates a single decision-making unit, which in turn becomes a multi-member unit when marriage takes place.

Of course, it must be emphasized that not all individuals have a complete freedom of choice (Bassett and Short, 1980; Wiseman and Roseman, 1979). In the past slaves were forced to move and taken to a new destination, whilst even today refugees are forced from their homeland, although sometimes they may retain some choice of destination. Similarly, many people are forced to move because of land use conversion projects such as new road schemes, dam and reservoir construction, urban renewal, etc. In many of the poor rural areas of both the developed and developing world householders may perceive no choice but to move to the city, or even emigrate. In contrast the wealthy classes have much greater freedom to move or stay, and often are able to choose destinations at will (Bell, 1958). The wealthy have a much greater choice within the housing market than the poorer and minority groups, whose access is limited by economic and racial discrimination. In other words, the decision to migrate takes place within a highly constrained situation, which inevitably determines the individuals involved and the likely destination chosen (see Chapter 9).

According to Wilber (1963), the decision to migrate may be simplified into three interrelated elements: firstly, the resolution of the choice between the *acts* of moving and not moving; secondly, the decision to move might only be made after additional information about an *event*, for example, housing, jobs, etc.; and thirdly, both the act and the event have a *consequence* for the decision-maker. In the application of this theory the complex psychological factors which motivate an individual to move have been highly simplified by conceiving them as a utility function. Wolpert (1964; 1965; 1966), in a series of pioneering papers, developed this within a geographical context by the introduction of the concept of 'place utility', defined as 'the net composite of utilities which are derived from the individual's integration at some time in space . . . it may be expressed as a positive or negative quality, expressing respectively the individual's satisfaction or dissatisfaction with respect to that place' (Wolpert, 1965, 60). Where migration is intended and not forced, the argument goes, the migrant will tend to resettle at a destination which offers a relatively higher level of utility than both the place or origin and the alternative place of destination. This higher utility may be expressed in terms of actual characteristics of the place, or it may be the potential of the place as perceived by the migrant. The 'subjective expected utility' of a decision was expressed by Graves (1966) to be a function of personal expectations that the decision would lead to various outcomes, and of the utility values, both positive and negative, of those outcomes. Thus place utility enters the migration decision in respect of the potential migrant's decision to seek a new residential site arising from dissatisfaction with present utility or perceived improved utility, and as part of the decision as to actually where to search for a new residence.

If economic rationality is assumed in migration behaviour (as was implied by the original gravity models), then the logical end of such behaviour is a resolution of behaviour and aspirations in an optimum location where utility or revenue are maximized. The rationality of human behaviour, however, is limited, and man is frequently satisfied with less than the maximum obtainable. As a development of this theme, Wolpert introduced Simon's (1957) 'satisficer' concept to his work, a concept which suggests that 'aspiration levels tend to adjust to the attainable, to past achievement levels, and to levels achieved by other individuals with whom the aspirant compares himself' (Wolpert, 1964, 543). In other words, the individual's evaluative mechanism of utilities is a self-adjusting process because aspirations tend to adjust to the attainable.

Further, Wolpert (1966) argued that individuals tend to choose locations of relative certainty. This can be achieved either by postponing the move or by acquiring more information by greater search and feedback. Although an individual may have a wide knowledge of locations, in general only a small number will be relevant to the migration decision. This is often referred to as an individual's 'action space', or a set of places for which expected utilities have been defined by the individual. The search for greater information tends to enlarge an individual's action space and enables the potential migrant to develop a place utility idea for a range of competing places. Also uncertainty can be reduced by the individual joining a well established migration channel. Therefore the individual's physical and behavioural environment is constrained by his perception of the structures around him just as his activities are constrained by the 'activity spaces' or 'action spaces' as he perceives them. Migration is a process of adjustment to better satisfy the needs and desires of each intended migrant, that is to increase the utility space of the migrant. Images rather than concrete facts are seen by some to control spatial activities, including all kinds of movement, searches and location choices, while information is seen to be transmitted through 'community' or 'mean information fields' based on the perceptual structures of the individual (Lieber, 1978).

A Migration Decision-making Model

Arising from Wolpert's introduction of the concept of place utility, there have been several attempts to model the migration decision-making process. In Figure 8.1, for example, the migration decision is presented within a highly simplified man-environment decision-making system. Assuming that there is a desire to move, then a household's information about opportunities in the real world will be evaluated by their value system into a set of images, or subjective utilities. It is on the basis of these images that the migration decision is made, which involves either moving to a new location or remaining in the present one or continue the search in order to enlarge their subjective utilities. Such a decision-making process formed the basis of Brown and Moore's (1970) sequential residential decision-making model, which distinguishes between the decision to move and the decision where to move to (Figure 8.2). Following Wolpert's (1966) elaboration of his idea of place utility in which mobility was conceived as a form of adaption to stress in the environment, the model argues that the decision to move is determined by the severity of those stressors. Stress can involve changes in the needs and expectations of the household as well as changes in the characteristics of the dwelling and the environment. Only when the place utility is reduced either by internal or external sources of stress,

Figure 8.1: A Simplified Man-environment Decision-making System

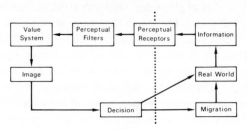

Figure 8.2: A Behavioural Model of Residential Relocation

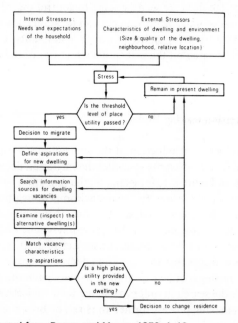

Source: Adapted from Brown and Moore, 1970, 1-13.

or both, below a certain threshold level, will the household decide to move. But this does not necessarily mean that a move will be made, since the stress can be overcome by the household either by being satisfied with less or by improving its existing circumstances. The decision where to move to involves searching information sources about likely vacancies and matching these with the household's aspirations. If a high place utility is provided by the new location then there is a

Figure 8.3: Generalized Locational Decision Scheme

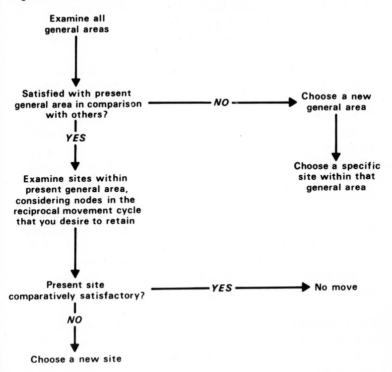

Source: After Roseman, 1971, 589-98.

decision to migrate. If not, a decision to remain in the present location or continue the search is made.

Since the appearance of this model there have been several attempts to broaden its perspective and make it more realistic. For example, Roseman (1971) has conceived the migration decision in a wider context than residence location by suggesting that even the relocation decision is itself made up of two successive steps (Figure 8.3). In the first step, a decision is made about the desired general area of residence. If a high evaluation is placed upon the present area and the current job, then migration beyond the commuting field of the place of work is unlikely. On the other hand, if a high evaluation is placed upon a better job or better environment, in another area, then migration may take place. After this first decision has been made, another has to be made regarding the location of the home within the general area. This time the decision is based upon a comparative evaluation of the site and neighbourhood attributes of the present home with those of the potential alternative home. Migration does not take place if both the general area and the house site decisions favour the present situation. Of the two types of migrant, total displacement and partial displacement migrants, it is only the former who have to change their location as a result of both steps; the latter form of migration is based solely on the site and neighbourhood attributes of the home.

Recently, in an interesting elaboration of the Brown and Moore model, Popp (1976) has suggested that there are at least three ways in which it may not be fully operative; firstly, migrations are not always the result of a reduction in place utility; secondly, the decision to seek a new residence (phase I) and the relocation decision (phase II) need not always follow one another chronologically; and thirdly, not only phase I but also phase II may not take place. From an empirical investigation of migrants in Erlangen (West Germany), five variations of the decision process were identified, of which only one, by far the most important since it formed 58.9 per cent of the sample, corresponded with the model of Brown and Moore. The others included:

(a) The household is caused to leave its present dwelling against its will, yet before it has even started to look for a new dwelling, it is offered alternative accommodation, which it accepts (3.5 per cent of the sample).
(b) The household must leave its present dwelling against its will, and the household now looks for a new residential location (7.8 per cent).
(c) Although the household is to some extent dissatisfied with its accommodation, it has not yet reached the decision to move. In this situation a new dwelling, which would provide it with a considerably higher place utility, is offered by personal contact. It decides to change its residential location, but no longer needs to go through the phase of search for a new residence (7.8 per cent).
(d) The household may decide to change its dwelling and has already reached the decision to move. It has, however, not yet actually begun to search for a new dwelling. The household is then in conversation offered alternative accommodation which it accepts and moves into (22.0 per cent).

In view of the fact that not all decisions are free and that a wide variety of constraints upon movement operate within all societies, many have suggested that the Brown and Moore model is rather unrealistic. Essentially what is being argued is that the migration decision is a process which must pass through a series of filters which act as constraints, any one of which can affect its outcome, and indeed prevent its completion. According to Murie (1975) these include (a) household preferences based on values, income and occupation which affect the interpretation of opportunities and their changing character; (b) search and information gathering, which affects a household's perception; (c) access to housing, which affects the eventual outcome since both the public and private sector have 'rules' of access; and (d) availability of the type of dwelling required. Clearly the first two of these form an integral part of the behavioural approach to decision-making; on the other hand, the remaining two focus on the institutional role in restricting migration opportunities. In other words, what is being emphasized is that all households make decisions about migration within a set of individual and societal constraints, which due to the fact that they are differently located in space and society results in a marked selectivity of migrants (Chapter 6). For ease of discussion, therefore, the remainder of this chapter will focus on the preference and search components of the migration process. Then in the succeeding chapter the role of institutional and societal constraints in determining migration will be discussed.

Components of Migration Decisions

Despite the original stress-threshold model being the basis of considerable research activity, no attempt has been made to operationalize it fully, apart from a few experimental approaches (Lieber, 1979; Smith, Clark, Huff and Shapiro, 1979; Clark, Huff and Burt, 1979). In fact, the major focus of the research has been upon the model's component parts, and for our purposes three are worthy of some further attention:

(1) the manner in which a household's dissatisfaction with their existing place-utility provides the basis for a decision to move;
(2) the way in which households evaluate aspects of the environment for alternative courses of action; and
(3) the knowledge that households have about opportunities, areas, etc., and the actual process in which the environment is searched.

Stress and Satisfaction

The basis of any decision to migrate is the household's belief that the level of satisfaction obtainable elsewhere is greater than its present level of satisfaction. The difference between the two levels can be regarded as a measure of stress and, therefore, a decision to move may be viewed as an adjustment to stress (Wolpert, 1966). Obviously, the perception of, and response to, stress situations will vary between individuals and not every experience of stress will result in migration since stress may be expressed as violent frustration, or just as general discontent (Brown and Moore, 1970). According to Murie (1975) stress is set in motion by 'trigger-like' mechanisms, of which four are the most significant: (a) changes in income; (b) changes in family life cycle; (c) changes in place of work; and (d) changes in the environment, for example a renewal scheme or an invasion by incompatible households.

Despite the importance of the stress-threshold concept in an understanding of the migration decision, it is, however, extremely difficult to measure and operationalize (Brummell, 1981). For example, a pioneering effort to delineate the concept was Brown and Longbrake's (1970) study of residential mobility between 1966 and 1967 for 64 origins and destinations in Cedar Rapids, United States. A principal component analysis revealed that over 64 per cent of the migration could be explained in terms of family status, income levels, housing quality, residential density and site selection quality, from which it was inferred that place utilities leading to migration are more likely to occur in those districts which were 'deprived' in comparison to the norm of their type of area. In other words, the nature of the district was not necessarily significant but rather how it related to the norm of other similar districts. Unfortunately, such a measure of stress tells us little as to its content and the way in which it affects the migration decision. More recently, however, Clark and Cadwallader (1973a) have suggested indicators for the identification of different levels of stress in the urban environment. Among the indicators chosen included (1) the size and facilities of the dwelling unit; (2) the kind of people living in the neighbourhood; (3) proximity of friends and relations; (4) proximity to work; and (5) levels of air pollution. The significance of these were tested in Los Angeles where a sample of households were asked to rate on the basis of the five indicators how easy or difficult it would be to find a more desirable location elsewhere as well as evaluate its present level of satisfaction with the present location. A correlation of .384 significant at the .001 level, between a desire to move and locational stress was achieved. Therefore, most

Figure 8.4: The Relationship between Socio-economic Variables, Satisfaction Index, Wish to Move, and Mobility in Rhode Island, 1969. Included are all paths where the correlation coefficients are statistically significant at p < .05 based on two-tailed test. Intercorrelations of less than .2 between socio-economic variables are not shown

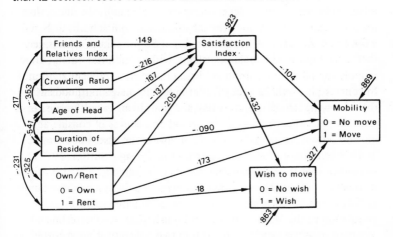

Source: After Speare, 1974, 173–88.

stress was experienced by those households who thought they could find a better residence elsewhere and were the least satisfied with their present location. Apart from the pollution stressors each of the other four were important in creating household stress, although the size and facilities of the dwelling unit was the most significant and proximity to work the least. Similarly, Speare (1974) developed an index of residential satisfaction based on housing and neighbourhood characteristics, and found among a sample of households in Rhode Island that it provided a meaningful measure of whether the households wished to migrate and whether they moved the following year. It was also found that individual attributes acted indirectly through the residential satisfaction index to affect mobility potential (Figure 8.4). The only exception was home ownership, which had a significant effect on both mobility variables. Clearly, both of these studies identified housing as the crucial variable in determining household stress and, therefore, provide support for the findings of those studies more directly concerned with the causes of residential mobility (Chapter 7).

Such findings must, however, not be overemphasized since there is more to residential satisfaction than housing and family requirements.

Individuals identify with their residential location and endow it with some social meaning. It also provides a means of social interaction as well as being a symbol of social standing in Western society, for example, suburban residence appears to symbolize all the values of 'good' living. For example, Michelson (1977) found among a sample of inhabitants in Toronto a higher rating for single-family dwellings than high-rise apartments. Among the inhabitants of four suburbs in New York State, Zehner (1972) calculated that 86 per cent of them rated their neighbourhood as being excellent, with friendliness, safety, good schools and pleasant environment being the most significant attributes. In contrast, it would be thought that inner city neighbourhoods with their decaying fabric, overcrowding and poor living conditions, often referred to by the media as slums, would be a source of considerable dissatisfaction. Surprisingly, this is not always the case. For example, in his classic study of the Adams district in Chicago, Suttles (1972) has shown that the slum can generate its own subculture, which can be sufficient to offset the many disadvantages of a decaying fabric. Ley (1974) found a similar high level of satisfaction among the black population of the Monroe district of Philadelphia. An interesting comparison of the satisfaction levels in two contrasting neighbourhoods has recently been undertaken by Herbert (1975) in Cardiff. It was found that over two-thirds of the residents of Adamsdown, the inner terraced housing neighbourhood, were satisfied with their area compared to 96 per cent of those resident in the middle-class suburb in Rhiwbina. The higher rating of Rhiwbina was particularly marked in terms of cleanliness, safety, play facilities, open space and social facilities. Essentially, what has been shown here is that differences in the physical condition of the slum and the suburb is not always matched by differences in residential satisfaction levels. In other words, satisfaction is purely relative, since it can vary according to the needs and aspirations of particular individuals and groups. For example, Onibokun (1976) found that satisfaction levels among Canadian public housing estates varied significantly with the social attributes of the population. It was shown that residential satisfaction was, in general, low among large households, one-parent families, unemployed tenants, tenants of high socio-economic status, recent immigrants from Europe, tenants with lengthy residence in public housing, tenants who had moved from owner-occupied properties, tenants who had moved from town, semi-detached, or single family 'dwellings', tenants who perceived their neighbourhood as lower- or upper-class in status, and tenants who perceived themselves as lower- or upper-class in status. In conclusion, then, residential satisfaction is a multi-faceted concept, which means that in some social settings a particular background variable might have an effect opposite to the effect it has in other settings (Fried and Gleicher, 1961). This emphasizes the need in any consideration of the migration decision to look more closely at how individuals evaluate and perceive their residential location.

Evaluation and Preference

Individuals and groups have different levels of residential satisfaction, which is the summation of their evaluation of the different components of the environment (Flowerdew, 1973). In the decision to migrate individuals have to 'trade-off' some components of the environment against others within an overall utility context. A number of attempts have been made to determine how individuals evaluate their residential environments within different 'trade-off' situations, and so provide some clues as to the manner in which the migration decision is made. One of the earliest was Wilson's (1962) determination of the criteria employed by the residents of two small cities in North Carolina to evaluate their residential environments. The respondents were asked to evaluate their neighbourhood as well as a number of photographs of residential areas in terms of 15 qualities of the environment. On the basis of the aggregate scores for both photographs and neighbourhoods, the qualities were ranked in importance thus:

1. Spaciousness
2. Beauty
3. A character which is
   good for children
4. Exclusiveness
5. A country-like
   character
   ↓

11. Cleanliness
12. Newness
13. Friendliness
14. Crowdedness
15. Dirtiness

Yet, when the responses were ranked in terms of neighbourhood attributes only, then a differing ordering was achieved:

1. Friendliness
2. Homeliness
3. Quietness
4. Greenery
5. Cleanliness
   ↓

12. Beauty
13. Exclusiveness
14. A country-like
    character
15. Spaciousness

From this evidence it would appear that the respondents were reasonably satisfied with residence in neighbourhoods which they considered unsatisfactory in a number of ways. Such a paradox can be resolved, however, if it is realized that the choice of residence is made within a highly constrained situation rather than the freedom to discriminate allowed by the first evaluation. Under 'real-world' conditions the majority of householders have insufficient wealth to even approximate what they ideally desire and so the less attainable qualities are set aside and choice made in terms of those which may be realized.

In order to illustrate the way in which a household's limited resources influences its evaluation of the residential environment, a simulation exercise was carried out among a sample of Leicester residents. Each respondent was asked to 'spend' a given amount of money on some combination of residential density and access to urban facilities. Since the 'game' precluded the attainment of low density residence and good access to services the respondents were, therefore, forced to isolate their main priorities. Over 75 per cent of the respondents chose moderately low residential density, which since it was 'expensive', meant that only basic services could be 'afforded': primary school, bus stop, grocery store, newsagent and post office. Only when the respondents were allowed to choose with unlimited resources did cultural and recreational facilities become significant. Therefore, constrained choices tend to focus on basic needs, while free choices lead towards consideration of what may be described as 'luxury'. Such a 'game' can, however, be criticized for its unrealistic context and so in order to overcome this weakness the respondents were further requested to characterize their current house and neighbourhood in terms of a series of qualities, which were then weighted and aggregated to provide a 'sum' to spend. The results obtained emphasized the significance of 'constraints' in the evaluation of residential environments (Rowley and Wilson, 1975). However, according to Balderson (1981), the criteria often employed to evaluate the urban environment are not independent but often associated, and sometimes synonymous. When a group of respondents were asked to rate the residential areas of Leicester on the basis of 20 qualities, a factor analysis of the responses concluded that over 68 per cent of the variance could be 'explained' by three qualities: 'physical', 'social' and 'accessibility'.

The significance of these criteria within an actual migratory context has been analyzed by Gustavus and Brown (1977), employing four different methodologies, for a sample of migrants into Columbus, Ohio. Briefly, they suggest that a two-stage process seems to operate. In the first, a set of alternative destinations is identified, which involves comparisons with the former place of residence on the basis of attributes such as the 13 used in the study. Although in the abstract all 13 attributes were significant, in a trade-off situation, housing, jobs, schools and health care facilities were particularly critical. The second stage of the process involves choosing from among the alternative destinations identified. The authors emphasize that it is an extremely complex process to measure accurately and objectively the suitability of one place against another. It is likely, then, that places are evaluated in terms of threshold levels rather than on a continuous scale. This would explain why Columbus and the second choice place were both perceived as dramatically different from the former place of residence but nearly identical to each other. Since all the respondents chose Columbus it would appear that personal contacts, not isolated by the 13 attributes used in the study, provided the migrant with accurate information and a means of adjusting relatively easily into a new environment.

Such evaluations form the basis of individual preferences for different places and locations, which provide the initial context for the decision to migrate (Demko, 1974). This theme has been the source of considerable research activity, the majority of which emphasizes marked variation in people's preference for places (Svart, 1976; Hanson, 1977). Within an urban context such biases may be illustrated from a study carried out in Leicester. A sample of the residents was asked to rank order 30 of its residential districts as desirable places to live, and after scaling the derived scores a trend surface analysis was employed to aid interpretation. Figure 8.5 reveals a large zone of indifference stretching across the centre of the city from southwest to northeast, which coincides with the areas of terraced housing and council estates. The favoured districts around the edge of the city include the newer, private housing estates, as well as some council housing areas, yet the most favoured district of all forms a distinct sector to the southeast. This high-status sector stretches from the large, late nineteenth-century housing of the inner city to the modern single-family dwellings of the suburban villages of Oadby, Wigston and Thurnby. When the preferences of individual districts are considered a similar pattern is replicated in association with a strong local preference bias (Figure 8.6). Briefly, this study has emphasized the occurrence of three tendencies in urban preferences: firstly, a high local preference,

Figure 8.5: Residential Desirability Surface of Leicester Residents, 1976. Preferences are scaled from low (−30) to high (+30)

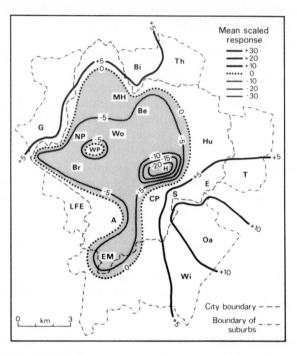

Source: After Budd, 1979.

often creating a sectoral bias; secondly, preference for high status residences, although attenuated to a certain extent by income levels; and thirdly, the operation of social distance, most vividly instanced by the low preference scores for the immigrant districts east of the city centre. Several other studies have confirmed these conclusions in different circumstances and in a more specific manner. For example, Johnston (1973) found that in Christchurch, New Zealand, a high degree of consensus among his sample of respondents as to the status of the city's nine residential districts as well as a local preference dome extending outwards in a sectoral fashion and an overriding preference for the northwest district irrespective of status and location. More specifically, Clark and Cadwallader (1973b), as part of their study in the Los Angeles metropolitan area, tested the effect of income and ethnic differentials upon residential preferences. A number of

Figure 8.6: Residential Desirability Surfaces of the Residents of Two
Neighbourhoods in Leicester, 1976. Evington is a middle-class suburb,
and Eyres Monsell an inter-war local authority housing estate.
Preferences are scaled from low (−30) to high (+30)

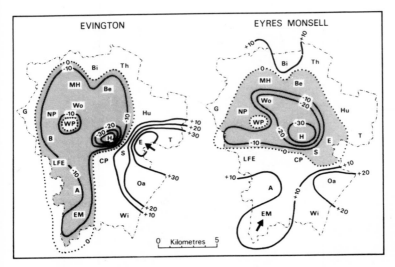

Source: After Budd, 1979.

interesting variations in the first choice district of the four income
groups were identified: the low-income groups favouring centrally
located communities as well as Long Beach, Santa Monica and
Hollywood; the two middle-income groups preferred suburban
communities including those in the San Fernando valley; and the high-
income group had the most restricted locational preference of all.
Both the Blacks and Mexican–Americans exhibited a high degree of
correspondence between their location preferences and present
distribution. On a wider scale such spatial biases also occur in people's
preferences. For example, Gould and White (1968) have shown that the
residential desire of pupils about to leave school in England and Wales
had marked local preferences within an overall bias towards the
pleasanter coastal and suburban areas (Figure 8.7). Such preferences
with their social and spatial biases will of course play an important role
in the decision to migrate and in the selection of likely destinations.

Figure 8.7: Residential Desirability Surface of Inverness School
Leavers, 1966

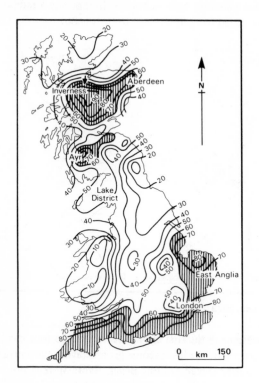

Source: After Gould and White, 1968, 161–82.

Information and Searching

The comparative evaluation of the present location and potential
future location is based upon the knowledge a migrant has concerning
each alternative. The procedure by which an individual gathers such
information is guided by the extent and content of his information
field, or the set of places about which he has knowledge. Such a field
can be divided into two: an activity space and an indirect contact space
(Wolpert, 1965). Activity space is made up of all those locations with
which an individual has regular, almost day-to-day contact, resulting
in a fairly accurate knowledge of the area involved, although it may
be spatially restricted. For example, Figure 8.8 reveals the contacts of
members of two families in Leicester during a 25-day surveillance. It
would appear that the observed differences reflect the influence of

Figure 8.8: A Simplified Representation of the Contact Pattern of Two Families from the Knighton District of Leicester, 1976: (a) a household with a high level of contacts; (b) a household with a low level of contacts. Journeys to work and school have been omitted

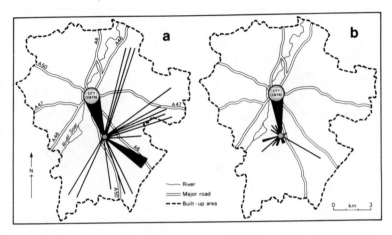

family life cycle and socio-economic factors. Such personal knowledge forms the basis of the partial displacement migrant's decision. In contrast indirect contact space lies beyond the area of the individual's day-to-day contacts, and partly depends upon information from the mass media and other people about alternative locations. Even the mass media have a certain degree of spatial bias, both in terms of information reported and in the areas covered (Walmsley, 1980). The total displacement migrant's decision is more likely to be based upon this type of knowledge. The nature of such knowledge tends to make his site and neighbourhood decision less efficient than that of the partial displacement migrant's, and so increases the possibility that he himself will make a further partial displacement movement shortly after the initial move.

Within such an information-gathering process there tends to be a decay in the accuracy and content of the information an individual possesses with distance, often referred to as an information field (Marble and Nystuen, 1963; Morrill and Pitts, 1967). For example, within cities it has been argued that the activity spaces of individuals bias the information pattern of potential movers. Adams (1969) has claimed that the general sectoral movement of households from their homes to the city centre influences any relocation decision. Two case-studies may be used to illustrate some of the spatial biases in

Figure 8.9: Levels of Familiarity with the Residential Districts of
Leicester, 1976: (a) Woodgate — an inner city terraced housing area;
(b) Oadby — a post-war suburban area

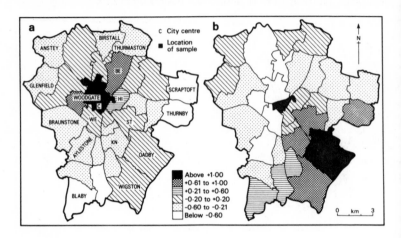

individual information about the city. Following Horton and Reynolds
(1971), two groups of householders, one from a low-income district
near the city centre and another from an upper-middle income
district in the suburbs, were interviewed in Leicester in order to
determine their familiarity with the city. Each respondent was asked to
indicate on a five-point scale (0–unfamiliar to 4–very familiar) his level
of familiarity with each of the city's residential districts. The results
obtained reveal that the low-income residents of Woodgate had a
pronounced familiarity with the home area and the adjacent city
centre, and decreasing familiarity with increasing distance from the
home district (Figure 8.9). On the other hand, the residents of Oadby,
the middle-income group, had not only a more pronounced overall
level of familiarity but also a marked linear rather than concentric
pattern. Similarly, Boyle and Robinson (1978) employing cloze
procedures, have identified some interesting variations in the knowledge
that the residents of Sunderland have about their town. Based on the
number of successful clozures, the middle-class residents of Alexandra
Road exhibited a widespread information within which the best-known
areas were the home and the town centre (Figure 8.10). In contrast,
the residents of Pennywell, a working-class council estate, had a more
restricted pattern of knowledge, yet, surprisingly, the highest level of
clozure success occurred around the town centre and not around the

Figure 8.10: Residential Familiarity in Sunderland as Revealed by Cloze Procedures: (a) the percentage of Alexandra Road residents making at least one successful replacement in each square; (b) the percentage of Pennywell residents making at least one successful replacement in each square

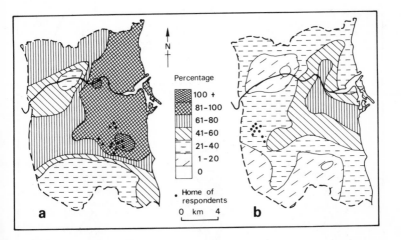

Source: After Boyle and Robinson, 1978, 11 and 12.

home. The authors suggest that this is a reflection, apart from generally lower levels of spatial knowledge, of their strong dependence on public transport and consequent travel patterns which are inevitably directed towards the town centre, rather than laterally. At the wider scale evidence seems to indicate the existence of some spatial bias also (Pacione, 1978). For example, Gould (1975) has determined the information levels of Swedish schoolchildren by asking them to write down in the space of 5 minutes the names of all the villages, towns and cities in Sweden that they could remember. From Figure 8.11 it is apparent that the configuration of the resultant information surface was influenced by distance from the home town of the children and the population size of the settlements. Similar findings have also been reported in a study of information about 30 cities in the Los Angeles region by Cadwallader (1978). The respondents were asked to rate their familiarity with each city against a standard measure, and again the pattern of information scores could be satisfactorily accounted for by population and distance variables. Such factors have also been significant in determining the accuracy of information, rather than

Figure 8.11: The Information Surfaces of Schoolchildren in Skövde, Sweden: (a) nine-and-a-half year olds; (b) sixteen-and-a-half year olds; (c) eighteen-and-a-half year olds

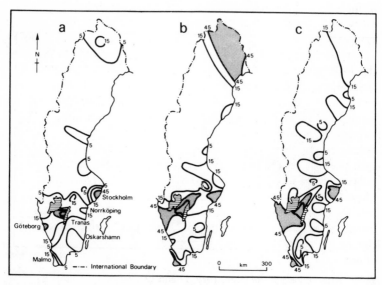

Source: After Gould, 1975, 87–100.

quantity (Webber, Symanski and Root, 1975). In broad terms, therefore, it would appear that the differences and similarities in the spatial configuration of individual information about places conform fairly closely to their activity and indirect contact spaces.

The search for a new job or another house depends not only on the household's knowledge of alternative opportunities or location but also on the types of available information. In his study of residential mobility in Baltimore, Rossi (1955; 1980) found that the most successfully used source was essentially informal whilst estate agents, who might have been expected to be the main source of information, are in fact the least important as well as the least effective. Similar conclusions were reached by Herbert (1973b) in Swansea where for a high-cost neighbourhood the chosen vacancies were discovered by 'looking around' by 39 per cent of the respondents and a further 25 per cent were found through family and friends, whereas only 11 per cent were found through newspapers and 17 per cent through estate agents; and the difference was even more striking for a low-cost neighbourhood, for which the respective percentages were 21 per cent and 58 per cent as against 13 per cent and 8 per cent. The importance of the more casual channels suggests that it is more likely that households will search areas with which they are already familiar and, if this is so, then the action space of households will play a not inconsiderable part in their selection of the area to which they eventually move.

Due to the fragmentary nature of information about places beyond the 'local' space, migrants have, therefore, to rely heavily on specific channels of information about opportunities whether they be employment or housing. One of the most significant channels is that formed by friends and relatives, who not only provide detailed information about their home location but also can assist the assimilation of the newcomer into a strange community. The effect of such information feedback is to create a distinctive migration stream between two places. Hillery and Brown (1965, 47) have shown that 'the southern Appalachians is not a region in the sense of its parts belonging to the same migration system. Rather it is a collection of fringes, or, as it has often been put, of "backyards"', which are connected to non-Appallachian areas, often distant cities, as a result of migration. 'The kinship structure provides a highly persuasive line of communication between kinsfolk in the home and the new community which channels information about available job opportunities, and living standards directly . . . (to rural) families. Thus, kinship linkage tends to direct migrants to those areas where their groups are already established.' (Brown, Schwarzweller and Mangalam, 1963, 53-4). Similarly, Caldwell (1969) found that of those migrants who left his case-study area in rural Ghana for an urban destination, less than one-fifth searched for accommodation on their own. In addition, the migrants who remain in the towns maintain contact with their families by sending home money even after long absences from their villages. However, there is a tendency within migration literature to overemphasize this type of connection at the expense of other information channels. In the Welsh Borderlands, it has been shown that between 1966-76 the information source upon which a community was selected depended on the type of migration (Lewis, 1981a). Since rural-to-rural migration was predominantly local, personal experience was the most significant source. Surprisingly, those who migrated from the rural areas to the towns and cities based their information overwhelmingly upon the mass media; the feedback of knowledge by friends and relatives was of little significance. The onset of the mass media seems to have superseded the traditional information source because of its ability to disseminate greater and more detailed knowledge about locational opportunities. The channel of information used in the urban-to-rural migration in the Welsh Borderlands varied with the move's purpose. Generally, those families who had settled in the region upon retirement based their decision on knowledge derived either from previous residence or holiday visits, whilst those who moved out from the adjacent towns were guided by their personal knowledge. Clearly the manner in which a rural migrant chooses his new home location is as complex as that revealed for the intra-urban migrant (Adams and Gilder, 1976).

So far the spatial distribution of information has been conceived as static space, but, of course, in reality it changes in time and space. From our activity space and indirect contact space we learn about the environment; this learning, in turn, can be reinforced by searching the environment, particularly if it is purposeful, such as searching for a new residential location. Unfortunately, the operation of learning and searching from a spatial viewpoint is exceedingly limited (Silk, 1971). A major contribution, however, was Gould's (1975) study of the spatial information of Swedish schoolchildren of different ages. From Figure 8.11 it can be seen that knowledge of places in Sweden increases with age, although by the late teens there appears to be some information saturation. Irrespective of age there is again a clear distance decay from Skövde, the home town of the children, in the level of their information, as well as considerable knowledge about the larger towns and cities. Essentially, this changing information level reflects not only increased mobility by the children but also greater awareness as a result of education and the mass media.

Of late the changing information pattern of individuals as a result of purposeful search has become a source of investigation, particularly residential mobility and consumer behaviour within the city (Brown and Holmes, 1971; Hudson, 1975). Schneider (1975), Flowerdew (1976) and Meyer (1980) have also considered the nature of search models and suggested their applicability in a spatial context. The search for a new residence in the city will be concentrated near to the home or in other accessible areas simply because an individual's activity and awareness space are so highly localized (Barrett, 1973; 1976). Any extension of the search space will be attenuated by economic and psychological costs. Balderson (1981), in an interesting study of house search among middle-income groups in Leicester, has suggested that the process tends to operate in a series of stages. In the first stage the

Figure 8.12: Inspected House Vacancies for a Middle-income Sample of Migrants in Leicester. The inspected properties were plotted relative to both the original residence and to the one they finally chose. The shape of the area searched is compared by drawing the ellipses for both initial and new residence sites using the same reference node and orientation to the city centre

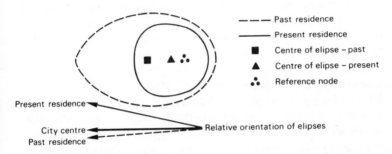

Source: After Balderson, 1981.

search tends to be space-covering and generally covers a wide area, with the home areas being the focal point. At the second stage, space-organizing, the search will focus on a small area where a satisfactory vacancy is likely to be found. If a suitable vacancy is not found then a third stage is initiated, in which the intensity of the search is increased and, possibly, a widening of the search space again. Finally, as time runs out and still no suitable vacancy has been found, the strategy then is for the household to redefine its strategy either by changing its house and neighbourhood requirements or even by reversing the decision to move.

The spatial bias in the process of house search has been analyzed in some detail in three studies (Brown and Holmes, 1971; Whitelaw and Gregson, 1972; Balderson, 1981). By collecting information on respondent's previous place of residence as well as all locations of houses which they had inspected, it is possible to determine migrant search spaces. By then constructing standard ellipses which best fit the resulting aggregate distribution, some spatial biases may be discerned. Figure 8.12 reveals the distribution of the inspected vacancies with reference to both past and present residence sites in Leicester. The distribution around the present site is both smaller and more circular than that around the past site. This indicates that households selected a relatively small area within that with which they were familiar and searched it for suitable vacancies. The site chosen was generally quite close to the centre of the area searched. The degree of ellipticity around the past home shows a directional bias in the search pattern and the orientation of the ellipse almost exactly towards the city centre shows that the bias is sectoral. Brown and Holmes (1971) also found differences in the distribution of the search space of inner and outer city residents in Cedar Rapids. With reference to the home from which they had moved the inner-city migrants had searched an almost circular area whereas the outer-city migrants' search was sectorally biased. Also it has been demonstrated in Melbourne by Whitelaw and Gregson (1972) that the most crucial variable in a successful search for a house vacancy is length of residence; it not only provides the basis of accurate information but also shortens the length of the search. Clearly, information restriction prevents individuals from searching the whole area which is potentially available to them, which results in a distance and directional bias of search space (McCracken, 1975). In aggregate the spatial form of search space appears to conform with the mental map of the city (Lloyd, 1976).

Over a decade ago Mangalam (1968, 16) complained that 'migration is practically a virgin area for those who want to study the phenomenon from a behavioural point of view'. From the evidence reviewed in this chapter the present decade has seen a proliferation of attempts to conceive the migration process within a decision-making framework. But since much of the research has been based on residential mobility, our understanding of how other migrants decide to move and how they choose their destinations is still far from complete. Yet from the limited available evidence it would appear that among longer-distance migrants there is also considerable social and spatial bias. More recently, however, the behavioural approach to migration study has been criticized for its tendency to view decisions within a context where there is ample choice, a context which many consider to be only true for the wealthy groups in Western society (Bassett and Short, 1980). What is being suggested is that for the majority of the population the choice of a new destination is highly constrained, not only by their own economic and cultural circumstances but also by the way in which society and its institutions determine opportunities. In such circumstances there is a marked selection of migrants, and even among those who do migrate there is institutional control on likely destinations.

9 CONSTRAINTS ON MIGRATION

Most attempts to explain migration have assumed that the decision to migrate and the choice of destination are made freely by the individual within, of course, the context of the existing economic order, the degree of social and cultural ties, and the level of available information. In other words, the decision to migrate is conceived within a 'free market' situation in which choice is made between a set of alternative opportunities. In general, it is assumed that there is an all-pervading migration process, varying in its intensity for different members of society, thus generating differential rates of migration for different age groups, occupations and levels of education. Apart from forced migration, voluntary movement is conceived as the norm, a view which has been reinforced by a tendency for even micro-level studies to focus their attention upon those groups with the greatest choice — the middle- and upper-income households. However, it is self-evident that not all individuals have the same opportunities, whether it be in employment or housing; therefore, as suggested in Chapter 8, freedom of choice is an unrealistic concept in the real world (Murie, 1975; Humphreys and Whitelaw, 1979). Rather, the decision to migrate depends upon the access that individuals and households have to the opportunities that exist within society (Gray, 1975; Thorns, 1980a). If the migration process is conceived in this way, then the stayer is one who is either satisfied with his present situation or is constrained from moving in some way despite high levels of dissatisfaction, a form of latent migration potential (Davies, 1966). Even among those who do move, some have greater choice than others, no doubt reflecting differential accessibility to available opportunities. Such a migration decision-making situation has been described by Morgan (1973) as one where choice is made within a framework of a set of personal and institutional constraints (Figure 9.1). Similarly Short (1978b) sees migration as a form of adaptive behaviour, in that households are not autonomous decision-making units, since their decisions are dependent upon the supply of opportunities and the 'rules' controlling their allocation. Such a situation is one of differential access to scarce resources, which is, of course, dependent upon wider society (Thorns, 1980b).

In recent years there has been a growing awareness of the

151

Figure 9.1: A Simplified Representation of the Migration Process
Within the Context of Opportunities and Constraints

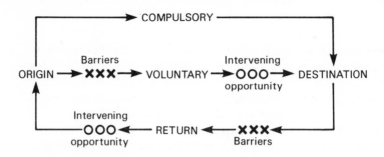

significance of differential access to resources in structuring migratory
movements, which has resulted in a proliferation of studies focusing
upon the supply side of the migration equation. Throughout the focus
has been upon the supply of opportunities, how much and where, and
who controls its supply and allocation. Most attention has been upon
the way in which the structuring of society can determine the supply
of resources, often debated in terms of different ideological
perspectives (Harloe, 1977; Bassett and Short, 1980; Johnston, 1980);
on the other hand, the relationship between society and resources,
and migratory behaviour still needs to be developed. Although most of
the research on this theme has been involved with housing as a resource,
many of the structures identified and the processes involved have much
wider relevance.

In this chapter, then, the focus will be upon the constraints
operating within society which can structure the migration process. In
order to illustrate the basis of these constraints two of the underlying
forces of modern society — the market situation and the operation of
public policy — will be considered initially. The way in which these
can influence 'who gets what where' will then be analyzed in terms of
labour migration and urban residential mobility. In view of the limited
range of detailed studies on this theme the discussion that follows will
be suggestive, rather than comprehensive.

Access to Resources

To many an understanding of the migration process can only be
achieved if it is viewed in terms of the life chances of individuals in

different competitive circumstances. The market situation focuses attention on the criteria that determine 'success' in different markets and, therefore, constrains our ability to choose scarce and desirable resources such as employment and housing. Such differential access to resources has been conceived in terms of a struggle between classes (Castells, 1977; Harvey, 1973). According to Marx, class is 'a group of people [who] share a common relationship to property, perform the same function in the organization of production, have similar relations to power in society and have a tendency to common behaviour patterns, as determined by their objective behaviour' (Marquand and Clegg, 1969, 6). Therefore, the social position of an individual in such an economically based class system involves his relations to the means of production, which can be either by controlling the means of production (bourgeois or capitalist) or by selling his labour (proletarian or worker) (Howard and King, 1975). Many have criticized this interpretation since it is a too-simplistic view of modern society, particularly its failure to consider important cultural forces such as status. Despite Harvey's (1973, 281) counter-argument that 'these are orderings very important to the self-respect of people, but are irrelevant to the basic economic structure of society', many still feel that such orderings play a significant role in determining an individual's social and spatial position. Such a view is similar to that of Weber, who conceived power as being not only economically based but also differentiated and reinforced by cultural and political values such as prestige, honour and political affiliation. This class situation is 'the typical chance for a supply of goods, external living conditions, and personal life experiences in so far as this chance is determined by the amount and kind of power, or lack of such, to dispose of goods and skills for the sake of income in a given order' (Gerth and Mills, 1948, 181). Therefore, Weber has argued that it is possible for propertied and unpropertied households to belong to the same status group, since status involves 'every typical component of the life and fate of men that is determined by specific, positive or negative, social estimation of honour' (Gerth and Mills, 1948, 186–7). Essentially, despite these different interpretations, class membership restricts our range of choice, although it is important to remember that this range can be enlarged by those responsible in supplying and allocating resources.

The supply and allocation of resources plays a crucial role in determining the life chances of individuals, a theme which has aroused considerable research interest of late (Cox, 1978; Bassett and Short, 1980; Pahl, 1977a). What has been argued is that the supply of resources is not the result of the multiplicity of decisions of individuals and households in a 'free' market, but rather the result of competition and conflict between 'interest' groups with differing degrees of power (Cox, 1979). Modern society is conceived as being dominated by a number of interacting organizations, including big business and industries, local and national governments, financial institutions, real estate and building concerns, etc., which 'control' the opportunities available to the individual. Essentially, then, the availability of resources is the outcome of conflict and bargaining between these organizations (Harloe, 1977). In turn the life chances of individuals are affected by the way these resources are allocated, and the focus here is on who decides how to allocate these resources. A myriad of individuals are involved in the management of resources, ranging from those at the head of a large business or government to those operating at a local scale.

The role and effects of individuals and institutions involved in the supply and allocation of resources such as employment and housing and the interaction between them provide the framework in which households make their decision to migrate. Hence, when viewed in such a light the migration process is highly structured.

Public Policy

A major influence on migratory movement is that of public policy and, in view of its increasing significance in altering market forces it is worthy of separate consideration (Pryor, 1976; Clark and Moore, 1980). Although government is rarely concerned with migration *per se*, it, however, seeks to influence migration as a means of effecting some policy goal. Usually such a policy is developed for the benefit of society as a whole rather than the personal objectives of its members (Houston, 1979). According to Farooq (1975) migration policy can involve remedial policies dealing with the existing population as well as redirectional policies designed to achieve a more efficient population distribution. For example, in many West European countries policies have been developed to reduce the depopulation of their less prosperous regions, which take the form of measures to improve their economic base as well as measures to induce people to remain. At times measures of a more general nature have been used to lubricate the labour market and, hopefully, this would be of some benefit to the poorer regions. These measures take the form of 'carrots', to encourage

new developments such as improvements to a region's social and
economic infrastructure, and encourage industrialists to set up new
factories.

Governments can also induce migratory movements, whether
intended or not, by a series of what may be described as 'hidden'
policies. Morrison (1975, 5) has suggested that 'agencies that build
highways, award defence contracts, and choose locations for federal
installations are simultaneously redistributing employment and altering
incentives for private investment'. For example, in the United States
the interstate highway programme not only improved the transport
system but also fostered new growth potential for some major cities
and metropolitan areas, and the vast expenditure on defence and
aerospace has attracted population to the Gulf Coast and California
(Friedman, 1966). Similarly, the various welfare programmes to
support the poor and ethnic minorities in American cities have been
the basis for increased residential mobility. In Britain income tax
deductions on mortgage repayments for home owners has not only
improved the housing stock but also become an incentive for middle-
class families to move to single-family dwellings in the suburbs. State-
subsidized public housing has also encouraged a dispersal of low-income
households away from the older high-density residences of the inner
city to other parts of the urban area, including the suburbs (Murie,
Niner and Watson, 1976). On the basis of such evidence, Morrison
(1975) has attempted to classify migration policies by the mode of
government intervention:

(1) Direct payments to individuals and households
(2) Grants to local authorities, public facilities and welfare services
(3) Subsidies to producers, such as road, rail, agriculture,
    industry, etc.
(4) Subsidies to consumers, such as subsidized rents, income tax
    deductions, etc.
(5) Government programmes, such as defence, public works, etc.
(6) Government regulations and laws, which can either, directly or
    indirectly, control migration, for example, immigration laws.

Hence public policy can influence the movement of people in a variety
of different ways; it can dampen down migration potential as well as
encourage it, both in terms of the population as a whole and individual
groups.

Labour Migration

As a result of post-war changes in the employment structure of all
modern economies, many labour economists have begun to question
the assumptions implicit in economic-based migration models (Shaw,
1975). Among these changes probably the most significant include the
emergence of segmented labour markets and the growth in the
significance of large private and public multi-locational organizations,
both of which have imposed considerable constraints on migration
potential. The segmenting of the labour market has emerged as a result
of the formal and informal rules of entry into various occupations
imposed by employers and trade unions and, therefore, makes it
difficult for workers to move between occupations. Broadly, such a
labour market may be divided into a primary segment, which has job
security, high wages and prospects for advancement, and a secondary
one with low wages, less job security and little promotional prospects.
Gordon (1972) has suggested that this distinction is not analogous with
the usual white- and blue-collar division since many white-collar
occupations, for example, some office jobs, are as routinized and
lacking in prospects as blue-collar ones. Such a labour market is
increasingly being dominated by a small number of large firms and
businesses, usually multi-functional and often located in a number
of countries. Even many national and state governments are organized
in a similar fashion to that of multi-national firms. The spatial
configuration of these organizations will depend upon their function
and the degree to which they have to be near their markets. According
to McKay and Whitelaw (1977), at least three forms of spatial
configuration can be recognized: firstly, the scale and contact
dependent organizations, which depend upon external and internal
economies of scale; secondly, market-dependent organizations, such
as government departments of welfare, whose distribution will reflect
that of the population; and thirdly, resource-dependent organizations,
such as mining companies, the location of part of whose activities is
determined by the occurrence of minerals. Again it is suggested that
the policy and spatial configuration of these organizations will
influence migration patterns since they can determine the migration
potential and the destinations involved of an increasing proportion of
the population. Let us, therefore, at this juncture illustrate the role
of government and private organizations in determining the level and
spatial patterning of labour migration.

The most obvious role of government in the migration process is

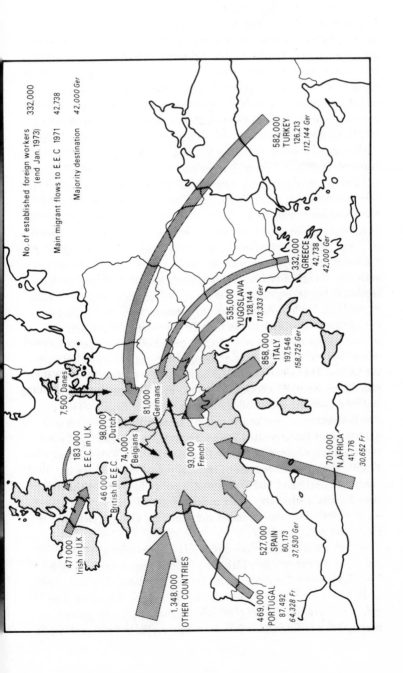

No. of established foreign workers (end Jan. 1973)   332,000

Main migrant flows to E.E.C 1971   42,738

Majority destination   *42,000 Ger*

582,000
TURKEY
126,213
112,144 Ger

332,000
GREECE
42,738
42,000 Ger

535,000
YUGOSLAVIA
128,144
113,333 Ger

858,000
ITALY
197,546
158,725 Ger

7,500 Danes

81,000
Germans

98,000
Dutch

74,000
Belgians

93,000
French

183 000
E.E.C. in U.K.

46 000
British in E.E.C.

471 000
Irish in U.K.

1,348,000
OTHER COUNTRIES

527,000
SPAIN
60,173
37,530 Ger

469,000
PORTUGAL
87,492
64,328 Fr

701,000
N.AFRICA
41,776
30,652 Fr

the direct manner in which it controls the level of immigration. Compared with the situation during the late nineteenth century, strict immigration laws have reduced the number of migrants entering a country today down to a trickle (OECD, 1975). At present immigrants are only accepted into a country if they are skilled and can contribute to its more effective development, although at times of labour shortages some of these laws are relaxed. For example, in order to create demand and therefore to expand the economy Australia allowed in 'permanent' migrants, mostly from southern Europe, during the 1960s (Roberts, 1972). During the same period the countries of the Common Market alleviated their labour problems by encouraging 'short-term' immigrants from North Africa, Greece, Turkey and Yugoslavia on limited-period work perimits (Figure 9.2). After the 1973 oil crisis the economies of Western Europe began to falter, and with the consequent fall in labour requirements, the amount of labour migration has fallen quite sharply (Klaassen and Drewe, 1973). At the regional scale most governments of advanced economies have developed policies which have aimed at dispersing populations in order to alleviate the overconcentration of activities in certain regions and to provide growth potential in those regions experiencing decline (De Jong, 1975; Sundquist, 1975). For example, in the Mid-Wales region government assistance to factory development according to the then Development Commission between 1961 and 1971 retained just over 3,000 people, over half of whom were in the child-bearing ages, who might otherwise have left the region. The effect of this was to reduce the decline in Mid-Wales's population from 4.3 per cent to 2.3 per cent between 1961 and 1971, and to reduce the excess of deaths over births by nearly 40 per cent. The designation of one of the region's small towns, Newtown, as a growth-point has generated further factory development, and even the beginning of some migration from outside Mid-Wales (Jones, 1976). Despite the apparent success of regional policy in stemming the continued decline of Mid-Wales, such a policy has been the source of considerable controversy, since many argue that it is nothing more than 'spitting into the wind' of social and economic change (Heidenheimer, Heclo and Adams, 1975).

Governments play a more direct role in determining labour migration by the way in which their various agencies are organized. For example, the National Health Service stipulates the number of general practitioners that each area health authority is allowed to employ. Therefore, Davies (1966) has argued that many general practitioners in England and Wales would prefer to be in practice in the southeast region. Between 1953 and 1957 the number of doctors applying for a vacancy in practices of 2,000 or more patients in the north of England averaged 27, whereas similar practices in southern England received on average 53 applications. This effectively proves the spatial preferences of doctors for the south, and since the economic motive, financial gain, is standardized, other factors are needed to explain the pattern. In other words, doctors' migration desires are being constrained by an insufficiency of opportunities in the south, and are thus creating a migration potential of doctors in the remaining regions. Similarly, in Australia government agencies control not only the mobility level of their employees but also by being state-based confine movements to those within states. According to McKay and Whitelaw (1977), those employed in health care, education and local government formed the predominant element of intra-state migration between 1966–71 in Australia. In contrast, the same paper revealed that inter-state moves were dominated by those involved in manufacturing and financial institutions moving between metropolitan centres, largely as a part of career opportunities. For those employed in the secondary segment of the labour market the major flow was to the state capitals with little backflow to the more peripheral regions. Such differential movement reflects quite clearly the different spatial configuration of various organizations: the state government agencies provide facilities for the whole state, while private institutions are market oriented and, therefore, are attracted to the infra-structural advantages of the metropolitan areas. Such patterns are becoming increasingly apparent elsewhere in advanced economies (Keowan, 1971; Johnson, Salt and Wood, 1974).

What has been illustrated here is the fact that a growing proportion of migrants involve those who move or are moved by their employer for career opportunities. According to Whyte (1956, 304), such a migrant 'Keeps on moving — year after year, until perhaps, that distant day when he is summoned back to Rome' and, therefore, has little choice when the move is to take place and where to. Since the organizations, whether public or private, are multi-locational, distance and size of the urban areas are not significant constraints on migration. Often these 'organizational' migrants are assisted in their removal expenses, information about vacancies, and even in some cases the provision of housing.

Yet for the majority of potential migrants the availability of housing forms a major constraint to movement. From their study of housing and labour mobility in England and Wales, Johnson, Salt and

Wood (1974) concluded that the housing market was a major influence on the migration of labour. Housing acted as a constraint on movement not only by its supply but also by differential access to its various tenures. For example, as a result of these constraints owner-occupiers were more mobile over long distances than were those in private and public renting, thus hindering the flows of workers to those regions in need of labour. In other words, the structure of the housing market discriminates between households in their potential to migrate.

Residential Mobility

A glance at the housing market of most societies reveals that access to housing is not universal for all households even when income differences are taken into account (e.g. Gilbert and Ward, 1978; Ducland-Williams, 1978; Niner and Watson, 1978). In the competition for housing some individuals have greater power than others to choose, and even those who share the same position in the labour market sometimes differ in their access to housing space. However, the range of housing choice can be enlarged by financial credit being made available to a greater number of households and by builders constructing more cheap housing for sale. As suggested in Figure 9.3, access to housing and, therefore, migration potential, is a reflection not only of individual constraints but also the operation of those involved in organizing the housing market (Kirby, 1976; Duncan, 1976a).

In Britain there are three ways in which households can gain access to housing: by credit or capital accumulation, by obtaining a public housing tenancy, and by renting in the private sector. In such a situation households can be seen competing for limited resources, particularly mortgage capital and subsidized public housing, which results, according to Rex and Moore (1967), in the emergence of 'classes' with different access to these resources. Briefly, these 'housing classes' include:

(1) Outright owners of large houses in desirable areas.
(2) Mortgage-payers who 'own' houses in desirable areas.
(3) Council tenants in council-built houses.
(4) Council tenants in slum houses awaiting demolition.
(5) Tenants of private house-owners, usually in the inner ring.
(6) House-owners who must take in lodgers to meet loan repayments.
(7) Lodgers in rooms.

Figure 9.3: Residential Mobility and Access to Housing in Britain

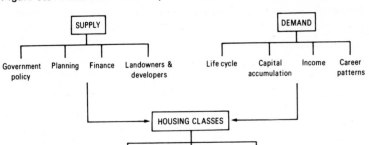

Despite considerable controversy over the details of these categorizations (Couper and Brindley, 1975; Bell, 1977), the schema does, however, emphasize that 'class' membership acts as an increasing constraint from the first to the seventh in the selection of housing, with the most fundamental division being between access to mortgage capital and obtaining a public housing tenancy. But, of course, there is no clear-cut correspondence between a particular tenure and a particular class, since owner-occupation has become more widespread and socially dispersed; for example, in Leicester only 5 per cent of the housing was owner-occupied in 1914, while by 1975 it had risen to 53 per cent. Yet the spread of owner-occupation down the social ladder has its limits since in Britain in 1975 only 19 per cent of unskilled workers owned their own house compared to 85 per cent of professional workers (Social Trends, 1978). Further, according to Cullingworth (1965), there is little movement between the various tenures. Between 1958 and 1962, most 'new' households entered privately rented accommodation, although nearly as many entered the owner-occupied sector, yet private tenancies were only a temporary phase because large numbers of tenants moved into owner-occupation or public housing. Owner-occupation and public housing appeared to be the final state, and both were growing at the expense of private tenancies.

The consumption, exchange and production of housing is organized and controlled by a variety of individuals and institutions (Ambrose and Colenutt, 1975; Williams, 1976). Government housing and taxation policies in general, financial institutions (Williams, 1978;

Figure 9.4: The interrelationship between Agents in the British Housing Market

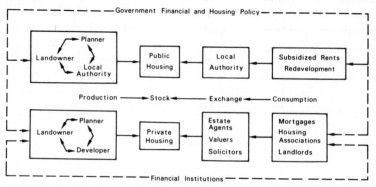

Harvey and Chatterjee, 1974), planning policies (Gans, 1972; Dennis, 1970), and the practice of estate agents (Palm, 1976; Ford, 1975) are but a few of the institutions that influence what housing is available, where and for whom (Figure 9.4). The operators of these institutions have been described by Pahl (1977b) as 'urban managers', or 'gatekeepers', in that they determine the amount of housing available, 'the gate', as well as the 'rules' of entry into the various tenures, 'the keepers'. For example, access to owner-occupation, apart from an accumulation of capital, is dependent upon mortgage finance, and in Britain building societies provide the largest amount of such credit (Boddy, 1976; Duncan, 1976b). A major qualifying criterion is security of income as well as its size; Barbolet (1969) has shown that for manual and clerical workers earning similar incomes, the latter obtain higher mortgages because of greater job security. Also mortgages are easier to obtain on new properties, except where the applicant is particularly credit-worthy (Williams, 1978). Often this means that those of lower income have to resort to insurance or local authority mortgages, with their larger interest rates, and hence are forced into older, smaller housing (Karn, 1976). This policy means that owner-occupation is discriminated against in the oldest and most deprived part of the city, 'the inner city', a tendency which is further accentuated by restrictions on local authority lending, the result of which is to militate against any possibility of a reversal of recent trends (Lambert, 1976; Boddy and Gray, 1979).

In Britain entry into public housing is dependent on housing 'needs', usually preference being given to large families and those affected by slum clearance, with a residential qualification of about five years duration (Niner, 1975). In the allocation of public housing, impressionistic evidence points towards a tendency for certain local authorities to grade their tenants and prospective tenants on the grounds of cleanliness and regularity of their rent payments. Such a grading results in the segregating of 'bad' tenants into older, poorer housing (Gray, 1976). Those households who fail to qualify for a mortgage or a public housing tenancy are forced to live in the private rented sector, which in 1975 occupied only 16 per cent of all housing in Britain compared with 45 per cent in 1950. Access to the private rented sector is based upon the production of a week's or month's rent only, yet here again there are constraints. Landlords have considerable influence over the kind of person to whom they are prepared to rent their property, and even estate agents when acting on behalf of a landlord can discriminate against certain people. In addition the various rent control acts have not only brought about a control of rents but also led to the sale of properties and their transfer to the owner-occupier sector, thus reducing the housing stock available for renting.

So far we have been concerned with those controlling the consumption and exchange of housing; other institutions control the amount of housing that is available (Bourne, 1976). These include landowners (Mortimore, 1969), builders and developers (Craven, 1969), and politicians and planners (Dennis, 1970; Simmie, 1974), whose actions are highly interdependent and often constrain the range of housing choices. For examples, development control policies devised by politicians and operated locally by planners, indirectly influence the actions of landowners and builders (Hall, Gracey, Drewett and Thomas, 1973).

Let us conclude by illustrating how some of these housing institutions have influenced residential mobility in the city by reference to two brief examples. Firstly, the phenomenon of 'gentrification', which involves the buying up and modernization of working-class housing by or for middle-class households (Hamnett, 1973; Williams, 1976), is a process which became apparent in the inner parts of London during the early sixties, and more particularly after the 1969 Housing Act, as a result of the availability of standard improvement grants and local authority expenditure on environmental improvements. Since there was no check on owners selling their improved houses, these grants could add both extra financial incentive to the activities of property companies and the promise of capital gain to private owners. A change in the law by the 1974 Housing Act, and in the availability of improvement grants, though it has reduced opportunities for speculation, has not completely removed it (Bassett and Short, 1978). Essentially, 'gentrification' has been initiated by the middle classes and several institutions involved in housing within the context of the government's overall housing policy, and though it has achieved the worthwhile objective of improving existing housing, it has done so at the expense of those least able to compete. The second example involves the operation of housing institutions towards ethnic and other minorities. In the United States there is much evidence to suggest that the availability of housing is determined according to white preferences. 'The practitioners of exclusion see as the outcome for themselves a clear conscience, peace of mind, and personal satisfaction in knowing that they are not hurting people by lowering the value of their property, giving them unwanted neighbours, or starting their neighbourhood on the downgrade, and knowing that their reputation, their status in the community and their business itself will not be harmed' (Helper, 1969, 69). Such discrimination results in black households paying up to 20 per cent more than white for the same type of housing (Kain and Quigley, 1972), consuming less housing when measured in terms of neighbourhood attributes and housing quality at any given income level (Straszheim, 1972), and being less likely to be house-owners (Kain, 1973). In Britain there is evidence to suggest that some estate agents try to guide immigrants to certain districts and away from others. Building societies, by refusing mortgages on older properties in the inner city, often called 'red-lining', and the residential qualification adopted by local authorities for entry to public housing, effectively discriminate against recent immigrants. Local authorities have certainly treated the prospects of allocating immigrants to public housing with some caution and, even in drawing up plans for the redevelopment of the inner city, have tended to avoid areas of denser colour settlement.

Essentially, what has been illustrated here is that migration takes place within the context not only of imperfect knowledge but one of considerable constraint. These constraints reflect the structured nature of society and manifest themselves locally in terms of differential access to employment and housing. The availability and access to these resources result from the interaction of several institutions and organizations, which operate within their own social and spatial bias, to provide a highly structured framework for household decision-making. However, despite considerable research on the nature and operation of these institutions involved in employment and housing, so far little attention has been given as to how they directly influence the decision whether to move, and if so, where to.

10 CONSEQUENCES OF MIGRATION

Although the preceding discussion has been concerned with the nature of migration as a response to social, political, economic and cultural changes within society, it is quite clear that migration can also be viewed as an independant variable, since it can initiate change itself (Figure 10.1). In other words, given a pattern of geographical mobility, what social, political, economic and cultural consequences ensue? However, it should be borne in mind that migration is only one of many agents which can initiate change. Among others which are of considerable significance are the dissemination of new ideas, information and techniques by means of spatial diffusion (Hägerstrand, 1967; Lewis, 1979b).

It is generally assumed that migration has a beneficial effect on economic development (Gaude and Peek, 1970). Such an assessment is based upon economic criteria, and, despite considerable research, the non-economic consequences of migration have too often been overlooked. This is rather surprising, when it is recalled that the greater part of this research has emphasized that migrants tend to experience considerable problems of adjustment and conflict as well as personal and community disorganization (Rose, 1969). Clearly, before a meaningful assessment can be made of the benefits of migration its effect upon those societies and individuals involved need to be discussed. Such a theme therefore necessitates a detailed examination in its own right.

Mabogunje (1970), in his systems approach to the migration process, suggested that when an individual leaves the countryside for the town, the former has to adjust to the loss of a member and the latter to an addition (Figure 2.10). At the same time the individual himself has to adjust to a new way of life, and his experiences when fed back to the countryside become the basis of accelerating or dampening down further movement. When viewed in these terms migration has an effect on many aspects of human activity and at several geographical scales. These interrelationships can be represented in a simplified framework (Table 10.1), which suggests that migration can bring about changes in several spheres — demographic, economic, social, cultural, political, etc. — and at several scales of analysis — societal, community and individual. Briefly, from such a framework it is evident that there are

Figure 10.1: A Simplified Representation of the Relationship between Selective Immigration and Changes in Britain's Social Structure within a Time Perspective

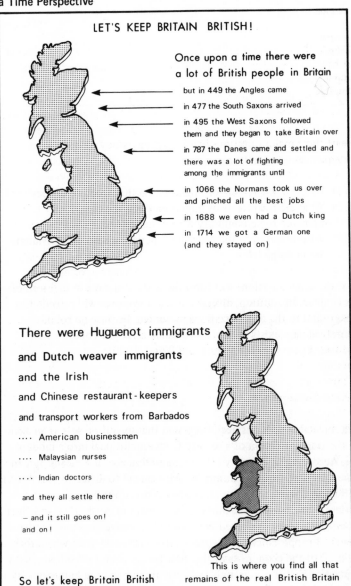

Source: Based on Kendall, 1977, 8-10.

Table 10.1: A Simplified Framework for the Study of the
Consequences of Migration

Dimension	Scale		
	Individual	Community	Societal
Demographic			
Economic			
Social			
Cultural			
Political			

at least three major questions involved in any study of the
consequences of migration:

(1) What are the effects of migration on the structure of society?
(2) What are the effects of migration upon the community of
     origin and the community of destination?
(3) What effect does the process of migrating have on individuals
     who undergo it?

These three questions will form the basis of the major divisions of
this chapter. In addition, diverse empirical evidence will provide the
background to the generalizations presented, because no sound
theoretical base exists on which we can analyze the consequences of
migration (Lewis, 1974b; White and Wood, 1980).

Societal Consequences

At a societal scale it has been suggested that migration acts as an agent
for the transformation of a society from a traditional into a modern
one. According to Zelinsky (1971), migration acts as a means by which
more advanced forms of human activity spread to different parts of the
world and, therefore, forms an essential part of the modernization
process. For example, the initial development of Australasia and North
America has to be explained in terms of successive migrations from
Western Europe, since the migrants took with them skills which formed
the basis of the economies of the 'new lands'. Even the contemporary
population distributions, political systems and cultural heterogeneity of
these countries are inexplicable without some reference to European
migrations during the last 200 years (Kovacs and Cropley, 1975). Of

late, however, the role of migration as an agent of the transformation of society has been a source of considerable discussion and controversy. The basis of such a controversy may best be illustrated with reference to three examples.

The first argues that such transformations are based on two assumptions – political continuity and cultural homogeneity – which are rare in historically complex European states. In a study of territories formerly under Austro-Hungarian and Turkish rule, Thomas (1980) has shown that the emergence from feudalism through capitalism to socialism exhibited regional contrasts resulting from environmental variety, diversity of antecedents, and the strength of cultural continuity. From the analysis it was concluded that migration is not in itself a primary cause of social and economic change but rather one mechanism whereby adaptations made necessary by other factors are achieved.

The second example illustrates the point that even when migration is generated by economic development it can in turn create problems and difficulties for the societies involved (Böhning, 1972; Paine, 1974). Since the Second World War to the onset of the general economic recession in 1974 the countries of Western Europe had experienced a vast influx of labour migrants from Greece, Spain, Portugal, Turkey and North Africa (Figure 9.2). Such migratory flows were explained in terms of the needs of Europe's 'booming' industries for labour to undertake unskilled tasks. In 1973 it was estimated that there were as many as eight million temporary migrants in Europe, although by now this figure has fallen sharply (Lewis, 1974b). Even prior to the present recession there was a good deal of discussion as to the efficiency of this labour system both for the countries of Western Europe and the native lands of the migrants. In 1973 it was estimated that these labour migrants earned about £2,000 million, about a half of which they sent home and the remainder was left on deposit in Europe. Although the money sent home was a vital contribution to the economies of their native countries, the remainder could also have been vital capital for further economic development. For other reasons, too, a number of countries by the late 1960s were already beginning to question the value of letting so many of their best workers (for example, 30 per cent of Yugoslavia's emigrants are skilled) leave for Western Europe. In Turkey there is a shortage of skilled foremen and supervisors and small entrepreneurs, whilst in Athens building labour is so difficult to find that Egyptians are being brought in to replace the locals who have left for West Germany and elsewhere.

Such a migration pattern is analogous to a series of 'waves' directed towards the major centres of commerce and industry. However, even for the countries of Western Europe an overdependence on such labour may prove to be a short-sighted policy, since stricter emigration policies in the native countries of the temporary migrants may easily induce economic difficulties and, at times of recession, the migrants may well be a source of conflict. With the onset of the recession, anti-immigration tension along with the new-found voice of the migrants themselves has led to considerable social and political difficulties. For some time those migrants already in Western Europe have demanded a better way of life, being increasingly prepared to fight as a group for opportunities to rise above the lowest jobs. But the more the migrants have struggled to better themselves, the more they are seen as a threat by the natives. The ability of the migrant workers to act as a group is illustrated by the case of the protest strike by North Africans in France in 1973: 'Nearly 30,000 North African workers began a 24-hour strike in and around Marseilles . . . in protest at the recent wave of anti-Arab violence, in which seven Algerians have died. The violence followed the murder of a Marseilles bus driver by a deranged Algerian 10 days ago' (*Guardian*, 4 September 1973). In 1973, as a result of serious race riots in the Netherlands, Rotterdam put a ceiling on the number of migrants who can work there. Despite restrictions of this kind, there is a dawning realization in most of Western Europe that the migrants may be permanent, and so the call to 'send them home' is spreading rapidly among the lower-paid natives.

An even greater source of controversy involves the role of migrants in the economic development of third world countries. Some of these controversies may be illustrated with reference to recent migratory movements in Ghana. According to Caldwell (1969, 139), '. . . migration has profoundly affected Ghana and its effect is a reflection of the depth of the economic and social changes which have occurred this century. It, in its turn, is an agent of further change'. A primary demographic consequence of migration has been to redistribute the population, particularly in the direction of the urban areas. In fact, about two-thirds of urban growth in Ghana during recent decades is a function of internal and external migration. Moreover, it is becoming apparent that the younger and more skilled members of the society are more concentrated in towns than in rural village areas. However, Caldwell (1969) has argued that the high rates of natural increase in rural areas and high rates of return migration reduce the equilibrium function of migration. In other words, the reduction in the excess rural population through mobility to urban areas has been less than dramatic.

Many scholars view the migrant labour system in Ghana and other West African states as an efficient adaption to a changing economy and one which exhibits little sign of decreasing. Migration has permitted such countries to experience more rapid economic growth than might otherwise have been possible. Berg (1965) has gone as far as to argue that labour migration has been an economic benefit not only to recipient areas but also to the labour-exporting villages. Nevertheless, others claim that temporary migration makes labour productivity lower than it would be if the same labour force were permanent: temporary migration prevents the establishment of a permanent industrial labour force, discourages the acquisition of skills and the development of labour organization, and may lead to social problems in recipient areas where migrants of different origins are brought together. Further, it can also be argued that seasonal migration is detrimental to the labour-exporting rural communities. Skinner (1966) has shown that among the Mossi of the Upper Volta region migration has affected agricultural practices, the types of crops grown, and work patterns. Seasonal migration has resulted in the discontinuance of family farming, since every hand available was required to make it operative. In addition, attitudes towards farming have changed, from the pursuit of subsistence to commercial ideals. As a result, many of the Mossi have given up agriculture in order to engage in local and regional trading. Although labour migration has changed the economic and material life of the Mossi, it is far from clear whether it has resulted in any substantial improvement in their standard of living.

On the other hand, migration strengthens the economic infrastructure through the need to develop roads and transportation facilities. As a result of migration between rural and urban areas in Ghana, the cash economy is beginning to spread to the rural districts, and Goldscheider (1971) has gone so far as to claim that migration may prove instrumental in stimulating industrialization in the larger towns: 'Rather than serving as a response to rapid industrialization and the need for an urban labour supply, migration in Africa may stimulate industrialization and generate economic development' (Goldscheider, 1971, 210).

However, despite the apparent economic advantages of labour migration, seasonal movements can cause considerable social and political problems. This temporary migration means the disruption of agricultural production and authority structure in rural areas. In the towns, it means the establishment of a permanent unskilled labour force, and a young, male, potentially violent population. For society as a whole it may mean unemployment and group tension. One such tension associated with migration is the discord it engenders in authority, family and kinship relationships.

Evidence such as that discussed above has formed the basis for the questioning of the role of migration as an effective agent in the transformation of society. It would appear that there exists a variety of intervening factors which results in a number of instances in migration actually attenuating the change process. In other words, migration sets up so many social and political problems that attempts to solve them leads to a slowing-down in the development process. The continuation of a migration stream after the demand for labour has declined can also reduce the rate of economic change.

Community Consequences

The community consequences of migration depend upon the intensity of the migration, its differential nature and the social composition of the communities involved (Hunter, 1974). It is now well established that, of the three components of population change (births, deaths and migration), it is migration which is by far the most significant at the community level. Not only does migration bring about a net gain or loss of population, but by its selectivity, particularly of the young, it can also indirectly affect a community's population growth rate. A continuous in-migration of young migrants can accelerate the birth-rate of the community involved; conversely, a large out-flow of young migrants contributes to a falling birth-rate. In the former case an accelerating natural increase will develop, whilst in the latter there will be a falling natural increase, or even a natural decrease.

In Chapter 6 it was revealed that migration tends to be selective of certain individuals, so giving rise to the likely modification of the social structure of the communities involved in the process. Among the differentiating factors which have been shown to generate social change are included socio-economic status, education, ethnicity, occupation, language and religion. More often than not migrants are innovators and prospective leaders within a community, although Galtung (1971, 191) has suggested that someone who may have been an innovator in his home community may be more conservative in the host community. In order to illustrate these points, three examples of spatial change will now be considered: urban growth and spatial segregation; depopulation and the declining rural community; and commuting and the metropolitan village.

Urban Growth and Spatial Segregation

The migratory movement of individuals is, by definition, a mechanism by which the spatial distribution of population is altered or transformed (Greenwood, 1973). According to Gibbs (1963), the redistribution of population in industrialized societies during the past 200 years or so has been characterized by considerable spatial order. He maintains that urbanization involves, not only an increase in the size of towns and cities, but also a tendency towards a concentration of population in certain parts of countries. According to Gibbs (1963), such population redistribution takes place in a series of distinct stages:

(1) Cities comes into being but the percentage increase of the rural population equals or exceeds that of the urban population at the time that cities first appear.
(2) The percentage increase of the urban population comes to exceed the percentage increase of the rural population.
(3) The rural population undergoes an absolute decline.
(4) The population of small cities undergoes an absolute decline.
(5) The difference among the territorial divisions with regard to population density declines, i.e. a more even spatial distribution of population develops.

Of course such stages are not mutually exclusive; consequently, it is logically possible for a society to be at two or more of the stages simultaneously. Aldkogius (1970), in a study of population change and urban growth in Sweden, was able to identify several of these patterns. For example, during the 1950s the population of urban places increased by 800,000 persons whilst that of rural declined by 350,000. The actual population increase was concentrated, however, in very restricted areas in the central and southern parts of the country: mainly in the larger urban centres. Urban places with more than 50,000 inhabitants were expected to increase their population by 50 per cent between 1950 and 1980, while the population of Sweden was expected to grow only 20 per cent during the same period. Smaller urban places, as well as the rural areas, were expected to lose population. However, during the 1960s in Europe and North America further changes have taken place in the population growth patterns of communities as a result of

Figure 10.2: Population Changes by Sub-divisions of Economic Planning Regions in England and Wales, 1966–71: a — total change; b — net migration

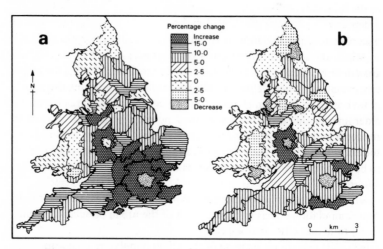

Source: Calculated from tables in Central Statistical Office *Abstract of Reginal Statistics 1973*, HMSO, London, 1973.

differential migration (Figure 10.2). Among these trends are included:

(a) an outward migration from conurbations and major cities;
(b) an inward migration to the smaller cities;
(c) a rural increase in population.

Despite the continued increase in employment opportunities within the conurbations and major cities, the outward migration is a reflection of an increased divorce between place of work and residence. This is partly because rural areas and towns peripheral to the conurbations have become foci for in-migrants who work in the conurbations themselves. But there are also additional groups of out-migrants from the conurbations and major cities who have made moves beyond their orbit. Firstly, there are retired people who have located themselves in coastal districts or in the countryside; secondly, there are many single persons who were previously attracted to large cities, but who upon marriage and parenthood have found the economies and social stresses of raising a family so considerable that they have migrated out to the smaller cities. As a third case, Lind (1969, 85) has argued that in Britain a typical 'inter-regional migrant seems very likely to be someone leaving one of the Northern conurbations and moving to a small town in the Midlands or South. This is very different from the normally accepted stereotype of migration which is of people leaving the uncongested north and moving to London'.

Migration not only contributes significantly to the differential growth of towns and cities but also it is the mechanism through which a city expands spatially. When the industrial cities were undergoing rapid growth through migration, the majority of the newcomers settled in the older inner areas of the city, which were vacated by the long-established residents in favour of the suburbs. After a period of adjustment and socialization, lasting one or more generations, the migrants would move to better housing areas on the periphery (Goldstein and Mayer, 1965; Moore, 1978). Such a pattern of growth and social change seems to have been the typical one for many European immigrants in North American cities, although, despite considerable social and geographical mobility, most American cities have retained a series of 'ethnic' neighbourhoods. In recent years, however, many scholars have begun to question the validity of this classical theory of migration and urban growth, on two major grounds:

(1) The pattern of migration into the city envisaged by the theory does not correspond with the reality of the situation in cities experiencing high rates of in- and out-migration. Different groups of in-migrants move directly into different zones within the city: for example, the high-status migrants from other urban areas tend to locate themselves on the suburban fringes whilst young adults, both the unmarried and those married but without children, select the inner-city because they have certain economic and cultural advantages (Figure 10.3).
(2) Increasingly, evidence is being gathered which conclusively shows that not all migrants are able to achieve social and spatial mobility (Taeuber and Taeuber, 1964; Rose, 1972). A number of groups find it difficult, and in some cases almost impossible, to leave the inner city (Chapter 9). According to Eisenstadt (1954) the development of this segregation is determined by changes in the role-allocation structure of both the migrant groups and the host society. In such a schema the formation on the one hand of groups with common cultural origins and of specialized religious, educational or other institutions serving migrants, and the existence on the other hand of community patterns of residential, occupational or social segregation, are both

Figure 10.3: Distribution of Social Groups in Leicester, 1966: Socio-economic Status (Component 1) and Life Cycle (Component 3)

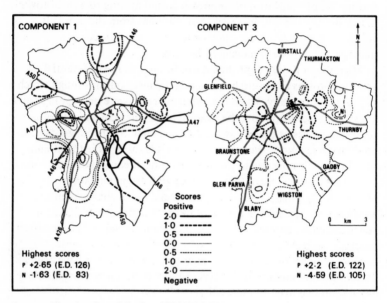

Source: After Lewis and Davies, 1974, 194–207.

subsumed under the rubric of differences in roles allotted to, and performed by, migrants and non-migrants respectively. Therefore, community change may tend either towards convergence of role distribution (the filtering process) or towards the stabilization of separate, pluralistic role structures (the segregation process). To many the development of such processes have to be interpreted within the context of the structure of modern society (Chapter 9).

Depopulation and the Declining Rural Community

The depopulation of rural areas within the developed world remains a paradoxical phenomenon, when one considers that the majority of developed nations are still experiencing considerable population growth (Lowenthal and Comitas, 1962). In a study of rural population change in the United States, Beale (1964) claimed that more counties had lost population during a period of high national population growth (the 1950s) than did so during the period of lowest national growth (the 1930s). In addition, it was shown that between 1920 and 1960 the proportion of losing counties that have been heavy losers has grown:

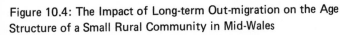

Figure 10.4: The Impact of Long-term Out-migration on the Age
Structure of a Small Rural Community in Mid-Wales

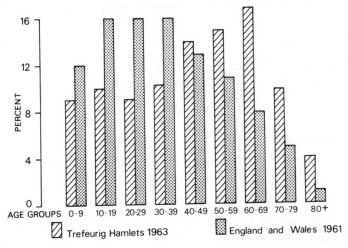

in the 1920s little more than a fourth of the declining counties fell in
population by more than 10 per cent, but by the 1950s the proportion
of losers in this category exceeded one-half. During the past two
decades these trends have begun to be reversed, particulary in those
rural areas accessible to metropolitan centres and small cities (Roseman,
1977; Lamb, 1975). This rural 'turnaround' is taking place not only
in the United States but also in Britain and other countries in Western
Europe. The major agent of this differential pattern of rural population
change has been migration, which has resulted in the countryside being
divided into at least two demographic areas: an inner or pressured
countryside, and an outer or declining countryside. In the latter
depopulation still continues, and as a result of a prolonged and
increasingly high net out-migration of young rural adults (25–45 year
olds), a condition has been reached in many rural communities in which
births are exceeded by the number of deaths taking place (Drudy,
1978). In such communities there exists a distorted age structure, and
an accelerating depopulation (Figure 10.4). However, of late, there is
evidence to suggest that even this decline is beginning to slow down as
a result of a repopulation of the remoter countryside by a number of
'new' migrant groups (Nicholson, 1975). For example, in the Colwyn
district of the Welsh Borderland these in-migrants were made up of at
least four groups (Lewis, 1981a). Firstly, there were the second home
owners who occupied their properties for only a part of the year and,

Figure 10.5: Arson Attacks in Rural Wales Reported between 1977 and 1979

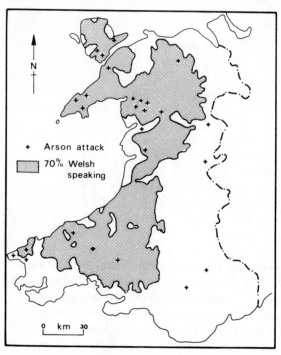

were the source of considerable antagonism, which in certain parts of Wales has resulted in several arson attacks (Figure 10.5). A growing number of retirement migrants formed a distinguishable second group; in general, they comprised of those returning to their home area and 'second homers' who had reached retirement age. The third group, although small, included those who could divorce place of residence from that of work in both time and space. In effect they were those who did not have to travel to work on a daily basis, e.g. company directors, or could carry out their work from home, e.g. authors, broadcasters, etc. The final group were those who had left the city for the 'tranquillity' of rural life. These 'urban drop-outs' had given up professional-type occupations and taken up small-scale farming or craftwork. Quite often these four groups were a source of discussion within the host communities: some viewed them as the cause of local housing shortages whilst others were critical of their failure to contribute fully to community social life.

A continuous out-migration of young adults has had a marked effect upon the social structure of the rural communities involved (Leonard and Hannon, 1977). According to Mitchell (1950) a falling population, and the selective nature of the decline, contributes to a disintegration of traditional rural life. The removal of the relatively young, often the more able and articulate, reduces the number of potential leaders within the community, and this, allied to a falling and ageing population, makes the maintenance of a varied social life extremely difficult. Frankenberg (1957) has shown that small communities such as the one he studied in North Wales can sustain only a limited number of social organizations. In 'Pentrediwaith' during the 1950s only one major social organization could be sustained at any one time: during this period the football club declined and was replaced by the carnival as the major focus of the community interest. Mitchell (1950) has shown that in such ageing communities inter-personal contact is extremely strong; social life, however, becomes increasingly dependent on such relationships.

The effect of long-term depopulation has been to erode the service infrastructure of the remoter communities. The closure of schools, banks, shops, post offices, doctors' surgeries, etc., has meant that the residual populations have been forced to become highly dependent upon more distant centres for their basic needs. At the same time low levels of car ownership and a decline in public transport have exacerbated the situation by making access to services even more problematic. Rural accessibility is now a serious problem, particularly for the elderly, teenagers and young housewives (Moseley, 1979). In turn, these changes make the rural community less attractive to potential in-migrants; for example, there is evidence to suggest that those villages without a school are not attractive to young families.

In order to reverse these trends, then, there is a need for more employment opportunities. In rural Wales and the highlands of Scotland two development boards have been concerned with rural decline for some time. Among their many activities one of the most significant has been concerned with attracting new forms of industrial employment into the two regions. Despite the regions' distance from market and the dispersed nature of their population, considerable success has been achieved in bringing in industrial employment. Yet, in general, industrialists have been cautious about locating in rural regions often because of a lack of labour with sufficient skills. In other words, the continuing out-migration is itself making the regions less and less attractive to industrial and other forms of employment.

Commuting and the Metrpolitan Village

Despite the general decline of rural population by migration, those areas adjacent to the major cities are today actually experiencing growth. Between 1951 and 1971 in England and Wales there was a considerable net in-migration into rural districts adjacent not only to the major metropolitan centres but also to small towns. Lewis (1979b) and Maund (1976) have shown that there was considerable sub-urban growth even around the towns of Aberystwyth and Hereford. The development of such population growth is due, on the one hand, to an out-migration by urban dwellers into the countryside and, on the other, to an increasing dependence of the rural dwellers on the town for employment. This increasing divorce of place of work from place of residence has been analyzed by Lawton (1968) for the period since 1921. Essentially, it was shown that the length of the journey to work had increased to such an extent that virtually the whole of rural Britain was dependent upon urban areas for employment.

Such population growth brings about not only an enlargement of the rural communities but also significant changes in their social structure. It results in an introduction of upper-middle- and middle-class inhabitants with different attitudes and values, and it creates a marked polarization of the community into 'newcomers' and the 'established'. Although these terms imply a differentiation based upon length of residence, they essentially reflect a class distinction. According to Pahl (1975, 66–8) the social structure of rural communities in Hertfordshire can be subdivided into additional groups:

1. Large property owners
2. Salaried in-migrants with some capital
3. Spiralists
4. Those with limited income and little capital
5. The retired
6. Council-house tenants
7. Tied cottages and other tenants
8. Local tradesmen and owners of small businesses

Such a social structure is not, however, uniform among all the rural communities located adjacent to large cities. A major contributor to social differentiation among these communities is the way in which the 'key village' planning policy results in a selectivity of in-migrants (Figure 10.6). Such a policy involves the designation of each community's growth potential (Cloke, 1979); in general, where a

Figure 10.6: 'Key' Village Policy in Leicestershire, 1973

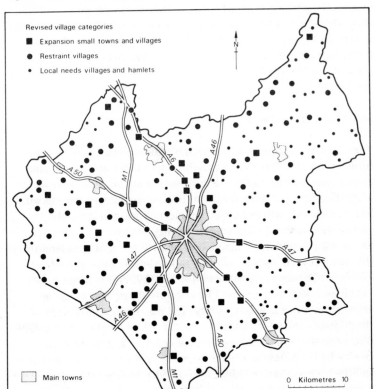

community is designated for 'non-growth' then there is a tendency for it to be attractive for upper-middle-class residence. These groups are attracted by the community's continuing rural character and, of course, have the wealth to 'gentrify' the housing.

Among the newcomers to these 'metropolitan' villages, distinction must be made between 'reluctant' and 'community' migrants, since the latter involve those who have chosen rural residence deliberately whilst the former have been 'forced' to reside in the countryside. Often these 'reluctant' migrants eventually leave to reside within the confines of the city when suitable housing becomes available. On the other hand, the 'community' migrants, when seeking new housing do so within the same village or a nearby one, because of their desire for community involvement. In general, these newcomers are a stimulus to the development of a whole series of new social organizations which involves the whole community. But, as the community grows and the 'newcomers' increase in number, there is a tendency for social activities to fragment along class lines. In other words, inter-personal contact becomes more difficult and personal assessment gives way to class as the basis for the identification of status.

Individual Consequences

The effect of migration upon the individual involved can take many forms, much of it being related to the extent to which his needs and aspirations are being met in the host community as well as his own adaptation to new surroundings. In the host community the migrant has to adapt to a 'new' social, economic, political and cultural environment, although this adaptation may be eased if he joins a group with a similar cultural background to himself. Much of the literature on this theme, beginning with Thomas and Znaniecki's classic study of *The Polish Peasant in Europe and America* (1927), has focused upon the discontinuities experienced by migrants during the process of assimilation into a new community. The major concern has been upon the prejudice and discrimination experienced by migrants, particularly their exclusion from certain spheres of activities and the problems created by the differences in norms, values and customs between them and the host population (Abu Lughod, 1961; McGhee, 1975). An understanding of the assimilation process is necessary since it not only affects the wellbeing of the individual but also later migrations.

The assimilation of the migrant into the receiving community, according to Germani (1965), involves three, often interrelated, processes: adjustment, participation and acculturation. In order to avoid terminological confusion such processes will be defined along the lines suggested by Germani:

   (a) Acculturation — 'the process (and the degree) of acquisition and learning by the migrant of ways of behaviour (including roles, habits, attitudes, values, knowledge) of the receiving society' (p. 164).
   (b) Adjustment — 'the manner in which the migrant is able to perform his roles in the various spheres of activity in which he participates' (p. 163).
   (c) Participation — 'How many and in which roles [he is]

Table 10.2: The Assimilation Process

	Sub-process or condition	Type of Assimilation
1	Change of cultural patterns to those of host society	Cultural or behavioural assimilation (acculturation)
2	Large-scale entrance into host society's primary groups (cliques, clubs, etc)	Structural assimilation (participation)
3	Large-scale inter-marriage	Marital assimilation (amalgamation)
4	Development of sense of peoplehood based on host society	Identification assimilation (adjustment)
5	Absence of prejudice	Attitude receptional assimilation
6	Absence of discrimination	Behaviour receptional assimilation
7	Absence of value or power conflict	Civil assimilation

Source: Gordon (1964).

performing within the institutions, social groups, and various sections of the host community' (p. 164).

In his study of *Assimilation in American Life* (1964), Gordon goes a stage further by identifying the processes which bring about the assimilation of the migrant into the host society. By relating the processes involved ('sub-processes' or 'conditions') to different types of assimilation, he builds up a form of classification of the 'assimilation process' (Table 10.2).

Implicit within such a classification is the existence of a temporal component in the assimilation process. Gordon has hypothesized that the sequential nature of assimilation may take the following forms:

(i) 'Cultural assimilation, or acculturation, is likely to be the first of the types of assimilation to occur when a minority group arrives on the scene' (p. 73).

(ii) 'Cultural assimilation, or acculturation, of the minority group may take place even when none of the other types of assimilation occurs simultaneously or later, and this condition of "acculturation only" may continue indefinitely' (p. 77).

(iii) 'Once structural assimilation has occurred, either simultaneously with or subsequent to acculturation, all of the other types of assimilation will naturally follow' (p. 81).

These hypotheses clearly emphasize the point that the components of assimilation do not necessarily all occur simultaneously. A given degree of adjustment (or participation, or acculturation) may be achieved in one sphere of activity but not in another (Goldlust and Richmond, 1974). For example, a migrant may feel adjusted to the needs of his new job, and yet be unable to bear the psychological stress introduced by impersonal human relations in the new community. However, it is true, at least with regard to certain spheres of activity, adjustment, participation and acculturation will usually go together, though incongruities between different spheres of activities may be quite frequent, as has been illustrated by several studies of immigrants to Australia (Borrie, 1954; Cronin, 1972; Kuber, 1977). After this brief outline of the process of assimilation it is now opportune to discuss the nature of the prejudice and discrimination experienced by migrants during their assimilation into the host society within the context of its three component parts.

Acculturation, or the acquisition of new cultural traits by the migrant, may take place in various ways: it may consist of relatively superficial learning, or it may penetrate deeply into his personality. According to Price (1969, 196), 'in the new setting the migrant is confronted with the need of acquiring new knowledge, and also new attitudes and new values. But in such re-socialization . . . [it] . . . may lead to a deep involvement and identification with the new pattern, to a very superficial acceptance, or to a more or less complete rejection. The recognition of such different forms and degrees of acculturation is sometimes of paramount importance'.

Traditionally, studies of acculturation have emphasized the isolation of the newcomer from the host society as a result of differences in norms, values and customs. As Louis Wirth (1945, 64) wrote: '. . . as newer immigrant groups followed older ways, the latest comers increasingly became the objects of prejudice and discrimination on the part of natives and older immigrants alike . . . Although the ethnic minorities in the United States suffer mainly from private prejudices rather than restrictive public policies, their path of assimilation is not without its serious obstacles'. Similar forms of prejudice and discrimination in British cities have been revealed by a number of studies, in particular Richmond's (1973) analysis of race relations in Bristol. Of course, if such segregation involves a sufficient number of migrants they will form a distinctive minority group within the host society located within easily identifiable territorial limits (Henderson, 1978).

In any discussion of a migrant's adjustment to his changed circumstances, the main concern is with his ability to perform various roles without excessive or unbearable stress. A number of studies have identified a relationship between migration and family disorganization, mental illness, delinquency, poverty, etc. The findings have stressed that migrants tend to have higher rates of these problems than do the host population. For example, Park described the adjustment difficulties of the in-migrants to American cities in the following manner: '. . . the enormous amount of delinquency, juvenile and adult, that exists today in the Negro communities in northern cities is due in part, though not entirely, to the fact that migrants are not able to accommodate themselves at once to a new and relatively strange environment. The same thing may be said of the immigrants from Europe, or of the younger generations of women who are just entering in such large numbers into the new occupations and the freer life which the great cities offer them' (Park, 1925, 37). Similarly Bonilla (1970, 72) describes the *favelado* of Rio de Janeiro as being '. . . plagued by all the ills that beset his kind everywhere. As a group, the favela population is on the wrong side of every standard index of social disorganization whether it be illiteracy, malnutrition, disease, job instability, irregular sexual unions, alcoholism, criminal violence, or about any other on the familiar list'.

An explanation of such social disorganization is complex, and it is difficult to generalize. For example, Bogue has gone as far as to suggest four possible reasons as to why migrants are more prone to mental disorders than non-migrants. Briefly, they are:

1. . . . a lack of a supportive receiving population that favours rapid and easy social adjustments lead to mental stress and disorder.
2. Aggravated hostility, prejudice, and highly inconsistent behaviour on the part of the receiving community may be conducive to mental disorders.
3. In some situations migrants leave their homeland gladly and without great mental stress, but in others their movement is forced by tragic circumstances, so that the separation is a very traumatic one.
4. . . . migration may involve a dramatic transition that requires a complete reorganization of the personality (Bogue, 1969, 800).

The above may be an over-elaborate way of stating the obvious: i.e. that the mental health of migrants is a function of the amount of stress they must undergo in the process of separating themselves from their community or origin and of gaining the status of accepted members of their community of destination. It is also very plausible to suppose that it is often persons in a state of deep anxiety and stress who will seek to migrate in an effort to resolve their problems. A similar pattern of relationship exists between migration and other forms of adjustment.

In a study of migrants' participation in the social and economic structure of the host community it is necessary to distinguish at least three different dimensions. Firstly, how many, and which, roles is the migrant performing within the institutions, social groups and various sectors of the receiving community? Secondly, how efficiently are such roles being performed by the migrant, particularly as viewed from the standpoint of the receiving institutions and groups and of the values of the receiving community? And thirdly, how do the social groups and institutions of the receiving society react with regard to the migrants and their participation? Often in this context the term integration is used to refer specifically to the degree of accepted and/or non-conflictual participation. Thus the degree of participation of the migrant in the various social groups and institutions of the host society, can really be assessed only when it is compared with that of the native population. Although a migrant may be participating very fully within the host community, he may still not be fully adjusted or acculturated. The nature of differential rates of participation has been revealed by a number of studies. For example, Zimmer (1970) has carried out a detailed study of migrant participation in an American Midwestern urban community (population 20,000). By use of such indices as membership of formal organizations, offices held in formal organizations and registration to vote, Zimmer revealed lower rates of participation among the migrants than among the native population. However, the migrants' rates of participation increased with their length of residence in the host community, and the greater the similarity of the migrants' social and economic background to that of the receiving society, the more quickly they came to participate in the activities of that society; for example, it was found that urban migrants tended to enter the activities of the community more rapidly than farm migrants. Such conclusions are readily supported by a wide variety of other studies of migrant participation (Lewis, 1979b).

There have been many attempts to identify the stages which an individual goes through during his assimilation into a host society. Broadly speaking, there are two major theories – the 'melting-pot' and 'ethnic-pluralities' theories – which attempt to explain the assimilation process, and in many ways these correspond to the 'filtering' and 'segregation' process discussed earlier. Essentially, the first theory looks towards the eventual conformity of the immigrant within the host community; the second assumes that differences will harden into permanent distinct groups. A wide variety of sequences generalizing the process of assimilation have been described, and since these have been well documented elsewhere (Price, 1969), reference will here be made only to two examples which stand midway between the two theories.

According to Duncan (1933) the assimilation process involves at least three generations, which may be summarized as follows:

  (a) *First generation* — although a few immigrants assimilate completely, the overwhelming majority adopt only a limited number of the host society's social and economic values, and so form ethnic groups and institutions to maintain their original culture.
  (b) *Bridge generation* — there is a tendency for this generation to preserve the 'old' culture at home as a result of parental pressure and to acquire the 'host' culture outside the home, so forming a mixed set of values and a dual culture.
  (c) *Assimilated generation* — under pressure from the host society this generation rejects the 'old' culture and adopts all the values and customs of the 'host' culture. Thus the process of assimilation is complete.

There has been considerable criticism of these stages by a number of scholars (Price, 1969). Some have argued that during the third generation there is a tendency to revert back to the 'old' culture, whilst others, basing themselves upon American evidence, have emphasized the tendency for ethnic differences to wane within the triple contexts of Protestantism, Catholicism and Judaism. As a result of these criticisms a further modification to the process of assimilation has been suggested by Glazer and Moynihan (1963) along the following lines:

  (a) First stage — the creation of ethnic groups and organizations but a gradual disappearance of ethnic culture and language.
  (b) Second stage — beginning of the transformation of the ethnic groups into 'interest' groups distinguished by colour and religion, by attitudes to education, politics and family life.
  (c) Third stage — the disappearance of the ethnic groups into divisions of colour and religion.

Unfortunately, the majority of studies of assimilation are based upon the North American experience where ethnic difference is the major source of differentiation. However, it could be argued that in any society the same processes operate, and that differences are only a matter of detail. In addition, it appears that the greater the initial differences, the greater the problem of assimilation; and where racial prejudice is significant then both the 'melting-pot' and 'ethnic-plualities' processes are operative, even during the latter stages.

This chapter has discussed and attempted to explain the important cultural, political and social consequences of migration at three societal scales. If such an approach is adopted, it becomes clear that any major societal shift of population has marked consequences for the communities and individuals involved. The nature of the social, political and cultural difficulties experienced by individuals and social groups, as a consequence of migration, may well lead to the questioning of the widely-held view that large-scale mobility is of considerable benefit for the regions and populations involved. Certainly such consequences need to be taken into account in determining priorities in any form of economic development.

11 CONCLUSION

This book has sought to examine the ways in which the process of migration may be analyzed within a geographical framework. Since research is an ongoing process a conclusion is often dated by the time the book is published; therefore, a passage such as this is more often than not an irrelevancy. But in view of the tentative and speculative nature of this book some concluding comments are needed. At least three themes suggest themselves for consideration: the greater realism in migration analysis, the changing view of the role of migration in the transformation of society, and the need for a better understanding by public policy-makers of the nature of migration.

The purpose of theory should be to provide a framework of variables and processes within which individual researchers can locate their findings. At one time it was thought that the underlying causes and effects of migration were fully understood, whether it was in terms of 'push-pull' factors, 'gravity' forces, and 'adaptation' processes. However, increasing empirical research has revealed the existence of a variety of migrant types and migration patterns which are not accounted for by early theories. Too often, theory has focused upon rural to urban migration, yet in the developed countries new patterns, such as urban to urban and urban to rural, have emerged, whilst in the third world it has been revealed that the temporary or periodic migrant is an integral part of the migration process. As a result there has been a shift towards a decision-making framework on the grounds 'that migration is a behavioural result of a complex set of decisions that are rational and irrational, conscious and unconscious, deliberate and impulsive' (Reissman, 1967, 212). Many researchers suggest, however, that the migrant does not have a complete choice since the structure of the society of which he is a part provides the basis of opportunities. On the other hand, several students of migration still maintain that potential migrants have considerable free choice whether to move or not, as well as to where to move to. From the available evidence it would appear that an individual is not inexorably locked into a system in which his actions are determined, though clearly there are constraints to which he is subject. In other words, migration is a 'holistic' system involving a set of interrelated, personal, socio-economic and situational elements.

This broadening of the geographical perspective has had a marked effect upon the interpretation of the role of migration in the transformation of society. According to Richmond (1969, 280), 'the migrants perform a catalytic function, instigating processes of change at the technological and social levels that have profound repercussions throughout society . . . [they are] agents of the post-industrial revolution itself'. For such a post-industrial society a 'McLuhanesque' interpretation of migration trends is envisaged since high levels of mobility become a norm of behaviour. Individuals will form a part of a worldwide communications network and will not be tied to any one locality. A better understanding of the migration process has resulted in many questioning the likelihood of this scenario, particularly arguing that age and occupational selectivity will persist and that the locality will remain a force in everyday life. In the contemporary third world the massive growth in urban population suggests that a transformation of society is taking place but, however, it does not mean a total break with the past since the migrant continues to have strong ties with his native land. This suggests that the view of Zelinsky (1971), that seasonal migration to urban areas is a temporary phase which eventually leads to permanent residence, has also to be questioned. In fact, the evidence indicates that these forms of movement do not show any signs of decreasing in intensity and so emphasizing continuity rather than discontinuity in the migration process.

Despite a greater understanding among social scientists of the nature of migration and its role as a force generating change, policy-makers continue to conceive migratory movements in a highly simplified way. Politicians still talk about the migration 'problem' and consequently initiate policy to 'reduce its impact', 'to control it', or 'keep 'em on the farm'. Such a conception is very much the 'outsider' attempting to look 'inside' without a clear understanding of the causes of the 'problem' and the likely effects of the policy adopted. Conversely those policy-makers who adopt the opposite stance — such as a British Prime Minister who has asserted that people should be prepared to move to find work — also reveals an ignorance of the migratory process. The naivity of this assertion is most vividly illustrated from a letter to the *Daily Telegraph* (1980): 'to be able to transfer from one council house to another must be a rarity indeed. To sell one's house and buy another elsewhere is at present fraught with difficulties and problems, because of the "chain reaction" in almost all house purchase/sale transactions'. Clearly politicians need to become aware of the complexities of the migration process as it affects different peoples at different times differently. Only by making policy-makers aware of these complexities will more realistic policies be adopted, which is essential for the world's future since the movement of people is the most universal and powerful force for change ever known.

BIBLIOGRAPHY

Abu Lughod, J. (1961) 'Migrant adjustment to city life: the Egyptian case', *American Journal of Sociology*, *67*, 22–72

Adams, J.S. (1969) 'Directional bias in intra-urban migration', *Economic Geography*, *45*, 302–23

—— and Gilder, K.A. (1976) 'Household location and intra-urban migration', in Herbert, D.T. and Johnston, R.J. (eds.), 159–92

Adams, R.B. (1969) 'United States Metropolitan migration: dimension and predictability', *Proceedings of the Association of American Geographers*, *1*, 1–6

Aldkogius, M. (1970) 'Population change and urban growth', *Geografiska Annaler*, *52B*, 131–40

Allon-Smith, R.D. (1978) *The Migration of the Elderly: a Social Geography*, unpublished Ph.D. thesis, University of Leicester

Alperovich, G., Bergsman, J. and Eheman, C. (1977) 'An econometric model of migration between United States metropolitan areas', *Urban Studies*, *14*, 135–45

Alvarez, J.H. (1967) *Return Migration to Puerto Rico*, University of California Press, Berkeley

Ambrose, P. and Colenutt, R. (1975) *The Property Machine*, Penguin, Harmondsworth

Amin, S. (ed.) (1974) *Modern Migrations in Western Africa*, Oxford University Press, London

Bachi, R. (1963) 'Standard distance measures and related methods for spatial analysis', *Regional Science Association, Papers and Proceedings*, *10*, 83–132

—— (1965) 'Analysis of geographical data on internal migration', Paper presented at United Nations World Population Conference, Belgrade, Yugoslavia

Balderson, W.A. (1981) *Aspects of Recent Residential Mobility in Leicester*, Ph.D. thesis in progress, University of Leicester

Barbolet, R. (1969) *Housing Classes and the Socio-ecological system*, Centre for Environmental Studies, U.W.P. No. 4, London

Barrett, F.A. (1973) *Residential Search Behaviour: A Study of Intra-Urban Relocation in Toronto*, Geographical Monographs No. 1, York University, Atkinson College, Toronto

—— (1976) 'The search process in residential relocation', *Environment and Behaviour*, *8*, 169–98

Bassett, K. and Short J.R. (1978) 'Housing improvements in the inner city: a case study of changes before and after 1974 Housing Act', *Urban Studies*, *15*, 333–42

—— and —— (1980) *Housing and Residential Structure*, Routledge and Kegan Paul, London

Beale, C.L. (1964) 'Rural depopulation in the United States: some demographic consequences of agricultural adjustments', *Demography*, *1*, 264–72

192

Beals, R.E., Levy, M.B. and Moses, L. (1967) 'Rationality and migration in Ghana', *Review of Economic Statistics*, *49*, 480–6

Beaujeau-Garnier, J. (1966) *Geography of Population*, Longman, London

Bedford, R.D. (1973) 'A transition in the circular mobility: population movement in the New Hebrides, 1800–1970', in Brookfield, H.C. (ed.), *The Pacific in Transition: Geographical Perspective on Adaptation and Change*, Arnold, London, 187–228

Bell, C. (1977) 'On housing classes', *Australian and New Zealand Journal of Sociology*, *13*, 36–40

Bell, D.N.F. and Kirwan, F.X. (1979) 'Return migration in a Scottish context', *Regional Studies*, *13*, 101–11

Bell, W. (1958) 'Social choice, life style and suburban residence', in Dobriner, W. (ed.), *The Suburban Community*, Putnam, New York, 225–47

Berg, E. (1965) 'The economics of the Migrant labour system', in Kuper, H. (ed.), *Urbanization and Migration in West Africa*, University of California Press, Los Angeles

Beshers, J.M. and Nishuira, E.N. (1961) 'A theory of internal migration differentials', *Social Forces*, *39*, 214–18

Board, C. (1976) *The spatial structure of labour migration*, Department of Geography Occasional Paper No. 6, Queen Mary College

Boddy, M. (1976) 'The structure of mortgage finance: building societies and the British social formation', *Transactions, Institute of British Geographers*, *N.S.I.*, 58–71

—— and Gray, F. (1979) 'Filtering theory, housing policy and legitimation of inequality', *Policy and Politics*, *7*, 39–54

Bogue, D.J. (1959) 'Internal migration', in Hauser P.M. and Duncan, O.D. (eds.), *The Study of Population: An Inventory and Appraisal*, University of Chicago Press, Chicago, 486–509

—— (1961) 'Techniques and hypotheses for the study of differential migration: some notes from an experiment with United States data', *Proceedings of the International Conference*, *2*, Session 4, No. 114

—— (1969) *Principles of Demography*, Wiley, New York

——, Shryock, H.S. and Hoermann, S.A. (1953) *Subregional Migration in the United States 1935–40*, Miami University Press, Oxford, Ohio

Böhning, W.R. (1972) *The Migration of Workers in the United Kingdom and the European Community*, Oxford University Press, London

—— (1979) 'International migration in Western Europe: reflections on the past five years', *International Labour Review*, *118*, 401–14

Bonilla, F. (1970) 'Rio's Favelas', in Mangin, W. (ed.), *Peasants in Cities: Readings in the Anthropology of Urbanization*, Houghton Mifflin, Boston

Bonnar, D.M. (1979) 'Migration in the south east of England: an analysis of the interrelationships of housing, socio-economic status and labour demand', *Regional Studies*, *13*, 345–59

Borrie, W.D. (1954) *Italians and Germans in Australia. A Study of Assimilation*, Cheshire, Melbourne

Bourne, L.S. (1976) 'Housing supply and housing market behaviour in residential development', in Herbert, D.T. and Johnston, R.J. (eds.), 111–58

Boyle, M.J. and Robinson, M.E. (1978) *Cloze procedure and spatial configuration: an experiment in Sunderland*, School of Geography Research Papers No. 4,

194   *Bibliography*

University of Manchester

Brandes, S.H. (1975) *Migration, Kinship and Community*, Academic Press, New York

Bright, M.L. and Thomas, D.S. (1941) 'Interstate migration and intervening opportunities', *American Sociological Review*, 6, 773-83

Broek, J.O.M. and Webb, J.W. (1968) *The Geography of Mankind*, McGraw Hill, New York

Brown, A.A. and Neuberger, E. (eds.) (1977) *Internal Migration: A Comparative Perspective*, Academic Press, New York

Brown, J.S., Schwarzweller, H.K. and Mangalam, J.J. (1963) 'Kentucky Mountain migration and the Stem family: an American variation on the theme of Le Play', *Rural Sociology*, 28, 53-4

Brown, L.A. (1970) 'On the use of Markov Chains in Movement Research', *Economic Geography*, 46, 393-403

—— and Holmes, J. (1971) 'Search behaviour in an intra-urban migration context: a spatial perspective', *Environment and Planning*, 3, 307-26

—— and Longbrake, D.B. (1970) 'Migration flows in intraurban space: place-utility considerations', *Annals, Association of American Geographers*, 60, 368-84

—— and Moore, E.G. (1970) 'The intra-urban migration process: a perspective', *Geografiska Annaler*, 52B, 1-13

——, Oldland, J. and Golledge, R. (1970) 'Migration, functional distance and the urban hierarchy', *Economic Geography*, 46, 472-85

Browning, H.L. and Fendt, W. (1968) 'Selectivity of migrants to a metropolis in a developing country: a Mexican case-study', *Demography*, 6, 347-57

Brummell, A.C. (1979) 'A model of intra-urban mobility', *Economic Geography*, 55, 338-52

—— (1981) 'A method of measuring stress', *Geographical Analysis*, 13, 248-61

Budd, J.L.S. (1979) *The Cognition of Residential Areas: a Study in Leicester*, unpublished Ph.D. thesis, University of Leicester

Bureau of Labour Statistics (1963) Special Labour Force Report, *Geographical Mobility and Employment Status*, 6, Washington, DC

Butler, E.W., Chapin, F.S., Hemmens, G.L., Kaiser, E.J., Steeman, M.A. and Weiss, S.F. (1969) *Moving Behaviour and Residential Choice: A National Survey*, National Co-operative Highway Research Program Report No. 81, Washington, DC

Cadwallader, M. (1978) 'Urban information and preference surfaces: their patterns, structures and interrelationships', *Geografiska Annaler*, 60N, 97-106

Caldwell, J.C. (1969) *African Rural-Urban Migration: The Movement to Ghana's Towns*, Australian National University Press, Canberra

Carr Hill, R.A. and MacDonald, K.I. (1973) 'Problems in the analysis of life histories', *The Sociological Review Monograph*, 19, 57-95

Carrothers, G.P. (1956) 'An historical review of the gravity and potential concepts of human interaction', *Journal of the American Institute of Planners*, 22, 94-102

Castells, M. (1977) *The Urban Question: A Marxist Approach*, Arnold, London

Cavalli-Sforza, H. (1962) 'The distribution of migration distances: models and applications to genetics', in Sutter, J. (ed.), *Human Displacements*, Hachette, Monaco

Cebula, R.J. (1980) *The Determinants of Human Migration*, Lexington Books, Lexington, Mass.

Cerase, F.P. (1974) 'Migration and social change: expectations and reality. A case study of return migration from the United States to Southern Italy', *International Migration Review*, *8*, 245–62

Champion, A.G. (1976) 'Evolving patterns of population distribution in England and Wales, 1951–71', *Transactions, Institute of British Geographers*, *N.S.I.*, 401–26

Chapman, M. (1976) 'Tribal mobility as circulation: a Solomon Islands example of micro/macro linkages', in Kosinski, L.A. and Webb, J.W., *Population at Microscale*, I.G.U. Commission on Population Geography and New Zealand Geographical Society, Hamilton

Chevan, A. and Fischer, L.R. (1979) 'Retirement and inter-state migration', *Social Forces*, *57*, 1365–80

Claeson, C.F. (1969) 'A two-stage model of in-migration to urban centres: deductive development of a variant of the gravity formulation', *Geografiska Annaler*, *51B*, 127–39

—— and Egero, B. (1972) *Migration in Tanzania: A Review Based on the 1967 Population Census*, Research Notes No. 11, University of Dar es Salaam, Bureau of Resource Assessment and Land Use Planning

Clark, W.A.V. (1971) 'A test for directional bias in residential mobility', in McConnell, H. and Yasheen, D.W. (eds.), *Models of Spatial Variation*, Illinois University Press, Illinois

—— (1972) 'Measurement and explanation in intra-urban residential mobility', *Tijdschrift voor Economische en Sociale Geografie*, *28*, 171–80

—— (1976) 'Migration in Milwaukee', *Economic Geography*, *52*, 48–70

—— and Avery, K. (1978) 'Patterns of migration: a Macroanalytic case study', in Herbert, D.T. and Johnston, R.J. (eds.), 135–96

—— and Cadwallader, M. (1973a) 'Locational stress and residential mobility', *Environment and Behaviour*, *5*, 29–41

—— and —— (1973b) 'Residential preference: an alternative view of intra-urban space', *Environment and Planning*, *5*, 693–703

—— and Huff, J.O. (1977) 'Some empirical tests of duration-of-stay effects in intra-urban migration', *Environment and Planning*, *9*, 1357–74

——, Huff, J.O. and Burt, J.E. (1979) 'Calibrating a model of the decision to move', *Environment and Planning*, *11*, 689–704

—— and Moore, E.G. (1978) *Population Mobility and Residential Change*, Studies in Geography No. 25, Northwestern University, Evanston, Illinois

—— and —— (eds.), (1980) *Residential Mobility and Public Policy*, Urban Affairs Annual Review, *19*, Sage, New York

Clarke, J.I. (1965) *Population Geography*, Pergamon, Oxford

—— (1973) 'Population in movement', in Chisholm, M. and Rodgers, B. (eds.), *Studies in Human Geography*, Heinemann, London

Cloke, P. (1979) *Key Settlements in Rural Areas*, Methuen, London

Collins, L. (1976) *Introduction to Markov Chain Analysis*, CATMOG No. 1, Geo Abstracts, Norwich

Compton, P.A. (1969) 'Internal migration and population change in Hungary between 1959 and 1965', *Transactions, Institute of British Geographers*, *47*, 111–30

Conaway, M.E. (1977) 'Circular migration: a summary and bibliography', *Council of Planning Librarians Exchange Bibliography, 1250*, Monticello, Illinois

Connell, J., Dasgupta, B., Laishley, R. and Lipton, M. (1976) *Migration from Rural Areas*, Oxford University Press, Delhi

Conway, D. (1980) 'Stepwise migration: toward a classification of the mechanism', *International Migration Review, 49*, 3–14

Cook, R.C. (1957) 'World Migration, 1946–55', *Population Bulletin, 13*, 77–94

Couper, M. and Brindley, T. (1975) 'Housing classes and housing values', *Sociological Review, 23*, 563–76

Courgeau, D. (1976) 'Quantitative, demographic and geographic approaches to internal migration', *Environment and Planning, 8*, 261–70

Cowie, W. and Giles, A. (1957) 'An enquiry into reasons for the drift from the land', *Selected papers in Agricultural Economics, University of Bristol, 5*, 70–113

Cox, K.R. (ed.) (1978) *Urbanisation and Conflict in Market Societies*, Methuen, London

—— (1979) *Location and Public Problems*, Blackwell, Oxford

Craven, E. (1969) 'Private residential expansion in Kent 1956–64: a study of pattern and process in urban growth', *Urban Studies, 6*, 1–16

Crawford, C. (1966) 'Family attachment, family support for migration and migration plans of young people', *Rural Sociology, 31*, 293–310

Cribier, F. (1975) 'Retirement migration in France', in Kosinski, L.A. and Prothero, R.M. (eds.), 361–73

Cronin, C. (1972) *The Sting of Change. The Sicilian Family in Sicily and Australia*, University of Chicago Press, Chicago

Cullingworth, J.B. (1965) *English Housing Trends*, Bell, London

Daily Telegraph (1980) 'Mobility impeded by housing', Letters to the Editor, 29 July 1980, 14

Da Vanzo, J. (1975) 'Differences between return and non-return migration: an econometric analysis', *Rand Paper Series, P-5408*, Rand Corporation, Santa Monica, California

—— and Morrison, P.A. (1978) 'Dynamics of return migration: descriptive findings from a longitudinal study', *Rand Paper Series, P-5514*, Rand Corporation, Santa Monica, California

Davies, J.G. (1972) *The Evangelistic Bureaucrat*, Tavistock, London

Davies, W.K. (1966) 'Latent migration potential and space preferences', *Professional Geographer, 18*, 300–4

Davis, V.C. (1945) 'Development of a scale to rate attitudes of community satisfaction', *Rural Sociology, 10*, 246–55

Deaton, B.J. and Anschel, K.R. (1974) 'Migration and return migration: a new look at the eastern Kentucky migration streams', *Southern Journal of Agricultural Economics, 6*, 185–91

de Castro Lopo, L. (1975) *Theory of Internal Migration: a Review*, Research Papers in Geography No. 5, University of Newcastle, New South Wales

De Jong, G.F. (1975) 'Population redistribution policies: alternatives from the Netherlands, Great Britain and Israel', *Social Science Quarterly, 56*, 261–73

Demko, D. (1974) 'Cognition of southern Ontario cities in a potential migration context', *Economic Geography, 50*, 20–34

Dennis, N. (1970) *People and Planning*, Faber and Faber, London

Department of the Environment (1972) *West Yorkshire Movers Survey 1969*, Housing Survey Report No. 8, London
—— (1978) *Social Trends*, HMSO, London
Deskins, D.R. (1972) *Residential Mobility of Negroes in Detroit, 1837-1965*, Michigan Geographical Publication No. 5, Ann Arbor
Diehl, W.D. (1966) 'Farm-nonfarm migration in the south-east: a cost-returns analysis', *Journal of Farm Economics*, *48*, 1-11
Douglas, J.W.B. and Blomfield, J.M. (1956) 'The reliability of longitudinal surveys', *Milbank Memorial Fund Quarterly*, *34*, 227-52
Drake, M. (1972) 'The census 1801-91', in Wrigley, E.A. (ed.), *Nineteenth Century Society*, Cambridge University Press, Cambridge, 7-46
Drudy, P.J. (1978) 'Depopulation in a prosperous agricultural sub-region', *Regional Studies*, *12*, 49-60
Ducland-Williams, R. (1978) *The Politics of Housing in Britain and France*, Heinemann, London
Duncan, H.G. (1933) *Immigration and Assimilation*, Wiley, New York
Duncan, S.S. (1976a) 'Research directions in social geography: housing opportunities and constraints', *Transactions, Institute of British Geographers*, *N.S.I.*, 10-19
—— (1976b) 'Self help: the allocation of mortgages and the formation of housing submarkets', *Area*, *8*, 307-16
Dunn, M.C. and Swindell, K. (1972) 'Electoral registers and rural migration: a case study from Herefordshire', *Area*, *4*, 39-42
Du Toit, B.M. and Safa, H.I. (1975) *Migration and Urbanization*, Hague: Mouton
Eisenstadt, S.N. (1953) 'Analysis of patterns of immigration and absorption of immigrants', *Population Studies*, 7, 167-80
—— (1954) *The Absorption of Immigrants*, Routledge and Kegan Paul, London
Elizaga, J.C. (1965) 'Internal migration in Latin America', *International Social Science Journal*, *17*, 213-31
—— (1966) 'A study of migration to Greater Santiago, Chile', *Demography*, *3*, 352-78
Eversley, Lord (1907) 'The decline in the number of agricultural labourers in Great Britain', *Journal of the Royal Statistical Society*, *70*, 280-3
Fairchild, H.P. (1925) *Immigration: A World Movement and its American Significance*, Putnam, New York
Farooq, G.M. (1975) 'Population distribution and migration', in Robinson, W.C. (ed.), *Population and Development Planning*, Population Council, London, 134-52
Farr, W. (1876) 'Birthplaces of the people and the laws of migration', *Geographical Magazine*, *3*, 35-7
Fielding, A.J. (1971) *Internal Migration in England and Wales*, Centre for Environmental Studies, U.W.P. No. 14, London
Flowerdew, R.T.N. (1973) 'Preference ranking on several attributes: applications in residential site selection', *Environment and Planning*, *5*, 601-10
—— (1976) 'Search strategies and stopping rules in residential mobility', *Transactions, Institute of British Geographers*, *NSI*, 47-57
—— and Salt, J. (1979) 'Migration between labour market areas in Great Britain 1970-71', *Regional Studies*, *13*, 211-31

Ford, J. (1975) 'The role of building society manager in the urban stratification system: autonomy versus constraint', *Urban Studies*, *12*, 295-302

Frankenberg, R. (1957) *The Village on the Border*, Cohen and West, London

Fried, M. and Gleicher, P. (1961) 'Some sources of residential satisfaction in an urban slum', *Journal of the American Institute of Planners*, *27*, 305-15

Friedlander, D. (1970) 'The spread of urbanization in England and Wales 1851-1951', *Population Studies*, *24*, 423-43

——— and Roshier, R.J. (1966) 'A study of internal migration in England and Wales, Part II: recent internal migrants — their movements and characteristics', *Population Studies*, *20*, 45-60

Friedman, J. (1966) *Regional Development Policy*, MIT Press, Cambridge, Mass.

Gale, S. (1973) 'Explanation theory and models of migration', *Economic Geography*, *49*, 257-74

Galle, O.R. and Taeuber, K.E. (1966) 'Metropolitan migration and intervening opportunities', *American Sociological Review*, *31*, 5-13

Galtung, J. (1971) *Members of Two Worlds: A Development Study of Three Villages in Western Sicily*, Universitetsforlaget, Oslo

Gans, H. (1972) *People and Class*, Penguin, Harmondsworth

Gaude, J. and Peek, P. (1970) 'The economic effects of rural-urban migration', *International Labour Review*, *114*, 329-38

George, M.V. (1970) *Internal Migration in Canada: Demographic Analyses*, 1961 Census Monograph, Dominion Bureau of Statistics, Ottawa

George, P. (1976) *Les Migrations Internationales*, Presses Universitaires de France, Paris

Germani, G. (1965) 'Migration and acculturation', in Hauswer, P.M. (ed.), *Handbook for Social Research in Urban Areas*, UNESCO, Ghent, 159-78

Gerth, H.H. and Mills, C.W. (1948) *From Max Weber: Essays in Sociology*, Routledge and Kegan Paul, London

Gibbs, J.P. (1963) 'The evolution of population concentrations', *Economic Geography*, *39*, 340-50

Gibson, J.G. (1975) 'The intervening opportunities model of migration: a critique', *Socio-Economic Planning Sciences*, *9*, 205-8

Gilbert, A.G. and Ward, P.M. (1978) 'Housing in Latin American Cities', in D.T. Herbert and R.J. Johnson (eds.), 285-318

Ginsberg, R. (1972) 'Critique of probablistic models: application of the semi-Markov model to migration', *Journal of Mathematical Sociology*, *2*, 63-82

——— (1973) 'Stochastic models of residential and geographic model for heterogeneous populations', *Environment and Planning*, *5*, 113-24

——— (1978) 'Probability models of residence histories: analysis of times between moves', in Clarke, W.A.V. and Moore, E.G., 233-62

Girard, A., Bastide, H. and Pourcher, G. (1970) 'Geographical mobility and urban concentration in France: a study in the provinces', in Jansen, A.J. (ed.), 203-55

Glazer, N. and Moynihan, D. (1963) *Beyond the Melting Pot*, MIT Press, Cambridge, Mass.

Gober-Meyers, P. (1978a) 'Employment-motivated migration and economic growth in post-industrial market economies', *Progress in Human Geography*, *2*, 207-29

——— (1978b) 'Interstate migration and economic growth: a simultaneous equation approach', *Environment and Planning, 10*, 1241-52

Goddard, A.D., Gould, W.T.S. and Masser, F.I. (1975) 'Census data and migration analysis in tropical Africa', *Geografiska Annaler, 57B*, 26-41

Golant, S.M. (1972) *The Residential Location and Spatial Behaviour of the Elderly. A Canadian Example.* Department of Georgraphy Research Paper No. 143, University of Chicago

Gold, J.R. (1980) *An Introduction to Behavioural Geography*, Oxford University Press, London

Goldlust, J. and Richmond, A.H. (1974) 'A multivariate model of immigrant adaptation', *International Migration Review, 8*, 193-225

Goldsheider, C. (1971) *Population, Modernization and Social Structure*, Little Brown, Boston

Goldstein, S. (1954) 'Repeated migration as a factor in high mobility rates', *American Sociological Review, 19*, 536-41

—— (1958) *Patterns of Mobility 1910-50. The Norristown Study*, University of Pennsylvania, Philadelphia

—— (1964) 'The extent of repeated migration: an analysis based on the Danish Population Register', *American Statistical Association Journal, 59*, 1121-32

—— (1978) *Circulation in the context of Total Mobility in Southeast Asia*, Papers of the East-West Population Institute, No. 53, Honolulu

—— and Mayer, K.B. (1963) *Residential Mobility, Migration and Commuting in Rhode Island*, Rhode Island Development Council, Providence

—— and —— (1965) 'The impact of migration on the socio-economic structure of cities and suburbia', *Sociology and Social Research, 50*, 5-23

Golledge, R.G. and Rushton, G. (eds.) (1976) *Spatial Choice and Spatial Behaviour*, Ohio State University Press, Columbus

Goodchild, F. and Smith, T.R. (1980) 'Intransitivity, the spatial interaction model and United Stated migration streams', *Environment and Planning, 12*, 1131-44

Gordon, D.M. (1972) *Theories of Poverty and Underemployment*, Lexington Books, Lexington

Gordon, M.M. (1964) *Assimilation in American Life*, Oxford University Press, New York

Gosal, G.S. and Krishan, G. (1975) 'Patterns of internal migration in India', in Kosinski, L.A. and Prothero, R.M. (eds.), 193-206

Gould, P.R. (1972) 'Pedagogic review: entropy in urban and regional modelling', *Annals of the Association of American Geographers, 62*, 689-700

—— (1975) 'Acquiring spatial information', *Economic Geography, 51*, 87-100

—— and White, R.R. (1968) 'The mental maps of British school leavers', *Regional Studies, 2*, 161-82

Gould, W.T.S. and Prothero, R.M. (1975) 'Space and time in African population mobility', in Kosinski, L.A. and Prothero, R.M. (eds.), 39-50

Grandstaff, P.J. (1975) 'Recent Soviet experience and western "laws" of population migration', *International Migration Review, 9*, 479-97

Graves, T.D. (1966) 'Alternative models for the study of urban migration', *Human Organisation, 25*, 295-99

Gray, F. (1975) 'Non-explanation in urban geography', *Area, 7*, 228-35

—— (1976) 'Selections and allocation in council housing', *Transactions, Institute of British Geographers, N.S.I.*, 34-46

Greenwood, M.J. (1968) 'An analysis of the determinants of geographical labour mobility in the United States', *Review of Economics and Statistics, 51*, 189–204

—— (1970) 'Lagged response in the decision to migrate', *Journal of Regional Science, 10*, 375–84

—— (1971) 'A regression analysis of migration to urban areas in a less developed country. The case of India', *Journal of Regional Science Association, 11*, 253–62

—— (1973) 'Urban growth and migration: their interaction', *Environment and Planning, 5*, 91–112

Grigg, D.B. (1977) 'E.G. Ravenstein and the "laws" of migration', *Journal of Historical Geography, 3*, 41–54

Guardian (1973), 4 September

Gustavus, S. and Brown, L.A. (1977) 'Place attributes in a migration decision context', *Environment and Planning, 9*, 529–48

Haenszel, W. (1967) 'Concert, measurement and data in migration analysis', *Demography, 4*, 253–62

Hägerstrand, T. (1957) 'Migration and area: survey of a sample of Swedish migration fields and hypothetical considerations of their genesis', in Hannerberg, D. *et al.* (1957), 27–158

—— (1967) *Innovation Diffusion as a Spatial Process*, University of Chicago Press, Chicago

—— (1970) 'What about people in regional science?' *Papers of the Regional Science Association, 24*, 7–21

—— (1975) 'On the definition of migration', in Jones, E. (ed.), *Readings in Social Geography*, Oxford University Press, London, 200–9

Haggett, P. (1965) *Locational Analysis in Human Geography*, Edward Arnold, London

Hall, P., Gracey, H., Drewett, R. and Thomas, R. (1973) *The Containment of Urban England*, P.E.P. and Allen & Unwin, London

Hamnett, C. (1973) 'Improvement grants as an indicator of gentrification in inner London', *Area, 5*, 252–61

Hannan, D. (1970) *Rural Exodus*, Chapman, London

Hannerberg, D., Hägerstrand, D.T. and Odeving, B. (1957) *Migration in Sweden: A Symposium*, Lund Studies in Geography, No. 13, Gleerup, Lund

Hanson, S. (1977) 'Measuring the cognitive levels of urban residents', *Geografiska Annaler, 59B*, 95–108

Harloe, M. (ed.) (1977) *Captive Cities: Studies in the Political Economy of Cities and Regions*, Wiley, New York

Harris, A.I. and Clausen, R. (1963) *Labour Mobility in Great Britain 1953-63*, HMSO, London

Harris, J.R. and Todaro, M.P. (1970) 'Migration, unemployment and development: a two sector analysis', *American Economic Review, 60*, 126–42

Hart, R.A. (1970) 'A model of inter-regional migration in England and Wales', *Regional Studies, 4*, 279–96

—— (1972) 'The economic influences on internal labour force migration', *Scottish Journal of Political Economy, 19*, 151–73

—— (1973) 'Economic expectations and the decision to migrate: an analysis by socio-economic groups', *Regional Studies, 7*, 271–85

Harvey, D. (1973) *Social Justice and the City*, Arnold, London
—— and Chatterjee, L. (1974) 'Absolute rent and the structuring of space by Government and Financial institutions', *Antipode*, *6*, 22–36
Harvey, M.E. and Riddell, J.B. (1975) 'Development, urbanization and migration: a test of a hypothesis in the third world', in Kosinski, L.A. and Protheroe, R.M. (eds.), 51–66
Hauser, D.P. (1974) 'Some problems in the use of stepwise regression techniques in geographical research', *Canadian Geographer*, *18*, 148–58
Heidenheimer, A., Heclo, H. and Adams, C. (1975) *Comparative Public Policy: The Politics of Social Change in Europe and Americas*, Macmillan, London
Helper, R. (1969) *Racial Policies and Practices of Real Estate Brokers*, Oxford University Press, London
Henderson, J.R. (1978) 'Spatial re-organization: a geographic dimension in acculturation', *Canadian Geographer*, *22*, 1–21
Herberle, R. (1938) 'The causes of the rural-urban migration: a survey of German theories', *American Journal of Sociology*, *43*, 932–50
Herbert, D.T. (1973a) 'Residential mobility and preference: a study of Swansea', in *Social Patterns in Cities*, Special Publication No. 5, Institute of British Geographers, 103–21
—— (1973b) 'The residential mobility process: some empirical observation', *Area*, *5*, 44–8
—— (1975) 'Urban neighbourhood and social geographical research', in Phillips, A.D.M. and Turton, B.J. (eds.), *Environment Man and Economic Change*, Longman, London, 459–78
—— and Johnston, R.J. (eds.) (1976) *Social Areas in Cities*, Vol. 1, Wiley, London
—— and —— (eds.) (1978) *Geography and the Urban Environment*, Vol. 1, Wiley, London
Herbst, P.G. (1964) 'Organisational commitment: a decision model', *Acta Sociologica*, *7*, 34–45
Herrick, B.H. (1965) *Urban Migration and Economic Development in Chile*, MIT Press, Cambridge, Mass.
Hillery, G.A. and Brown, J.S. (1965) 'Migrational systems of the southern Appalachians: some demographic observations', *Rural Sociology*, *30*, 3–48
Hirst, M.A. (1976) 'A Markovian analysis of inter-regional migration in Uganda', *Geografiska Annaler*, *58B*, 79–94
Hocking, R.R. (1976) 'The analysis and selection of variables in linear regression', *Biometrics*, *32*, 1–50
Hofstee, E.W. (1952) *Some Remarks on Selective Migration*, Research Group for European Migration Publications, 7, Nijhoff, The Hague
Hollingsworth, T.H. (1970) *Migration: A Study Based on Scottish Experience between 1939 and 1964*, University of Glasgow Social and Economic Studies, Occasional Papers No. 12, Oliver and Boyd, Edinburgh
—— and El Rouby, M.G. (1976) *Repeated migration and past migration frequency*, University of Glasgow, Department of Social and Economic Research, Discussion Paper, *14*
Horton, F.E. and Reynolds, D.R. (1971) 'Effects of urban spatial structure on individual behaviour', *Economic Geography*, *47*, 36–48
House, J.W. and Knight, E.M. (1965) *Migrants of North East England 1951-61:*

Character, Age and Sex, University of Newcastle-upon-Tyne, Department of
Geography, Papers on Migration and Mobility, *2*
—— and —— (1966) *People on the Move: the South Tyne in the Sixties*,
University of Newcastle-upon-Tyne, Department of Geography, Papers on
Migration and Mobility, *3*
Houston, C.J. (1979) 'Administrative control of migration to Moscow 1959–75',
Canadian Geographer, *23*, 32–44
Howard, M.C. and King, J.E. (1975) *The Political Economy of Marx*, Longman,
London
Hubert, J. (1965) 'Kinship and geographical mobility in a sample from a London
middle-class area', *International Journal of Comparative Sociology*, *6*, 61–80
Hudson, J.C. (1970) 'Migration to an American frontier', *Annals, Association of
American Geographers*, *66*, 242–65
Hudson, R. (1975) 'Patterns of Spatial Search', *Transactions, Institute of British
Geographers*, *65*, 141–54
—— (1976) 'Linking studies of the individual with models of aggregative
behaviour: an empirical example', *Transactions, Institute of British
Geographers*, *N.S.I.*, 159–74
Huff, D.L. (1960) 'A topographical model of consumer space preferences', *Papers
of the Regional Science Association*, *6*, 159–73
Huff, J.O. and Clark, W.A.V: (1978) 'The role of stationarity in Markov and
opportunity models of intra-urban migration', in Clark, W.A.V. and Moore,
E.G. (eds.), 183–213
Hugo, G.J. (1975) 'The motivation of aggregate/macro-data', in Pryor, R.J. (ed.),
54–65
Humphreys, J.S. and Whitelaw, J.S. (1979) 'Immigrants in an unfamiliar
environment. Locational decision-making under constrained circumstances',
Geografiska Annaler, *61B*, 8–18
Hunter, A. (1974) 'Community change', *American Journal of Sociology*, *79*,
923–47
Hyman, G. and Gleave, D. (1978) 'A reasonable theory of migration',
Transactions, Institute of British Geographers, *N.S. 3*, 179–201
Illsley, R., Finlayson, A. and Thompson, B. (1963) 'The motivation and
characteristics of internal migrants', Parts I and II, *Mellbank Memorial
Foundation Quarterly*, 115–43 and 217–47
Imogene, S.O. (1967) 'Psycho-social factors in rural-urban migration', *Nigerian
Journal of Economic and Social Studies*, *9*, 375–85
Isbell, E.C. (1944) 'Internal migration in Sweden and intervening opportunities',
American Sociological Review, *9*, 627–39
Jackson, J.A. (ed.) (1969) *Migration*, Sociological Studies 2, Cambridge
University Press, Cambridge
Jakle, J.A., Brunn, S. and Roseman, C.C. (1976) *Human Spatial Behaviour. A
Social Geography*, Duxbury, North Scituate, Mass.
Jansen, C.J. (1968) *Social Aspects of Internal Migration*, Bath University Press,
Bath
—— (ed.) (1970) *Readings in the Sociology of Migration*, Pergamon, Oxford
—— and King, R.C. (1968) 'Migrationes et "occasions intervenates" en
Belgique', *Recherches Economiques de Louvain*, *4*, 519–26
Jarvie, W.K. and Browett, J.G. (1980) 'Recent changes in migration patterns in

Australia', *Australian Geographical Studies, 18*, 135–45

Jenkins, J. (1976) 'Problems of assembling international migration data from census and other sources for use in migration models, population accounts and forecasts. A preliminary exploration', Department of Geography, Working Paper 161, University of Leeds

Jerome, H. (1926) *Migration and Business Cycles*, National Bureau of Economic Research, New York

Johnson, J.H., Salt, J. and Wood, P.A. (1974) *Housing and Migration of Labour in England and Wales*, Saxon House, Farnborough

Johnston, R.J. (1966) 'The location of high status residential areas', *Geografiska Annaler, 48B*, 23–35

—— (1971) 'Resistance to migration and the mover-stayer dichotomy: aspects of kinship and population stability in an English rural area', *Geografiska Annaler, 53B*, 16–27

—— (1973) 'Spatial patterns in suburban evaluations', *Environment and Planning, 5*, 385–95

—— (1980) *City and Society*, Penguin, Harmondsworth

Jones, D.W. (1975) *Migration and Urban Unemployed in Dualistic Economic Development*, Department of Geography Research Paper No. 165, University of Chicago

Jones, H.R. (1965) 'A study of rural migration in central Wales', *Transactions, Institute of British Geographers, 37*, 31–45

—— (1976) 'The structure of the migration process: findings from a growth point in Mid-Wales', *Transactions, Institute of British Geographers, N.S.I.*, 421–32

Jones, R.C. (1980) 'The role of perception in urban in-migration: a path analytic model', *Geographical Analysis, 12*, 98–108

—— and Zannaras, G. (1976) 'Perceived versus objective urban opportunities and the migration of Venezuela Youths', *Annals of Regional Science, 10*, 83–97

Joseph, G. (1975) 'A Markov analysis of age/sex differences in inter-regional migration in Great Britain', *Regional Studies, 9*, 69–78

Kain, J.F. (1973) *What should America's Housing Program Be?* Discussion Paper No. 82, Program on Regional and Urban Economics, Harvard University, Cambridge, Mass.

—— and Quigley, J.M. (1972) 'Housing market discrimination, homeownership and savings behaviour', *The American Economic Review, 62*, 263–77

Kalbach, W.E. (1970) *The Impact of Immigration on Canada's Population*, 1961 Census Monograph, Dominion Bureau of Statistics, Ottawa

Kant, K. (1962) 'Classification and problems in migration', in Wagner, P.L. and Mikesell, M.W. (eds.), *Readings in Cultural Geography*, University of Chicago Press, Chicago, 47–57

Kariel, H.G. (1963) 'Selected factors areally associated with population growth due to net migration', *Annals, Association of American Geographers, 53*, 210–23

Karn, V. (1970) *Crawley Housing Survey*, Centre for Urban and Regional Studies, Occasional Paper 11, University of Birmingham

—— (1976) *Priorities for Local Authority Mortgage Lending. A Case Study of Birmingham*, Centre for Urban and Regional Studies, Research

Memorandum No. 52, University of Birmingham

Karweit, N. (1973) 'Storage and retrieval of life history data', *Social Science Research*, *2*, 41–50

Kendall, G. (1977) '500 words on immigration', *Now, Journal of Methodist Missionary Society*, January, 8–10

Kennett, S. (1980) 'Migration within and between the Metropolitan Economic Labour Areas of Britain 1966–71', in Hobcroft, J. and Rees, P.H. (eds.), *Regional Demographic Development*, Croom Helm, London

Keowan, P.A. (1971) 'The career cycle and the stepwise migration process', *New Zealand Geographer*, *27*, 175–84

Kirby, A.M. (1976) 'Housing market studies: a critical review', *Transactions, Institute of British Geographers*, *N.S.I.*, 2–9

Klaassen, L.H. and Drewe, P. (1973) *Migration Policy in Europe*, Saxon House, Farnborough

Kosinski, L.A. and Prothero, R.M. (eds.) (1975) *People on the Move. Studies in Internal Migration*, Methuen, London

Kostanick, H.L. (ed.) (1977) *Population and Migration Trends in Eastern Europe*, Westview Press, Boulder, Colorado

Kovacs, M. and Cropley, A. (1975) *Immigrants and Society*, McGraw Hill, Sydney

Kuber, R. (1977) *From Pasta to Pavlova. A Comparative Study of Italian Settlers in Sydney and Griffith*, University of Queensland Press, Brisbane

Ladinsky, J. (1966) 'Sources of geographic mobility among professional workers', *Demography*, *3*, 47–57

Lamb, R. (1975) *Metropolitan Impacts on Rural America*, Department of Geography Research Paper No. 162, University of Chicago

Lambert, C. (1976) *Building Societies, Surveyors and the Older Areas of Birmingham*, Centre for Urban and Regional Studies Working Paper No. 3, University of Birmingham

Land, K. (1969) 'Duration of residence and prospective migration: further evidence', *Demography*, *6*, 133–40

Lansing, J.B. and Mueller, E. (1967) *The Geographical Mobility of Labor*, Survey Research Center, University of Michigan, Ann Arbor

Law, C.M. and Warnes, A.M. (1976) 'The changing geography of the elderly in England and Wales', *Transactions, Institute of British Geographers*, *N.S.I.*, 453–71

—— and —— (1980) 'The characteristics of retired migrants', in Herbert, D.T. and Johnson, R.J. (eds.), *Geography and the Urban Environment*, Vol. 3, Wiley, London, 175–222

Lawton, R. (1967) 'Rural depopulation in nineteenth-century England', in Steel, R.W. and Lawton, R. (eds.), *Liverpool Essays in Geography*, Longman, London, 227–55

—— (1968) 'The journey to work in Britain: some trends and problems', *Regional Studies*, *2*, 27–40

—— and Pooley, C.G. (1978) 'Problems and potentialities for the study of internal population mobility in nineeenth-century England', *Canadian Studies in Population*, *5*, 69–84

Lee, E.S. (1966) 'A theory of migration', *Demography*, *3*, 47–57

—— (1970) 'Migration in relation to education, intellect, and social structure',

Population Index, *36*, 437–44

Leicester City Council (1980) *Population Atlas of Leicester*, Leicester City Council, Leicester

Leonard, O.E. and Hannon, J.H. (1977) 'Those left behind: recent social changes in a heavy emigration of north central New Mexico', *Human Organisation*, *36*, 384–94

Leslie, G.R. and Richardson, A.H. (1961) 'Life cycle, career pattern, and the decision to move', *American Sociological Review*, *26*, 894–902

Lewis, G.J. (1974a) *Human Migration*, Unit 9, Regional Analysis and Development, Open University Press, Milton Keynes

——— (1974b) *The Consequences of Labour Migration*, Unit 10, Regional Analysis and Development, Open University Press, Milton Keynes

——— (1979a) 'Mobility, locality and demographic change: the case of north Cardiganshire, 1851–71', *Welsh History Review*, *9*, 347–61

——— (1979b) *Rural Communities. A Social Geography*, David & Charles, Newton Abbot

——— (1981a) *Rural Migration. A Study on the Welsh Borderlands*, unpublished paper, Department of Geography, University of Leicester

——— (1981b) 'Urban neighbourhood and community exploratory studies in Leicester', in Turnock, D. (ed.), *Leicestershire Geography Essays*, Department of Geography Occasional Papers No. 1, University of Leicester

——— and Davies, W.K. (1974) 'The social patterning of a British city. The case of Leicester 1966', *Tijdschrift voor Economische en Sociale Geografie*, *65*, 194–207

——— and Maund, D.J. (1976) 'The urbanization of the countryside: a framework for analysis', *Geografiska Annaler*, *58B*, 17–27

Lewis, W.C. (1977) 'The role of age in the decision to migrate', *Annals of Regional Science*, *11*, 51–60

Ley, D. (1974) *The Black Inner City as Frontier Outpost: Images and Behaviour of a Philadelphia Neighbourhood*. Association of American Geographers, Monograph Series No. 7, Washington, DC

Lieber, S.R. (1978) 'Place utility and migration', *Geografiska Annaler*, *60B*, 16–27

——— (1979) 'An experimental approach for the migration decision process', *Tijdschrift voor Economische en Sociale Geografie*, *70*, 75–85

Lind, H. (1969) 'Internal migration in Britain', in Jackson, J.A. (ed.), 74–99

Lindsay, I. and Barr, B.M. (1972) 'Two stochastic approaches to migration: comparison of Monte Carlo simulation and Markov Chain models', *Geografiska Annaler*, *54B*, 56–67

Lipset, S. and Bendix, R. (1952) 'Social mobility and occupational career paths', *American Journal of Sociology*, *57*, 366–74

Litwak, E. (1960) 'Geographic mobility and extended family cohesion', *American Sociological Review*, *25*, 385–94

Lloyd, R.E. (1976) 'Cognition, preference and behaviour in space: an examination of the structural linkages', *Economic Geography*, *52*, 241–53

Long, L. and Hansen, K. (1979) *Reasons for Interstate Migration*, United Bureau of the Census, Washington

Long, L.H. (1972) 'The influence of number and ages of children on residential mobility', *Demography*, *9*, 371–82

——— (1973) 'Migration differentials by education and occupation: trends and variations', *Demography*, *10*, 243–58

Lowenthal, D. and Comitas, L. (1962) 'Emigration and depopulation: some neglected aspects of population geography', *Geographical Review*, *52*, 195–210

Lowry, I.S. (1966) *Migration and Metropolitan Growth: Two Analytical Models*, Chandler, San Francisco

Mabogunje, A.K. (1970) 'A systems approach to a theory of rural-urban migration', *Geographical Analysis*, *2*, 1–18

McCracken, K.W.J. (1975) 'Household awareness spaces and intra-urban migration search behaviour', *Professional Geographer*, *27*, 166–70

Macdonald, L.J. and Macdonald, J. (1964) 'Chain Migration, ethnic neighbourhood formation and social networks', *Milbank Memorial Fund Quarterly*, *42*, 82–97

McFarland, D.D. (1970) 'Intra-generational social mobility as a Markov process', *American Sociological Review*, *35*, 463–76

McGhee, T.G. (1975) 'Malay migration to Kuala Lumpar city: individual adaptation to the city', in du Toit, B. and Safa, H. (eds.), 143–78

McGinnis, R. (1968) 'A stochastic model of social mobility', *American Sociological Review*, *33*, 712–21

McInnis, M. (1971) 'Age, education and occupational differentials in inter-regional migration: some evidence from Canada', *Demography*, *8*, 195–205

McKay, J. and Whitelaw, J.S. (1977) 'The role of large private and government organizations in generating flows of inter-regional migrants: the case of Australia', *Economic Geography*, *53*, 28–44

——— and ——— (1978) *Internal Migration and the Australian Urban System*, Progress in Planning, *10*, Pergamon, Oxford

McNeill, W.H. and Adams, R.S. (eds.) (1978) *Human Migration: patterns and Policies*, Indiana University Press, Bloomington

Mangalam, J.J. (1968) *Human Migration*, University of Kentucky Press, Lexington, Ky.

Mann, M. (1973) *Workers On the Move*, Cambridge University Press, London

Marble, D. and Nystuen, J.D. (1963) 'An approach to the direct measurement of community mean information fields', *Papers of Regional Science Association*, *11*, 99–109

Marquand, D. and Clegg, I. (1969) *Class and Power*, Routledge and Kegan Paul, London

Masser, I. (1970) *A test of some models for predicting inter-metropolitan movement of population in England and Wales*, Centre for Environmental Studies, UWP 9, London

——— and Gould, W.T.S. (1975) *Inter regional migration in tropical Africa*, Special publication No. 8, Institute of British Geographers

Maund, D.J. (1976) *The Urbanization of the Countryside: a Case Study in Herefordshire*, Unpublished M. Phil. thesis, University of Leicester

May, R.J. (ed.) (1977) *Change and Movement*, Australian National University Press, Canberra

Meyer, R. (1980) 'A descriptive model of constrained residential search', *Geographical Analysis*, *12*, 21–32

Michelson, W. (1977) *Environmental Choice, Human Behaviour, and Residential Satisfaction*, Oxford University Press, New York
—— (1980) 'Residential mobility as a dynamic process: a cross-cultural perspective', in Ungerson, C. and Karn, V. (eds.), 36–49
Miller, S.J. (1970) 'Family life cycle: extended family orientations and economic aspirations as factors in the propensity to move', *Sociological Quarterly*, *17*, 323-35
Mitchell, G.D. (1950) 'Depopulation and rural social structure', *Sociological Review*, *42*, 69–85
Mitchell, J.C. (1969) 'Structural plurality, urbanization and labour circulation in Southern Rhodesia', in Jackson, J.A. (ed.), 151–81
Moore, E.G. (1971) 'Comments on the use of ecological models in the study of residential mobility in the city', *Economic Geography*, *47*, 72–85
—— (1972) *Residential Mobility in the City*, College Geography Resource Paper 13, Association of American Geographers, Washington
—— (1978) 'The impact of residential mobility on population characteristics at the neighbourhood level', in Clark, W.A.V. and Moore, E.G. (eds.), 151–81
Morgan, B.S. (1973) 'Why families move: a re-examination', *Professional Geographer*, *25*, 124-9
—— (1976) 'The basis of family status segregation: a case study of Exeter', *Transactions, Institute of British Geographers, N.S. 1*, 83-107
Morgan, D.J. (1977) *Patterns of Population Distribution: A Residential Preference Model and its Dynamics*, Department of Geography Research Paper No. 176, University of Chicago
Morrill, R.L. (1960) 'The distribution of migration distances', *Papers and Proceedings of Regional Science Association*, *11*, 75-84
—— (1965a) *Migration and the Spread and Growth of Urban Settlement*, Lund Studies in Geography, Series B, No. 26
—— (1965b) 'The Negro ghetto: problems and alternatives', *Geographical Review*, *55*, 339-61
—— (1965c) 'Expansion of the urban fringe: a simulation experiment', *Paper and Proceedings of the Regional Science Association*, *15*, 185-202
—— and Pitts, F.R. (1967) 'Marriage, migration and mean information fields', *Annals, Association of American Geographers*, *57*, 401-22
Morrison, P.A. (1967) 'Duration of residence and prospective migration: the evaluation of a stochastic model', *Demography*, *4*, 553-61
—— (1970) 'Chronic movers and the future redistribution of population: a longitudinal analysis', *Rand Paper Series*, *P-4440*, Rand Corporation, Santa Monica, California
—— (1975) 'Toward a policy planner's view of the urban settlement system', *Rand Paper Series*, *P-5357*, Rand Corporation, Santa Monica, California
—— and Wheeler, J.P. (1976) 'Rural Renaissance in America? The revival of population growth in remote areas', *Population Bulletin*, *31*, Population Reference Bureau, Washington, DC
Mortimore, M.J. (1969) 'Landownership and urban growth in Bradford and its environs in the West Riding conurbations', *Transactions, Institute of the British Geographers*, *46*, 99-113
Moseley, M.J. (1979) *Accessibility: the Rural Challenge*, Methuen, London
Murie, A. (1975) *Household Movement and Housing*, Centre for Urban and

Regional Studies, Occational Paper 28, University of Birmingham
——, Niner, P. and Watson, C. (1976) *Housing Policy and the Housing System*, Allen and Unwin, London

Murphy, P.A. (1979) 'Migration of the elderly: a review', *Town Planning Review*, *50*, 84–93

Musgrave, F. (1963) *The Migratory Elite*, Heinemann, London

Myers, G.C., McGinnis, R. and Masnick, G. (1967) 'The duration of residence approach to a dynamic stochastic model of internal migration: a test of the axiom of cumulative inertia', *Eugenics Quarterly*, *14*, 121–6

Nalson, J.S. (1968) *The Mobility of Farm Families*, Manchester University Press, Manchester

Ng, R. (1969) 'Recent internal population movement in Thailand', *Annals, Association of American Geographers*, *59*, 710–30

Nicholson, B. (1975) 'Return migration to a marginal rural area – an example from northern Norway', *Sociologia Ruralis*, *15*, 227–44

Niner, P. (1975) *Local Authority Housing Policy and Practice*, Centre for Urban and Regional Studies, Occasional Paper 31, University of Birmingham
—— and Watson, C.J. (1978) 'Housing in British Cities', in Herbert, D.T. and Johnston, R.J. (eds.), 319–52

North Regional Planning Committee (1967) *Mobility and the North*, Newcastle

OECD (1975) *The OECD and International Migration*, Paris

Okun, B. and Richardson, R.W. (1961) 'Regional income inequality and internal population migration', *Economic Development and Cultural Change*, *9*, 128–43

Oliver, F. (1964) 'Inter-regional migration and unemployment 1951–61', *Journal of the Royal Statistical Society*, *127*, 42–75

Olsson, G. (1965) *Distance and Human Interaction: A Review and Bibliography*, Regional Science Research Institute, Bibliography Series No. 2, Philadelphia
—— (1967) 'Central place systems, spatial interaction and stochastic processes', *Papers of the Regional Science Association*, *18*, 13–45

Onibokun, A.G. (1976) 'Social system correlates of residential satisfaction', *Environment and Behaviour*, *8*, 323–44

Pacione, M. (1978) 'Information and morphology in cognitive maps', *Transactions, Institute of British Geographers*, *N.S. 3*, 548–68

Pahl, R.E. (1975) *Whose City*, Pelican, Harmondsworth
—— (1977a) 'Collective consumption and the state in capitalist and state capitalist societies', in Scase, R. (ed.), *Industrial Society. Class Cleavage and Control*, Allen and Unwin, London
—— (1977b) 'Managers, technical experts and the state: forms of mediation, manipulation and dominance in urban and regional development', in Harloe, M. (ed.), 91–114

Paine, S. (1974) *Exporting Workers: The Turkish Case*, Cambridge University Press, Cambridge

Palm, R. (1976) 'Real Estate Agents and Geographical Information', *Geographical Review*, *66*, 266–280

Park, R.E. (1925) *Human Communities*, Free Press, Glencoe

Parkes, D.N. and Thrift, N.J. (1980) *Times, Spaces and Places*, Wiley, London

Patten, J. (1976) 'Patterns of migration and movement of labour to three pre-industrial East Anglian towns', *Journal of Historical Geography*, *2*, 111–29

Perry, P.J. (1969) 'Working class isolation and mobility in rural Dorset, 1837–1936', *Transactions, Institute of British Geographers*, *46*, 115–35

Petersen, W. (1958) 'A general typology of migration', *American Sociological Review*, *23*, 256–66

Pickvance, C.G. (1974) 'Life cycle, housing tenure and residential mobility: a path analytic approach', *Urban Studies*, *11*, 171–88

Popp, H. (1976) 'The residential location decision process: some theoretical and empirical considerations', *Tijdschrift voor Economische en Sociale Geografie*, *67*, 300–5

Porter, R. (1956) 'Approach to migration through its mechanism', *Geografiska Annaler*, *38*, 317–43

Pourcher, G. (1970) 'The growing population of Paris', in Jansen, A.J. (ed.), 179–202

Power, J. and Hardman, A. (1976) *Western Europe's Migrant Workers*, Minority Rights Group Report No. 28, London

Price, C.A. (1963) *Southern Europeans in Australia*, Oxford University Press, Melbourne

——— (1969) 'The study of assimilation', in Jackson, J.A. (ed.), 181–237

Prothero, R.M. (1957) 'Migratory labour from North-Western Nigeria', *Africa*, *37*, 251–61

——— (1959) *Migrant Labour from Sokoto Province, Northern Nigeria*, Government Printer, Kaduna

——— (1968) 'Migration in tropical Africa', in Caldwell, J.C. and Okonjo, C. (eds.), *The Population of Tropical Africa*, Longman, London, 250–62

Pryor, R.J. (1971) *Internal Migration and Urbanization*, Geography Department James Cook University Monograph Series No. 2, Townsville

——— (1975a) 'Migration and the process of modernization', in Kosinski, L.A. and Prothero, R.M. (eds.), 23–8

——— (ed.), (1975b) *The Motivation of Migration*, Studies in Migration and Urbanization No. 1, Department of Demography, Australian National University, Canberra

——— (ed.) (1976) *Population Redistribution: Policy Research*, Studies in Migration and Urbanization No. 2, Department of Demography, Australian National University, Canberra

——— (ed.) (1979a) *Residence History Analysis*, Studies in Migration and Urbanization No. 3, Department of Demography, Australian National University, Canberra

——— (ed.) (1979b) *Migration and Development in South East Asia. A Demographic Perspective*, Oxford University Press, London

Ravenstein, E.G. (1885; 1889) 'The laws of migration', *Journal of the Royal Statistical Society*, *48* (1885), 167–235; and *52* (1889). 241–305

Redford, A. (1926) *Labour Migration in England, 1800–50*, Manchester University Press, Manchester

Rees, G. and Rees, T. (1977) 'Alternatives to the census: the example of sources of internal migration data', *Town Planning Review*, *48*, 123–40

Rees, P.H. (1976) 'The measurement of migration from census data and other sources', Department of Geography, Working Paper 162, University of Leeds

Reissman, L. (1967) 'The metrics of migration', *Pacific Viewpoint*, *8*, 211–2

Rempel, H. and Todaro, M.P. (1972) 'Rural-to-urban labour migration in Kenya', in Ominde, S.H. and Ejogu, C.N. (eds.), *Population Growth and Economic Development in Africa*, Heinemann, London

Rex, J.A. and Moore, R. (1967) *Race, Community and Conflict*, Oxford University Press, London

Rhoades, R.E. (1978) 'Intra-European return migration and rural development: lessons from the Spanish case', *Human Organization*, 37, 136–47

Richmond, A.H. (1968) 'Return migration of Britons from Canada', *Population Studies*, 22, 263–71

—— (1969) 'Sociology of migration in industrial and post-industrial societies', in Jackson, J.A. (ed.), 238–81

—— (1973) *Migration and Race Relations in an English City*, Oxford University Press, London

—— and Kubat, D. (eds.) (1976) *Internal Migration. The New World and Third World*, Sage, New York

Riddell, J.B. (1970) 'On structuring a migration model', *Geographical Analysis*, 2, 403–9

—— and Harvey, M.E. (1972) 'The urban system in the migration process: an evaluation of the step-wise migration in Sierra Leone', *Economic Geography*, 48, 270–83

Rider, R.V. and Badger, G.F. (1943) 'Family studies in the Eastern Health District (Baltimore). A consideration of issues involved in determining migration rates for families', *Human Biology*, 15, 101–26

Roberts, H. (1972) *Australia's Immigration Policy*, University of Western Australia Press, Perth

Rodgers, A. (1970) 'Migration and industrial development: the Southern Italian experience', *Economic Geography*, 46, 111–35

Rogers, A. (1967) 'A regression analysis of inter-regional migration in California', *Review of Economics and Statistics*, 49, 262–7

—— (1968) *Matrix Analysis of Inter regional Population Growth and Distribution*, University of California, Berkeley

Rogers, T.W. (1968) 'A stochastic process for determining migration probabilities', *Sociological Quarterly*, 9, 193–201

Rose, A. (1969) *Migrants in Europe, Problems of Acceptance and Adjustments*, Minnesota University Press, Minneapolis

Rose, A.M. (1958) 'Distance of migration and the socio-economic status of migrants', *American Sociological Review*, 23, 420–3

Rose, H.M. (1972) *Black Ghetto*, McGraw Hill, New York

Roseman, C.C. (1971) 'Migration as a spatial and temporal process', *Annals, Association of American Geographers*, 61, 589–98

—— (1977) *Changing Migration Patterns within the United States*, Resource Papers for College Geography No. 77-2. Association of American Geographers, Washington, DC

Rossi, P.H. (1955; 1980) *Why Families Move*, Free Press, Glencoe, Illinois

Rowland, D.T. (1976) 'Residence histories of internal migrants in Victoria', in Logan, M.I. (ed.), *Internal Migration and Policy Issues*, Department of Geography, Monash University, Melbourne

—— (1978) 'Internal migration as an exchange process: a study of Victoria', *Australian Geographical Studies*, 16, 15–28

—— (1979) *Internal Migration in Australia*, Australian Bureau of Statistics,

Canberra

Rowley, G. and Wilson, S. (1975) 'The analysis of housing and travel preferences: a gaming solution', *Environment and Planning*, 7, 171–8

Rowntree, J.A. (1957) *Internal Migration: A Study of Frequency of Movement of Migrants*, Studies on Medical and Population Subjects No. 11, HMSO, London

Sabagh, G. and Van Arsdol, M.D. (1969) 'Some determinants of intra-metropolitan residential mobility: conceptual considerations', *Social Forces*, 48, 88–98

Safa, H.I. and Du Toit, B.M. (eds.) (1975) *Migration and Development: Implications for Ethnic Identity and Political Conflict*, Mouton, Hague

Salt, J. and Clout, H. (1976) *Migration in Post-War Europe: Geographical Essays*, Oxford University Press, London

Saville, J. (1957) *Rural Depopulation in England and Wales, 1851–1951*, Routledge and Kegan Paul, London

Schneider, C.H.P. (1975) 'Models of space searching in urban areas', *Geographical Analysis*, 7, 173–86

Schwind, P.J. (1971) *Migration and Regional Development in the United States: 1950–60*, Department of Geography Research Paper No. 133, University of Chicago

—— (1975) 'A General Field Theory of Migration: United States, 1955–60', *Economic Geography*, 51, 1–16

Sharma, P.C. (1978) 'Population migration: a selected bibliographic research guide 1972–77', *Vance Bibliographies, Public Administrative Series Bibliography*, P-13

Shaw, R.P. (1974) 'A note on cost-relative calculations and decisions to migrate', *Population Studies*, 28, 167–9

—— (1975) *Migration Theory and Fact. A Review and Bibliography of Current Literature*, Regional Science Research Institute Bibliography Series No. 5, Philadelphia

Shimbel, A. (1953) 'Structural parameters of communication networks', *Bulletin of Mathematical Biophysics*, 15, 129–46

Short, J.R. (1978a) 'Residential mobility in private housing market of Bristol', *Transactions, Institute of British Geographers*, N.S. 3, 533–47

—— (1978b) 'Residential mobility', *Progress in Geography*, 2, 419–47

Shryock, H.S. and Larmon, E.A. (1965) 'Some longitudinal data on internal migration', *Demography*, 2, 579–92

—— and Nam, C. (1965) 'Educational selectivity of inter-regional migration', *Social Faces*, 43, 299–310

—— and Siegel, J.S. (1971) *The Methods and Materials of Demography*, United States Bureau of Census, Washington, DC

—— and —— (1976) condensed edn. by Stockwell, E.G., *The Methods and Materials of Demography*, Academic Press, New York

Siegel, J.S. and Hamilton, C.H. (1952) 'Some consideration in the use of the residual method of estimating net migration', *Journal of the American Statistical Association*, 47, 475–500

Silk, J. (1971) *Search behaviour: general characterization and review of the literature in the Social Sciences*, Geographical Papers No. 7, Department of Geography, University of Reading

Simmie, J.M. (1972) *The Sociology of Internal Migration*, Centre for
Environmental Studies, UWP 15, London
—— (1974) *Citizens in Conflict: The Sociology of Town Planning*, Hutchinson,
London
Simmons, J. (1968) 'Changing residence in the city: a review of intra-urban
mobility', *Geographical Review*, *58*, 621–51
—— (1974) *Patterns of Residential Movement in Metropolitan Toronto*,
Department of Geography Research Publication No. 13, University of Toronto
Simon, H.A. (1957) *Models of Man*, Wiley, New York
Sjastaad, L.A. (1962) 'The costs and returns of human migration', *Journal of
Political Economy*, *37*, 615–28
Skinner, E.P. (1964) *The Mossi of the Upper Volta: the Political Development of
a Sudanese People*, Stanford University Press, Stanford, California
—— (1966) 'Labour migration and its relationship to socio-cultural change
in Mossi society', in Wallerstein, I. (ed.), *Social Change*, Wiley, London
Smith, T.R. (1979) 'A note on the consequences of risk aversion and age for
duration of stay effects in a heterogeneous population', *Geographical Analysis*,
11, 183–8
——, Clark, W.A.V., Huff, J.O. and Shapiro, P. (1979) 'A decision making and
search model for intra-urban migration', *Geographical Analysis*, *11*, 1–22
Speare Jr., A. (1970) 'Home ownership, life cycle stage, and residential mobility',
Demography, *7*, 449–58
—— (1971) 'A cost-benefit model of rural to urban migration in Taiwan',
Population Studies, *25*, 117–30
—— (1974) 'Residential satisfaction as an intervening variable in residential
mobility', *Demography*, *11*, 173–88
——, Goldstein, S. and Frey, W.H. (1974) *Residential Mobility, Migration and
Metropolitan Growth*, Bellinger, Cambridge, Mass.
Spencer, R.F. (1970) *Migration and Anthropology*, University of Washington
Press, Seattle
Spilerman, S. (1972) 'The analysis of mobility processes by the introduction of
independent variables into a Markov chain', *American Sociological Review*, *37*,
277–94
Stewart, C.T. (1960) 'Migration as a function of population and distance',
American Sociological Review, *25*, 347–56
Stone, L.O. (1969) *Migration in Canada*, 1961 Census Monographs, Dominion
Bureau of Statistics, Ottawa
Stouffer, S.A. (1940) 'Intervening opportunities: a theory relating mobility and
distance', *American Sociological Review*, *5*, 845–67
—— (1960) 'Intervening opportunities and competing migrants', *Journal of
Regional Science Association*, *2*, 1–26
Straszheim, M. (1972) *An Economic Analysis of the Urban Housing Market*,
National Bureau of Economic Research, Washington
Stub, H.R. (1962) 'The occupational characteristics of migrants to Duluth: a
retest of Rose's hypothesis', *American Sociological Review*, *27*, 87–90
Sunday Times (1973) 'The Slave Workers of Europe', 22 July
Sundquist, J.L. (1975) *Dispersing Population. What America Can Learn from
Europe*, Brookings Institution, Washington DC
Suttles, G.D. (1972) *The Social Construction of Communities*, University of

Chicago Press, Chicago

Svart, L.M. (1976) 'Environmental preference migration: a review', *Geographical Review*, *66*, 314–30

Swindell, K. (1970) 'The distribution of age and sex characteristics in Sierra Leone and their relevance to a study of internal migration', *Tijdschrift voor Economishe en Sociale Geografie*, *61*, 366–74

—— (1979) 'Labour migration in underdeveloped countries: the case of sub-Saharan Africa', *Progress in Human Geography*, *3*, 239–59

—— and Ford, R.G. (1975) 'Places, migrants and organization: some observations on population mobility', *Geografiska Annaler*, *57B*, 69–76

Taeuber, K.E. (1966) 'Cohort Migration', *Demography*, *3*, 416–22

——, Chiazze, L. and Haenszel, W. (1968) *Migration in the United States: An Analysis of Residential Histories*, Health Monograph No. 77. Public Health Service, United States Department of Health, Education and Welfare, Washington, DC

——, Haenszel, W. and Sirken, M.G. (1961) 'Residence histories and exposure residences for the United States population', *Journal of American Statistical Association*, *56*, 824–34

—— and Taeuber, G.F. (1964) 'The negro as an immigrant group: recent trends in racial and ethnic segregation in Chicago', *American Journal of Sociology*, *64*, 374–82

Tarver, J.D. (1962) 'Evaluation of census survival rates in estimating intercensal state net migration', *Journal of the American Statistical Association*, *57*, 841–62

—— (1964) 'Occupational migration differentials', *Social Forces*, *43*, 231–41

—— and Gurley, W.R. (1965) 'A stochastic analysis of geographic mobility and population projections of the census divisions in the United States', *Demography*, *2*, 134–9

—— and McLeod, D.R. (1970) 'Trends in distances moved by inter state migrants', *Rural Sociology*, *32*, 523–33

—— and Skees, D.M. (1967) 'Vector representation of migration streams among selected statistical economic areas during 1955–60', *Demography*, *4*, 1–19

Taylor, P.J. (1975) *Distance Decay Models in Spatial Interaction*, CATMOG, No. 2, Geo Abstracts, Norwich

—— (1980) 'A pedagogic application of multiple regression analysis', *Geography*, *65*, 203–12

Taylor, R.C. (1969) 'Migration and motivation: a study of determinants and types', in Jackson, J.A. (ed.), 99–134

ter Heide, H. (1963) 'Migration models and their significance for population forecasts', *Milbank Memorial Fund Quarterly*, *41*, 56–76

Thomas, B. (1954) *Migration and Economic Growth*, Cambridge University Press, Cambridge

—— (1961) *International Migration and Economic Development: a Trend Report and Bibliography*. UNESCO, Paris

Thomas, C. (1979) 'Population mobility in frontier communities: examples from the Julian March, 1931–45', *Transactions, Institute of British Geographers*, *4*, 44–62

—— (1980) 'Internal migration and the transformation of rural communities in the north Balkans, 1869–1871', Paper read at the Institute of British Geographers' Population Study Group meeting, September 1980

Thomas, D.S. (1938) *Research Memorandum on Migration Differentials*, Social Science Research Council Bulletin No. 47, New York

—— (1941) *Social and Economic Aspects of Swedish Population Movements, 1750–1933*, Macmillan, New York

—— and Kuznets, S. (eds.) (1957, 1960, 1964) *Population Redistribution and Economic Growth, United States: 1870–1950*, 3 vols, American Philosophical Society, Philadelphia

Thomas, W.I. and Znaniecki, F. (1927) *The Polish Peasant in Europe and America*, Knopf, New York

Thorns, D.C. (1980a) 'Constraints versus choices in the analysis of housing allocation and residential mobility', in Ungerson, C. and Karn, V. (eds.), 50–68

—— (1980b) *The Role of the Family Life Cycle in Residential Mobility*, Centre for Urban and Regional Studies, Working Paper 69, University of Birmingham

Tilley, C. and Brown, C.H. (1967) 'On uprooting, kinship and the auspices of migration', *International Journal of Comparative Sociology*, 7, 139–64

Todaro, M.P. (1969) 'A model of labour migration and urban unemployment in less developed countries', *American Economic Review*, 59, 138–48

—— (1976) *Internal Migration in Developing Countries. A Review of Theory, Evidence, Methodology and Research Priorities*, International Labour Office, Geneva

Todd, D. (1980) 'Rural out-migration and economic standing in a prairie setting', *Transactions, Institute of British Geographers*, 5, 446–65

Tolley, G.S. (1963) 'Population adjustment and economic activity: three studies', *Papers, Regional Science Association*, 2, 84–98

Troy, P.N. (1973) 'Residents and their preferences: property prices and residential quality', *Regional Studies*, 7, 183–92

Turner, F.J. (1920) *The Frontier in American History*, Holt, Rinehart and Winston, New York

Ungerson, C. and Karn, V. (eds.) (1980) *The Consumer Experience of Housing*, Gower, Farnborough

United Nations (1949) *Problems of Migration Statistics*, Department of Social Affairs, Population Studies, No. 5, New York

—— (1953) *The Determinants and Consequences of Population Trends*, Department of Social Affairs, Population Trends No. 17, New York

—— (1955) *Analytical Bibliography of International Migrants: Statistics, 1925–50*, Department of Social Affairs, Population Studies No. 12, New York

—— (1970) *Methods of Measuring Internal Migration*, Department of Economic and Social Affairs, Population Studies No. 47, New York

—— (1973) *The Determinants and Consequences of Population Trends*, Department of Economic and Social Affairs, Population Studies No. 50, New York

—— (1978) *Trends and Characteristics of International Migration Since 1950*, Department of Economic and Social Affairs, Population Studies No. 61, New York

US Bureau of Census (1973) *Census of Population 1970. Detailed Characteristics*, Final Report PC (1)–D1, Washington DC

Van Arsdol, Jr, M.D., Sabagh, G. and Butler, E.W. (1968) 'Retrospective and subsequent metropolitan residential mobility', *Demography*, 5, 249–67

Van Binsbergen, W. and Meilink, H. (1978) *Migration and the Transformation of Modern African Society*, Afrika-Studiecentrum, Leiden

Van den Brink, T. (1954) 'Population registers and their significance for demographic statistics', *Proceedings of the World Population Conference 1954*, United Nations, No. 55, XIII 8/Vol 4, 917–18, New York

Wadycki, W.J. (1975) 'Stouffer's model of migration: a comparison of inter-state and metropolitan flows', *Demography*, 12, 121–8

Walmsley, D.J. (1973) 'The simple behaviour system: an appraisal and an elaboration', *Geografiska Annaler*, 55B, 49–56

—— (1980) 'Spatial bias in Australian News Reporting', *Australian Geographer*, 14, 342–9

Walter, B. (1980) 'Time-space patterns of second-wave Irish immigration into British towns', *Transactions, Institute of British Geographers*, N.S. 5, 297–317

Ward, B.J. (1975) 'The use of electoral rolls in the study of internal migration', *Australian Geographical Studies*, 13, 94–108

Ward, R.G. (1980) 'Migration, myth and magic in Papua New Guinea', *Australian Geographical Studies*, 18, 119–34

Webber, M.J., Symanski, R. and Root, J. (1975) 'Toward a Cognitive Spatial Theory', *Economic Geography*, 51, 100–16

Weeden, R. (1973) 'Inter-regional migration modes and their application to Great Britain', NIESR, Regional Papers 2, 51–67

Weinberg, A.A. (1961) *Migration and Belonging: a Study of Mental Health and Personal Adjustment in Israel*, Martinus Nijhoff, The Hague

Weinberg, D.H. (1979) 'The determinants of intra-urban household mobility', *Regional Science and Urban Economics*, 9, 219–46

Welch, R.L. (1970) *Migration Research and Migration in Britain*, Centre for Urban and Regional Studies, Occasional Paper No. 14, University of Birmingham

—— (1971) *Migration in Britain: Data Sources and Estimation Techniques*, Centre for Urban and Regional Studies, Occasional Paper No. 18, University of Birmingham

White, P. and Wood, R. (1980) *The Geographical Impact of Migration*, Longman, London

Whitelaw, J.S. and Gregson, J.S. (1972) *Search Procedures in the Intra-urban Migration Process*, Monash University Publication in Geography No. 2, Melbourne

—— and Robinson, G. (1972) 'A test for directional bias in intra-urban migration', *New Zealand Geographer*, 28, 181–93

Whyte, W.F. (1956) *The Organisation Man*, Simon and Shuster, New York

Wilber, G.L. (1963) 'Migration expectancy in the United States', *Journal of the American Statistical Association*, 58, 444–53

Williams, P.R. (1976) 'The role of institutions in the inner London housing market: the case of Islington', *Transactions, Institute of British Geographers*, N.S. 1, 72–82

—— (1978) 'Building societies and the inner city', *Transactions, Institute of British Geographers*, N.S. 3, 23–34

Willis, K.G. (1974) *Problems in Migration Analysis*, Saxon House, Farnborough,

1974
—— (1975) 'Regression models of migration', *Geografiska Annaler, 57B*, 42–54

Wilson, A.G. (1970) *Entropy in Urban and Regional Modelling*, Pion, London

Wilson, R.L. (1962) 'Livability of the city: attitudes and urban development', in Chapin, F.S. and Weiss, S. (eds.), *Urban Growth Dynamics*, Wiley, New York, 124–35

Wirth, L. (1945) 'The problems of minority groups' in Linton, R. (ed.), *The Science of Man in the World Crisis*, Columbia University Press, New York

Wiseman, R.F. (1978) *Spatial Aspect of Ageing*, Resource Papers for College Geography No. 78–4, Association of American Geographers, Washington, DC

—— and Roseman, C.C. (1979) 'A typology of elderly migration based on the decision-making process', *Economic Geography, 55*, 324–37

—— and Virden, M. (1977) 'Spatial and social dimensions of intra-urban elderly migration', *Economic Geography, 53*, 1–13

Wolpert, J. (1964) 'The decision process in spatial perspective', *Annals, Association of American Geographers, 54*, 220–9

—— (1965) 'Behavioural aspects of the decision to migrate', *Papers and Proceedings of Regional Science Association, 15*, 159–72

—— (1966) 'Migration as an adjustment to environmental stress', *Journal of Social Issues, 22*, 92–102

—— (1967) 'Distance and directional bias in inter-urban migratory streams', *Annals, Association of American Geographers, 57*, 605–16

—— (1969) 'The basis for stability of interregional transactions', *Geographical Analysis, 1*, 152–80

Woods, R. (1979) *Population Analysis in Geography*, Longman, London

Young, E.C. (1924) *The Movement of Farm Population*, Cornell Agricultural Experiment Station Bulletin, No. 426, Ithaca, New York

Young, M.L. (1979) 'Residence History Analysis: Malaysia', in Pryor, R.J. (ed.), 51–64

Zachariah, K.C. (1964) *An Historical Study of Internal Migration in the Indian Sub-continent 1901–31*, Asia Publishing House, Bombay

—— (1966) 'Bombay migration study: a pilot analysis of migration to an Asian metropolis', *Demography, 3*, 378–92

Zehner, R.B. (1972) 'Neighbourhood and community satisfaction', in Wohlwell, J.H. and Carson, D.H. (eds.), *Environment and the Social Sciences*, American Psychological Association, Washington, DC, 169–83

Zelinsky, W. (1962) 'Changes in the geographic patterns of rural population in the United States 1790–1960', *Geographical Review, 52*, 492–524

—— (1971) 'The hypothesis of the mobility transition', *Geographical Review, 61*, 219–49

Zimmer, R.G. (1970) 'Participation of migrants in urban structure', in Jansen, C.J. (ed.), 71–83

Zipf, G.K. (1946) 'The $P_1 P_2 /D$ hypothesis on the inner city movement of persons', *American Sociological Review, 11*, 677–86

INDEX

access 152-4, 160, 163, 164
accessibility 42, 66, 79, 120, 138, 141, 179
acculturation 182-4
action space 129, 147
activity space 129, 142, 143, 146
adjustment 31
adulthood 89
Africa 30, 31, 32, 36, 66, 110, 112, 171
Algeria 37
allocation 151, 152, 153
Americas 33, 34, 78
Anglo-Saxon 36
Appalachians 147
areal units 54
Asia 33, 66, 110
assimilation 29, 31, 147, 182-4, 186-8
Atlantic 105
Australia 3, 34, 47, 63, 75, 84, 96, 158, 159, 184
Automatic Interaction Detector 98

behavioural 4, 103, 126, 127, 150
Belgium 57
birth-rate 1, 172
Bombay 119
bourgeois 153
Brazil 36
Britain 3, 12, 18, 20, 36, 39, 40, 70, 84, 110, 111, 119, 155, 161, 164, 177
builders 163
building societies 162, 164
business cycle 104-5

California 55, 57, 109
Canada 18, 36, 41, 81, 87, 136
canomical analysis 115
capital cities 57, 96
career cycle 62, 63
  transients 91
census 12, 13, 61, 111, 113
central place 79
Chile 54, 84
circulation 23
city centre 90, 140
class 153, 184

cloze procedure 144
Common Market 158
community 26, 61, 69, 100, 120, 141, 166, 172-82
commuting 18, 131
conurbation 40, 50, 125, 174
cost-benefit analysis 105-6
counter stream 10, 15, 21, 36
cumulative inertia 70

data sources 12-15, 54, 61
death-rate 1
demographic equation 6
Denmark 69
depopulation 27, 123, 154, 176-9
destination 2, 10, 21, 25, 49, 54, 77, 79, 82, 96, 106, 168
developers 163
developing world 24, 42, 44, 47
Development Board 179
directional bias 51-3, 54
discriminant analysis 96
disorganization 166, 184
duration of residence 70-1, 72, 77, 78

East Africa 36
Eastern Europe 4
Economic
  development 22, 30, 42, 97, 104, 166, 169, 170, 188
  growth 104-5
  theory 4
Egypt 170
elderly 3, 94, 123
electoral registers 12
emigration 23, 70
England 14, 39, 54, 99, 110, 111, 122, 141, 158, 159
entropy 31-2, 58-60
established 69, 180-1
estate agents 146, 162, 163, 164
ethnic 87-9, 164, 172
evaluation 137-41
exposure residence 68

factorial analysis 115
familiarity 144-5
farmers 3, 123